Hardcore Java™

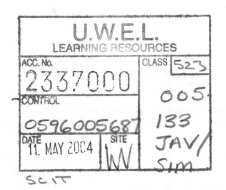

Robert Simmons, Jr.

O'REILLY®

Beijing · Cambridge · Farnham · Köln · Paris · Sebastopol · Taipei · Tokyo

Hardcore Java™
by Robert Simmons, Jr.

Copyright © 2004 O'Reilly Media, Inc. All rights reserved.
Printed in the United States of America.

Published by O'Reilly Media, Inc., 1005 Gravenstein Highway North, Sebastopol, CA 95472.

O'Reilly & Associates books may be purchased for educational, business, or sales promotional use. On-line editions are also available for most titles (*safari.oreilly.com*). For more information, contact our corporate/institutional sales department: (800) 998-9938 or *corporate@oreilly.com*.

Editor:	Brett McLaughlin
Production Editor:	Matt Hutchinson
Cover Designer:	Ellie Volckhausen
Interior Designer:	Melanie Wang

Printing History:

March 2004:	First Edition.

 This book uses RepKover™, a durable and flexible lay-flat binding.

ISBN: 0-596-00568-7

[M]

Table of Contents

Preface

Studying a computer language is a career-long process. Many developers make the mistake of thinking that they have learned enough. They get caught in the corporate cycle of build-and-deploy and don't seek to expand their knowledge. However, we can hardly blame them for that.

For one, the build-and-deploy cycle is intensive and carries with it a substantial amount of political pressure: managers don't want you to spend days reading a book or trying out code snippets when bugs and deadlines are looming. However, developers should take the time to experiment and learn more.

When you expand your skills as a developer, there is some initial time investment. However, this will rapidly pay off in increased productivity and quality. Instead of spending hundreds of hours debugging, you can implement coding standards that block bugs and spend a fraction of that time implementing new features. In the end, everyone wins; your company gets higher-quality code and quicker feature turnaround, and you get to spend more time playing Frisbee with your dog.

The second problem that the corporate developer has to deal with is that the majority of computer books are often not appropriate for the intermediate to advanced developer. When looking at my rather impressive computer book library, much of it from O'Reilly, I notice that my books tend to fall into two categories: many are introductions to concepts and most of the others are references to concepts. Although these books are very useful, there is a distinct lack of books that target the intermediate to advanced programmer. However, there is one shining exception in my library.

In a dusty corner of my desk is a book I bought several years ago. *Secrets of the C++ Masters* by Jeff Alger (Academic Press Limited) is absolutely essential for an intermediate C++ developer. It begins with the assumption that you know the language and then expands from there. The result is a book that can really transform a developer from the intermediate level to a true guru.

That is the goal of this book with regards to the Java™ language. Most of the material is meant to help you avoid many common mistakes made by Java developers.

We will also cover nuances of Java, idiosyncrasies of the JDK, and advanced techniques. With luck, this book will increase your productivity and your enjoyment of Java development.

Audience

This book is for the intermediate to advanced Java programmer. With that in mind, we can concentrate on the knowledge and techniques that go into some of the most advanced Java software available.

Prerequisites and Assumptions

Functional proficiency with Java

I will largely gloss over entire areas of Java. I assume that you understand Java-Beans™, bound properties, JDBC, and other basics.

Familiarity with basic computer science

I generally won't spend a lot of time on concepts such as scoping, logic operations, inheritance, and algorithm construction. These and similar concepts will be the basis for more detailed discussions.

Familiarity with UML

The Unified Modeling Language is the best way to express object-oriented engineering concepts in a manner that is familiar to all programmers, regardless of what language they speak. Most of the code diagrams in this book incorporate UML.

Familiarity with the JDK and the virtual machine

You should be familiar with the JDK and with how to compile a program and use its various tools in the JDK. However, expertise in all packages isn't necessary.

Typographical Conventions

This book uses the following font conventions:

Italic

Used for filenames, file extensions, URLs, application names, emphasis, and new terms when they are first introduced

`Constant width`

Used for Java class names, functions, variables, components, properties, data types, events, and snippets of code that appear in the text

`Constant width bold`

Used for commands you enter at the command line and to highlight new code inserted in a running example

This icon designates a note, which is an important aside to the nearby text.

 This icon designates a warning.

Code Samples

The code sample set for this book is massive. Almost every snippet of code from the book can be found in the downloadable source code (*http://www.oreilly.com/catalog/hardcorejv*). However, without a guide, you could get lost quickly when surfing through the examples.

Regarding the code itself, I will frequently snip out pieces you would need to get the code to compile and run. Copying this infrastructure code in the book would add unnecessary bulk and potentially cloud the issue being discussed. Since I assume you are experienced in Java, I will also assume you know the housekeeping procedures used to implement pertinent concepts.

One other tactic that I commonly use is to append a number to the name of a class or method. This is designed to show successive versions of the same class or method. The goal is to emphasize the development while allowing the user to look up the old version and play with it if he chooses. For example, you should read `Country4` as `Country`.

Finally, the code samples are very well-documented. However, for brevity's sake, I will usually slice out this documentation when presenting code examples. Although I firmly believe that good Javadoc documentation is important to good development, in this book such documentation would needlessly increase the page count without adding to the discussion.

One other thing to note about the examples is that you will often see the comment `//$NON-NLS-1$` imbedded within the code. This is merely a flagging comment that tells Eclipse not to internationalize a particular `String`. I have snipped these comments from the book, as they aren't relevant to the discussions.

Locating an Example in the Downloadable Code

Each example cited in the book is formatted as:

```java
package oreilly.hcj.review;
public class PointersAndReferences {
  public static void someMethod(Vector source) {
```

```
        Vector target = source;
        target.add("Swing");
    }
}
```

The emphasized lines show that you can find this code in the package `oreilly.hcj.`
`review` and the class `PointersAndReferences`. However, be aware that the code example cited may be embedded with other examples that are not relevant to that particular topic. In fact, I frequently combine several examples from a single subject into
one class file to reduce the housekeeping code needed to run the sample. Doing a
search on the method name will quickly locate the cited example.

Categories of Examples

The examples themselves can be divided into three categories. Each of these categories has a different usage paradigm that you should be aware of.

Syntax checkers

These are methods and snippets that were written solely for the purpose of checking
my syntax in the book. To check my syntax, I leverage the features of Eclipse 3.0M4.
However, be aware that the syntax checker examples will often be mixed with other
examples in the same class file.

Demonstrators

These examples demonstrate a specific concept but are not executed. They often
take the form of methods, which take a certain input and produce a certain output.
Mixed in with these samples, you will occasionally find little main( ) methods. I use
these simply to test things. If you want to play with them, feel free to do so; however, I do not discuss them in the book.

Some of the demonstrators are also used to demonstrate compiler errors when using
certain techniques. To use these examples, you can try changing the files and
rebuilding to demonstrate the concept. To compile a single file, there is a special Ant
target named `compile_example`. To use the target, simply pass the filename you want
to compile in the property example:

```
>ant -Dexample=oreilly/hcj/review/RTTIDemo.java compile_example
Buildfile: build.xml

init:

compile_example:
    [javac] Compiling 1 source file to C:\dev\hcj\bin
    [javac] C:\dev\hcj\src\oreilly\hcj\review\RTTIDemo.java:54: incompatible types
    [javac] found    : oreilly.hcj.review.RTTIDemo.A
    [javac] required: oreilly.hcj.review.RTTIDemo.B
```

```
[javac]     b = (A)a1;  // compiler error: a1 is not a B.
[javac]         ^
[javac] C:\dev\hcj\src\oreilly\hcj\review\RTTIDemo.java:55: inconvertible types
[javac] found   : oreilly.hcj.review.RTTIDemo.C
[javac] required: oreilly.hcj.review.RTTIDemo.B
[javac]     b = (B)c;  // compiler error: c is not a B.
[javac]           ^
[javac] 2 errors
```

Executables

Unlike demonstrators, executables are intended to be run and the output examined to demonstrate a concept or prove a point to a skeptical audience. When one of these programs is introduced, I will show you how to run it using Ant:

```
>ant -Dexample=oreilly.hcj.review.ObjectIsGod run_example
run_example:
    [java] class oreilly.hcj.review.ObjectIsGod$SomeClass --|> class
java.lang.Object
    [java] class oreilly.hcj.review.ObjectIsGod$SomeOtherClass --|> class
java.lang.Object
```

The emphasized line gives you the command needed to run the example after the prompt (>). The command is identical in most cases. The only difference is the name of the property example that you pass to the run_example target. While we are on the subject of running the sample code, there is one thing to note about the output. Since all of the examples are run with Ant to get the classpath and other housekeeping done, the actual output from the command will be much longer:

```
>ant -Dexample=oreilly.hcj.review.ObjectIsGod run_example
Buildfile: build.xml

init:

run_example:
    [java] class oreilly.hcj.review.ObjectIsGod$SomeClass --|> class
java.lang.Object
    [java] class oreilly.hcj.review.ObjectIsGod$SomeOtherClass --|> class
java.lang.Object
BUILD SUCCESSFUL
Total time: 1 second
```

Although this is the actual output, most of it is trivial and common to every use of Ant. Therefore, I snip out all of this housekeeping for the sake of brevity. The emphasized lines will be taken out when the run is presented in the book. Therefore, when you run the examples, be aware that Ant is a bit more verbose than I am.

Tools

One of the most important skills in professional development is knowing how to use tools. There are a wide variety of tools available, from the standard text editor and compiler to full-blown IDEs that do everything for you. Selecting the best tools for the job will make you a more productive developer.

UML Diagramming

For creating diagrams in UML, I use a product called Magic Draw UML, by No Magic, Inc. (*http://www.magicdraw.com/*). This tool is, without a doubt, the best professional UML modeling tool on the market. Rational Rose and Together can't even touch the functionality and quality of Magic Draw. I like it so much that I bought a copy of the Enterprise edition for myself. I highly recommend this product. Although it isn't free like other tools I recommend, it is well worth the price.

IDE

The IDE I use is Eclipse 3.0M4, which happens to be the IDE I use professionally as well. Eclipse simply has the single best development tool on the market. I don't know how I could live without my refactoring tools and the other goodies that come with Eclipse. You can find Eclipse at *http://www.eclipse.org/*. Also, I use many Eclipse plug-ins to make my job easier. They can be found in the Community section of eclipse.org, or you can surf the best directory of Eclipse plug-ins at *http://eclipse-plugins.2y.net/eclipse/index.jsp*.

Out-of-IDE Building

For building outside of my IDE and running examples, I use Apache Ant 1.5, which is available from *http://ant.apache.org/*. Ant is simply the best make program ever invented. I take my hat of to the folks at Apache.

Logging

I use Jakarta Log4J to do logging in my programs. Log4J is available from *http://jakarta.apache.org/log4j/docs/index.html*. In much of the sample code, there is little logging. However, in production systems, I am a logging fanatic.

 For those of you that are curious, I don't use the JDK 1.4 logging mechanism because it is, in my opinion, vastly inferior to Log4J on many levels.

Jakarta Commons

Another set of libraries that I often use in my professional code is the Jakarta Commons Libraries. These libraries are available from *http://jakarta.apache.org/commons/index.html*. They extend the JDK to include things that Sun either forgot to include or decided not to include in the JDK. Many of the common tools you will learn about later in the book, such as ConstantObject, will be submitted to Jakarta Commons after this book is published to make them more reusable. For now, though, you will find these tools in the *Hardcore Java* source code itself. If you haven't checked out the Commons Libraries, I strongly advise you to do so.

Using Code Examples

This book is here to help you get your job done. In general, you may use the code in this book in your programs and documentation. You do not need to contact O'Reilly for permission unless you're reproducing a significant portion of the code. For example, writing a program that uses several chunks of code from this book does not require permission. Selling or distributing a CD-ROM of examples from O'Reilly books *does* require permission. Answering a question by citing this book and quoting example code does not require permission. Incorporating a significant amount of example code from this book into your product's documentation *does* require permission.

We appreciate, but do not require, attribution. An attribution usually includes the title, author, publisher, and ISBN. For example: "*Hardcore Java*, by Robert Simmons, Jr. Copyright 2001 O'Reilly Media, Inc., 0-596-00568-7."

If you feel your use of code examples falls outside fair use or the permission given above, feel free to contact us at *permissions@oreilly.com*.

Comments and Questions

Please address comments and questions concerning this book to the publisher:

O'Reilly & Associates, Inc.
1005 Gravenstein Highway North
Sebastopol, CA 95472
(800) 998-9938 (in the United States or Canada)
(707) 829-0515 (international or local)
(707) 829-0104 (fax)

There's a web page for this book that lists errata, examples, and any additional information. You can access this page at:

http://www.oreilly.com/catalog/hardcorejv

To comment or ask technical questions about this book, send email to:

bookquestions@oreilly.com

For more information about books, conferences, Resource Centers, and the O'Reilly Network, see the O'Reilly web site at:

http://www.oreilly.com

Acknowledgments

I would like to thank all of the thousands of people who have answered my endless questions over the years in my quest to become a professional software engineer. Without these anonymous thousands on the Internet, the path would have been much more difficult.

I would also like to thank all of the junior programmers that have worked for me and kept my eyes open to new ideas. There is nothing like a fresh mind to suggest things that are radical, untried, and, in the end, brilliant. Certain people leap to mind, such as Bettina Linssen, now a senior developer. Even though I had considered myself something of a guru in Java GUI coding, her fresh insight and ideas taught me a thing or two. All you senior developers out there would be well advised to listen to the ideas of your junior developers. You never know what they might teach you.

I would also like to extend very special thanks to Marco Kukulies. Marco started his programming career as a junior developer working for me. He excelled beyond all expectations and demonstrated that he has that special gift that separates the normal programmers from the true gurus. Marco is now one of the best senior developers and architects I know. He has earned my respect, trust, and eternal friendship. Marco reviewed all of my book from a reader's perspective and gave me invaluable advice on what needed to be clarified, expanded on, or removed.

I would also like to thank one of my best friends who has little to do with programming but has provided endless moral support to keep me energized and working. Although my friend Saćir Husejnovic isn't a programmer, and generally doesn't understand much of my work, without his and Marco Kukulies' moral support, this book simply wouldn't have happened. My deepest respect goes out to these two gentlemen as well as to Saćir's wife Mirsada, and his three children Aida, Selma, and Amela. Thanks for being a second family to me!

I would like to take a moment to say "Hi" to my brother Paul and my sister Debbie. I currently live in Germany, and although I am very happy living here, I miss my brother and sister greatly.

On the publishing side of things, I would like to thank the artists at O'Reilly who did such a great job with my innumerable diagrams and drawings, not to mention the awesome cover. Also, I can't forget everyone who did such a good job publishing, distributing, and marketing this book. My compliments to you all.

Last, but definitely not least, I would like to thank my editor Brett McLaughlin, who can be found buried under piles of electronic chapters. Just look for the hand reaching up frantically for help. His editing prowess has increased the quality of my work to a level I never knew possible. When I proposed this book to O'Reilly, it was in a much rougher state than it is now. With many publishers, I would have been mostly on my own. However, O'Reilly has really worked hard to help me make this book one that I can be proud of. I have learned a lot, and Brett has truly converted me from a newbie author to a professional.

CHAPTER 1

Java in Review

I can hear the groans from here—a review on Java? Don't worry, I won't bore you with all of the gory syntax details or concepts of the Java language that you can easily pick up in other books. Instead, I will present a conceptual review that focuses on some various important issues that are often overlooked or underemphasized. The study of these issues will not only give you a better understanding of the Java language, but prepare you for what's covered in the rest of the book. You should think of this chapter as a roving spotlight, highlighting various issues of Java that are worthy of mention; even the intermediate and advanced programmer will benefit from the study of these issues.

Core Concepts

To understand the advanced concepts of the Java language, there are a few core concepts that you must have firmly in mind. Without these concepts, much of this book will not make a lot of sense. The concepts of pointers in Java, its class hierarchy, and RTTI (runtime type identification) are three of the most important on this list.

Constant Problems with Pointers

Java and C++ use a very analogous syntax to symbolize their instructions to the computer's CPU. In fact, there are probably more similarities between these languages than the two entrenched camps of supporters would like to admit. One difference between Java and C++ that is often mentioned, though, is that Java does not use *pointers*.

Pointers in C++ were a constant source of problems and were determined to be the programming equivalent of evil incarnate. There was, and is to this day, a large group of applications in C++ that suffer from the effects of this particular wrong. Therefore, Sun decided to leave them out of Java—at least that's the theory.

In reality, Java uses what C++ calls *references*. In fact, other than primitives, all variables in Java are references. References and pointers are very similar; both contain the memory location of a particular object. Pointers, however, allow you to do arithmetic whereas references do not. The fact that Java uses so many references introduces some difficulties that novice and proficient Java developers often get burned by. The code shown in Example 1-1 demonstrates one of these difficulties.

Example 1-1. Collections are passed as references

```
package oreilly.hcj.review;
public class PointersAndReferences {
  public static void someMethod(Vector source) {
    Vector target = source;
    target.add("Swing");
  }
}
```

Here, you simply copy the passed-in source vector and add a new element to the copy (named target); at least that is how it appears. Actually, something quite different happens. When you set target equal to source in the code, you copy a reference to the target vector, and not the contents of the vector itself. Since both variables now point to the same vector, this function actually adds an element to the source vector that was passed into the method; this was almost certainly not the desired effect! We will discuss how to prevent this problem in Chapter 2.

Since you can change the contents of an incoming collection, Java actually does have pointers—that is, Java references embody the same computer science principles that pointers do. So, when someone tells you that Java doesn't have pointers, you can correct them by saying, "Java has pointers, it just doesn't have pointer arithmetic."

Also, Java's use of references isn't a bad thing. In fact, the references are actually necessary to the Java language. Without them, you would have to pass everything by value. This would entail copying every single object each time an object was passed to a method. If the object were a String, this copying probably wouldn't be a big deal. However, if the object is a large array or set, the copy could take a long time. Therefore, passing everything by value would make Java code run extremely slowly. Furthermore, some objects simply don't make sense to copy at all. If you have a GUI panel and wish to pass the GUI panel to another component that needs to refer to it, you certainly don't want two copies of the panel floating around in memory. Instead, you want to send a reference to the existing panel. All of these issues point out the need for references in Java.

Everything Is a Class and Object Is God

In Java, all constructed types are regarded as objects. In fact, the only items in Java that are not objects are the primitive types, such as int and boolean; and even these primitive types can be treated as objects under some circumstances, such as when you use reflection.

I would expect that most Java programmers would find this trivial since they already know that every nonprimitive in Java is an object. The point that I am really trying to make, though, is that every constructed type in Java descends from the class java.lang.Object. Even if you don't declare a class as extending java.lang.Object, you still get this behavior. Example 1-2 shows a class that explicitly extends java.lang.Object, while Example 1-3 is a class that has no explicit extension.

Example 1-2. Explicitly extending java.lang.Object

```
public class SomeClass extends Object {
}
```

Example 1-3. Implicitly extending java.lang.Object

```
public class SomeClass {
}
```

In Example 1-2, SomeClass makes its object hierarchy clear; its superclass is Object.

Example 1-3, while visibly different, is actually equivalent to Example 1-2. The Java compiler will automatically assign the superclass of Object to this version of SomeClass.

In fact, even a class that implements interfaces instead of extending another class extends java.lang.Object. As a result, these two declarations are identical:

```
public class SomeClass extends Object implements Serializable {
}
```

```
public class SomeClass implements Serializable {
}
```

So, unlike C++, you cannot create a class that does not have a superclass. Object is the superclass to all classes in the entire language. In the example code for this book, you will find the class oreilly.hcj.review.ObjectIsGod, which demonstrates this concept:

```
> ant -Dexample=oreilly.hcj.review.ObjectIsGod run_example
run_example:
    [java] class oreilly.hcj.review.ObjectIsGod$SomeClass --|> class
java.lang.Object
    [java] class oreilly.hcj.review.ObjectIsGod$SomeOtherClass --|> class
java.lang.Object
```

There are three main reasons why java.lang.Object is always at the top of the inheritance tree:

- For Java to know the type of objects it must load, and to enforce type safety, it has to have some base type with which it can refer to all objects.

- Java currently lacks the concept of the *parameterized type* (also known as a *template*). This means that all the objects that are be stored in collection classes ultimately have to descend from one class.

- The fact that all objects have java.lang.Object as a superclass gives you supreme power when it comes to using reflection to turbocharge your code. Without this sort of inheritance, many techniques in reflection would be impractical. (We will discuss reflection in detail in Chapter 9.)

RTTI

Runtime type identification, or RTTI, is an extremely powerful tool. With RTTI, objects become very friendly and readily tell you what they are, how they are used, and more. In Java, RTTI is built right into the core of the virtual machine. You've almost certainly used RTTI, even if you don't realize it; it's all over the place. For example, consider that every object in Java can tell you what type it is through the getClass( ) method. Whenever you invoke getClass( ), you use RTTI. Example 1-4 shows the getclass( ) method in action.

Example 1-4. Demonstration of basic RTTI usage

```
package oreilly.hcj.review;
public class RTTIDemo {
  public final static void basicRTTIDemo () {
    Float y = new Float(15.0);
    String name = "Fred";
    System.out.println(y.getClass());
    System.out.println(name.getClass());
  }
}
```

This method will, quite politely, print the following:

```
>ant -Dexample=oreilly.hcj.review.RTTIDemo run_example
run_example:
     [java] class java.lang.Float
     [java] class java.lang.String
```

Since the getClass( ) method is a method defined by the class java.lang.Object, it is guaranteed to be there for all objects.

Java also uses RTTI to protect a programmer from her own errors, as Example 1-5 demonstrates.

Example 1-5. RTTI enforces type safety

```
package oreilly.hcj.review;
public class RTTIDemo {
  public static class A {
  }
```

Example 1-5. RTTI enforces type safety (continued)

```
public static class B extends A {
}

public static class C {
}


public final static void castingWithRTTI () {
  A a = null;
  A a1 = new A();
  B b = new B();
  C c = new C();

  a = (A)b; // no problem
  b = (B)a; // still no problem, casting back to what it was created as.
  a = a1; // Same type so no problem
  Object d = (Object)c; // no problem because of implicit inheritance
  c = (C)d; // casting back
  b = (A)a1; // compiler error: a1 is not a B.
  b = (B)c; // compiler error: c is not a B.
  }
}
```

This code shows how to create an object of a subclass, cast it to its base class, and then cast it back to the subclass. RTTI works in the background to ensure that your casting is always legal; in other words, an object can safely be cast only to its own type, or to a type that it is inherited from. In the sample code for the book, Example 1-5 is replicated with the bad casts commented out. If you uncomment these lines, you will see that the program won't even compile, and you will get errors such as those shown here:

```
>ant -Dexample=oreilly/hcj/review/RTTIDemo.java compile_example
compile_example:
    [javac] Compiling 1 source file to C:\dev\hcj\bin
    [javac] C:\dev\hcj\src\oreilly\hcj\review\RTTIDemo.java:54: incompatible types
    [javac] found    : oreilly.hcj.review.RTTIDemo.A
    [javac] required: oreilly.hcj.review.RTTIDemo.B
    [javac]     b = (A)a1;  // compiler error: a1 is not a B.
    [javac]         ^
    [javac] C:\dev\hcj\src\oreilly\hcj\review\RTTIDemo.java:55: inconvertible types
    [javac] found    : oreilly.hcj.review.RTTIDemo.C
    [javac] required: oreilly.hcj.review.RTTIDemo.B
    [javac]     b = (B)c;  // compiler error: c is not a B.
    [javac]         ^
    [javac] 2 errors
```

RTTI is useful for preventing common errors in programming. It also has many other uses; we will get to the juicy details of exploiting RTTI in Chapters 7 and 8.

Syntax Issues

When compared to languages such as C++, Java has a very simple syntax. However, there are some points of syntax that should be covered, even for the intermediate and advanced Java programmer.

Abbreviated if

One of the things that is not well understood about the if statement is that it abbreviates evaluations in order from left to right. For example, consider the following code:

```
package oreilly.hcj.review;

public class SyntaxIssues {
  public static void containsNested(final List list,
                                    final Object target) {
    Iterator iter = list.iterator();
    for (Set inner = null; iter.hasNext(); inner = (Set)iter.next()) {
      if (inner != null) {
        if (inner.contains(target)) {
          // do code.
        }
      }
    }
  }
}
```

In this code, the method is passed a list of sets to determine whether the targeted element is in one of the nested sets. Since a list can contain nulls, the method wisely checks for null before dereferencing inner. As long as inner isn't null, the method checks to see whether the set contains target. This code works, but the deep nesting is not necessary. You can write the code in another way:

```
package oreilly.hcj.review;

public class SyntaxIssues {
  public static void containsNested2(final List list,
                                     final Object target) {
    Iterator iter = list.iterator();
    for (Set inner = null; iter.hasNext(); inner = (Set)iter.next()) {
      if ((inner != null) && (inner.contains(target))) {
        // do code.
      }
    }
  }
}
```

In this version, the method checks for null and containment on the same line. This version of the method is in no danger of throwing NullPointerExceptions because the evaluation of the if statement is abbreviated at runtime. While evaluating an if

---

statement, the evaluations are run from left to right. Once the evaluation reaches a definitive condition that cannot be altered by any other evaluation, the remaining evaluations are skipped.

Ternary Expressions

Ternary expressions look a little strange at first. However, they can be useful in making code read better. For example, consider the following code:

```
package oreilly.hcj.review;

public class SyntaxIssues {
  public int someMethod(final Point p) {
    if (p == null) {
      return 0;
    } else {
      return p.x + p.y;
    }

  }
}
```

Although this method runs properly, it is unnecessarily wordy. The same thing could have been accomplished using a much simpler ternary expression:

```
package oreilly.hcj.review;

public class SyntaxIssues {
  public int someElegantMethod(final Point p) {
    return p == null ? 0 : p.x + p.y;
  }
}
```

The emphasized line is not as cryptic as it may appear at first. It is merely a large evaluation expression. If the given clause evaluates as true, then the value of the entire statement is in the ? clause. However, if the condition evaluates as false, then the value of the entire statement is in the : clause. The result of the evaluation is returned by the return statement.

Ternary statements are very useful for performing evaluations such as this. However, you have to be aware of a few gotchas. For example, the following code will not work:

```
p == null ? System.out.println("p is null!") : return p.x + p.y;
return 0;
```

In this statement, the user wants to make an if-then clause that would print a message if the point passed to the method was null or return the value if the point was not null. Basically, he is going for a less wordy version of the following code:

```
package oreilly.hcj.review;

public class SyntaxIssues {
  public static int someMethod(final Point p) {
```

```
      if (p == null) {
        System.out.println("p is null!")
      } else {
        return p.x + p.y;
      }
    }
    return 0;
  }
```

The problem is that a ternary expression is *not* an if-then clause. It is an evaluation clause. Both of the clauses in the ternary expression must evaluate to something. The statement System.out.println("p is null!") evaluates to void because the return of the println( ) method is void. Additionally, the statement return p.x + p.y is pure syntactical nonsense because return is a keyword that doesn't evaluate to anything.

Although ternary expressions are useful for shortening what would be an otherwise long and drawn-out piece of code, they can be cryptic to read if they are abused. I recommend that you use ternary expressions only for very small evaluations. If your evaluation is complex, you are better off going with the if-then structure.

Leveraging for Loops

The for loop is one of the most elegant and underused looping structures in the Java language. Most developers use only the basic concept of a for loop to iterate through a predefined series of numbers:

```
for (int idx = 0; idx < args.length; idx++) {
  // ...do something.
}
```

To the average reader, this code should be completely boring. However, to many developers, this is the pinnacle of for loop usage. But there are many more things that you can do with a for loop to make your code more elegant while dealing with some annoying programming issues.

Although the techniques in this section are not necessarily required, they do make your code look a lot nicer. However, if there is one concept that you should take from this section, it's that for loops can do much more than simply cycle through numbers.

for loop fundamentals

One recurring problem when dealing with collections is the need to iterate through the collection and keep track of an index at the same time. For example, you may need to copy all of the x coordinates from a List of Point objects into an array of ints. The following code represents a first attempt at implementing this method:

```
package oreilly.hcj.review;

import java.awt.Point;
import java.util.Iterator;
```

```java
import java.util.LinkedList;
import java.util.List;

public class SyntaxIssues {
  public static int[] extractXCoords(final List points) {
    int[] results = new int[points.size()];
    Point element = null;
    int idx = 0;
    Iterator iter = points.iterator();
    while (iter.hasNext()) {
      element = (Point)iter.next();
      results[idx] = element.x;
      idx++;
    }
    return results;
  }
}
```

Although this piece of code will work, it isn't very elegant. The code would look much neater written in the following way:

```java
package oreilly.hcj.review;

public class SyntaxIssues {
  public static int[] extractXCoords2(final List points) {
    int[] results = new int[points.size()];
    Point element = null;
    Iterator iter = points.iterator();
    for (int idx = 0; iter.hasNext(); idx++) {
      element = (Point)iter.next();
      results[idx] = element.x;
    }
    return results;
  }
}
```

This second example is much more elegant than the first. However, the important thing to note about the rewritten method is that the exit clause to the for loop has nothing to do with idx.

You can use the for loop structure in this manner because each of the statements inside the for loop are completely independent of each other. This is a fact that seems to escape many Java developers. The point is that the for loop has the following grammar:

```java
for (Allocation Statement; Expression; Iteration Statement)
```

The allocation statement in the for loop is executed when the loop is set up. At each iteration of the loop, the expression in the middle is evaluated and, if the expression is true, the iteration statement is run. You can stick any statement or expression in the for loop regardless of whether they are using the same variables. For example, the following is perfectly legal:

```
package oreilly.hcj.review;

public class ForLoops {
  public static void forWeird() {
    boolean exit = false;
    int idx = 0;

    for (System.setProperty("user.sanity", "minimal"); exit == false;
         System.out.println(System.currentTimeMillis())) {
      // do some code.
      idx++;
      if (idx == 10) {
        exit = true;
      }
    }
  }
}
```

When the loop is initialized, the system property user.sanity will be set to minimal. At each iteration of the loop, the current time in milliseconds will be printed as long as exit is false. This is a great demonstration of what you can do with for loops.

Now that you know just what is possible with for loops, you can leverage them even further to do things that are a bit more mainstream.

Collection iteration with for

Iterating through collections offers you another chance to have a bit of fun with the for loop. Let's begin with typical code used to iterate through a collection of objects:

```
package oreilly.hcj.review;

public class ForLoops {
  public static void forLong() {
    Properties props = System.getProperties();
    Iterator iter = props.keySet()
                         .iterator();

    String key = null;
    while (iter.hasNext()) {
      key = (String)iter.next();
      System.out.println(key + "=" + System.getProperty(key));
    }
  }
}
```

This snippet will iterate through all of the system properties and dump them to System.out. It works fine but it is very wordy and can be slightly problematic. For example, try the following bug on for size:

```
package oreilly.hcj.review;

public class ForLoops {
    public static void propsDump(final Set customKeys) {
        Properties props = System.getProperties();
        Iterator iter = props.keySet()
                             .iterator();

        String key = null;
        System.out.println("All Properties:");
        while (iter.hasNext()) {
          key = (String)iter.next();
          System.out.println(key + "=" + System.getProperty(key));
        }

        System.out.println("Custom Properties:");
        iter = customKeys.iterator();
        while (iter.hasNext()) {
          System.out.println(key + "=" + System.getProperty(key));
        }
      }
    }
  }
```

If you didn't see the bug in this piece of code instantly, then you are in trouble. The problem is that this code generates a logic error. In the second iteration, key = (String)iter.next() wasn't called. However, since key is still in scope from the previous loop, the code compiles and runs. Trivial errors such as this can consume tons of hours in complex applications.

It would be great if you could scope the key variable and the iter variable to the for loop where they are used. You can do this and make your program more elegant with the following code:

```
package oreilly.hcj.review;

public class ForLoops {
    public static void forShort() {
      Properties props = System.getProperties();
      for (Iterator iter = props.keySet().iterator(); iter.hasNext();) {
        String key = (String)iter.next();
        System.out.println(key + "=" + System.getProperty(key));
      }
    }
  }
```

In this example, the ability of for was leveraged to isolate your iteration variable. In this example, key is defined only within the for loop, and any attempt to access it outside the for loop will generate a compiler error. Additionally, the iterator itself is scoped to the for loop, which guards against a user that forgets to set up his iterator. Finally, the increment portion of the for loop has no value at all, which is completely legal.

When looking at forShort( ), you may be inclined to object that key is being allocated in a loop and that loop allocation is bad. In fact, in this example, the compiler notices that as well and optimizes out the variable to be allocated once while keeping it scoped to the for loop.

Abrupt Flow Control

Two of the more poorly understood pieces of Java syntax are the break and continue keywords. Both are used to control flow within loops or other complex statements. They can be very useful in some situations, but you need to be aware of their limitations.

break

The break keyword is probably familiar to most Java programers who have a flair for using switch statements. An example of a common usage is shown here:

```
package oreilly.hcj.review;

public class SyntaxIssues {
    public static String decode(final int input) {
        String decoded = null;
        switch (input) {
          case 1:
             decoded = "Option 1";
             break;
          case 2:
          case 3:
             decoded = "Option 2";
             break;
          default:
             return "Option 3";
        }
        return decoded;
    }
}
```

The break keyword tells the virtual machine to exit the switch statement. In this switch statement, if the user inputs a 1, the result will be "Option 1". If the user inputs a 2 or a 3, the result will be "Option 2". Finally, if she inputs anything else, the result will be "Option 4". The break statement lets certain cases, such as 2, fall through, but breaks out when it is done with the relevant logic. Without the break, you would always get "Option 4" as the result of the method because all lines inside the switch statement would run.

The break statement is a great way to make decisions such as those in the previous example. However, every now and then you get silly people that do something like the following:

```
package oreilly.hcj.review;

public class SyntaxIssues {
    public static String decode(final int input) {
        String decoded = null;
        switch (input) {
          case 1:
            decoded = "Option 1";
            break;
          case 2:
          case 3:
            decoded = "Option 2";
            break;
          default:
            return "Option 3";
            break; // <= someone doesn't get it!
        }
        return decoded;
    }
}
```

In this code, the final break statement is completely unnecessary, and also unreachable. The code will exit the switch statement regardless of whether the break was there. If you find it hard to believe people actually write code like this, the templates to generate switch statements that come with Eclipse do exactly this. However, this is a rather minor, if somewhat silly, problem. Some problems with break are a lot more serious. Consider the following code:

```
package oreilly.hcj.review;

public class SyntaxIssues {
    public static void matrixMeth(final Point[][] values) {
        for (int x = 0; x < values[0].length; x++) {
          for (int y = 0; y < values.length; y++) {
            if ((values[x][y].x < 0)
                 || (values[x][y].y < 0)) {
              break; // exit to the System.err line.
            }
            // do something with the value
          }
        }
        System.err.println("Invalid Point in Matrix");
        // cleanup processing resources
    }
}
```

In this piece of code, the developer wants the nested for loops to exit if a bad Point is detected in the matrix. However, the break statement doesn't do this. It merely breaks out of its *current* loop. The outer loop still runs, and the method processes bad data with potentially disastrous results.

When you use break in your code, you should be aware of these limitations and plan accordingly. The break keyword can be extremely useful for quick and abrupt termination of complex loops but its limitations can bite you if you aren't careful.

continue

The continue keyword is similar to break in that it abruptly changes the flow control of a method. However, whereas break exits a loop completely, continue merely skips back to the loop clause itself:

```
package oreilly.hcj.review;

public class SyntaxIssues {
  public static void continueFunc( ) {
    for (int idx = 0; idx < 1000; idx++) {
      // ...do some complex code.
      if (idx == 555) {
        break;
      }

      // ...processing code
    }

    for (int idx = 0; idx < 1000; idx++) {
      // ...do some complex code.
      if (idx == 555) {
        continue;
      }

      // ...processing code.
    }
  }
}
```

In the first loop, the processing code is executed only 554 times. When the value of idx is 555, the break statement is hit and the loop exits. However, in the second loop the processing code is executed 999 times. In this case, when idx is 555, the continue statement is hit, and the remainder of the logic inside the for loop is skipped. Subsequently, the loop then continues on normally with 556; therefore, the processing code is skipped only for element 555.

Although this example is trivial, the use of the continue statement can be a significant asset to your development when the code inside the loop is very complex. With many such possible "skip" conditions, your code can become deeply nested. The continue statement simplifies things dramatically. Without the continue statement, you would have to enclose the entire remainder of the for loop inside an if statement.

 The continue statement has the same semantics as the break statement in that it applies only to the loop in which the continue is enclosed.

Labels

Labels are one of those obscure pieces of Java syntax that you see only once in a blue moon. They are a way to mark a statement with an identifier to be used by a break or continue statement.

The following code declares labels on two different lines in a program:

```
LOGLINE: System.err.println("Invalid Point in Matrix");
LINE: for (int x = 0; x < values[0].length; x++) { ... }
```

The label is declared by simply prefacing the line with a legal variable name and then a colon. As usual with Java, any leading whitespace on the line will be ignored. However, keep in mind that you cannot declare a label unless it is the first statement on a line. The compiler would spit out all sorts of parsing errors if you tried something like the following:

```
System.err.println("Invalid Point in Matrix");   LOGLINE2:
```

Once you have declared the label, you can use it in a break or a continue statement. The following code shows how you can use break to repair a faulty matrix:

```
package oreilly.hcj.review;

public class SyntaxIssues {
  public static void matrixMeth2(final Point[][] values) {
    RESTART: {
      for (int x = 0; x < values[0].length; x++) {
        for (int y = 0; y < values.length; y++) {
          if ((values[x][y].x < 0) || (values[x][y].y < 0)) {
            values[x][y].x = Math.max(values[x][y].x, 0);
            values[x][y].y = Math.max(values[x][y].y, 0);
            break RESTART;   // Try to process again!
          }

          // do something with the value
        }
      }
    }
    // continue processing
  }
}
```

In this version, if an error condition is detected, the method will try to repair the error condition and then start to process the matrix all over again. This is accomplished by the break RESTART; statement. This statement tells the virtual machine to immediately transfer control to the statement labeled RESTART. This will work only if the break statement is nested inside the labeled statement. Otherwise, the compiler will just laugh at you sardonically and tell you that the label RESTART isn't declared.

Using labels with continue is slightly different. continue must be nested within the code block of any label to which it refers. Additionally, a continue can transfer control only to a label set on a looping construct such as a for, while, or do statement. For clarification on this rule, look at the following code:

```java
package oreilly.hcj.review;

public class SyntaxIssues {
  public static void matrixMeth3(final Point[][] values) {
    LINE: {
      for (int x = 0; x < values[0].length; x++) {
        COLUMN: for (int y = 0; y < values.length; y++) {
          if ((values[x][y].x < 0) || (values[x][y].y < 0)) {
            continue LINE;  // skip the rest of the line;
          }

          // do something with the value
        }
      }
    }
    LOGLINE: System.err.println("Invalid Point in Matrix");

    // continue processing

    PASS_TWO: for (int x = 0; x < values[0].length; x++) {
      // do some code.
    }
  }
}
```

In this example, instead of exiting to the log line, the programmer wants to simply skip the rest of the problematic line in the matrix. Using a continue statement without a label would have merely transferred control to the inner for loop. However, by telling the continue statement to continue at the LINE label, you can exit the inner for loop and skip the rest of the line properly. However, you could not use LOGLINE as a continue target because the statement after the label isn't a loop construct, such as a for, while, or do statement. You also couldn't use PASS_TWO as a target for the continue statement because although the label marks a looping statement, the continue statement is not nested in that looping statement. Furthermore, it would be impossible to break or continue to a label outside of the method.

Although labels can be useful in controlling the flow in a program, they can lead to a lot of confusion in development due to their idiosyncrasies. I recommend that you not use them as a rule; however, you should now be able to unwind the spaghetti code of another developer that did use them.

assert

The assert keyword is a new addition to Java that was introduced in JDK 1.4. It was a long overdue addition to the language, as it provides for error checking that C++ and other languages already have. However, since its introduction, I haven't seen it used nearly as much as it should be. The reason for this is a basic lack of understanding as to how assert works. The assert keyword has two forms. The first form of assertion uses the following grammar:

```
assert Boolean_Expression;
```

In this form, Expression is replaced by an expression that evaluates to a boolean result. If the result is false, then an AssertionError will be thrown by the compiler:

```
package oreilly.hcj.review;

public class Assertions {
  protected static void helperParseArgs (final String[] args) {
    assert (args != null);
    // ...code
  }
}
```

In this example, the programmer wants to make sure that the user of the helperParseArgs() method didn't send a null for the arguments parameter. To accomplish this, he uses the assert keyword. If the user passes a null, then the virtual machine will throw an AssertionError with no description, but with a stack trace to help the errant user figure out what he did wrong. If the developer of the method wants to provide an error message, he could have used the second form of assert:

```
package oreilly.hcj.review;

public class Assertions {
  protected static void helperParseArgs (final String[] args) {
    assert (args != null) : "args cannot be null.";
    // ...code
  }
}
```

In this case, if the assertion is thrown, the second expression is evaluated and the result of that evaluation is used for the detail message of the AssertionError. Keep in mind that you can use any expression that evaluates to anything other than void as the second expression. For example, the following would be illegal:

```
package oreilly.hcj.review;

public class Assertions {
  protected static void helperParseArgs (final String[] args) {
    assert (args != null) : String s = "args cannot be null.";
    // ...code
  }
}
```

An attempt to do something like this would be rejected by the compiler since the evaluation of the expression is void. Similarly, any method that returns void is off limits as well.

Assertions versus exceptions

One of the most common questions asked about assertions is why you should bother using them when you can perform these checks and indicate errors with exceptions.

First of all, the code doing the check may be far more complicated than a simple check for null. In fact, the body of assertion expressions can easily be as much work for the processor as the body of the method itself. If you use exceptions, then these checks will be performed every time the method is called. In a production system, this can add significant overhead.

On the other hand, with assertions, the virtual machine can be set to ignore the assertions. As a result, their processing time is near zero. In development mode, during testing, or during diagnosis of some nasty problem, you can turn on assertions and figure out the problems. Once the software is stable, you can turn off assertions and gain a performance boost. As a bonus, assertions offer a shorthand that makes your code look more elegant.

 Assertions are off by default and have to be turned on manually.

To assert or not to assert

Deciding whether to use assertions or exceptions is a decision that you have to take on a case-by-case basis. Here are some tips that will help you make the right decisions:

- Don't use assertions to validate parameters of public functions. These functions should throw NullPointerException, IllegalArgumentException, and other relevant exceptions instead. Since public functions will be used by other programmers, you should make sure that they get the right errors if they mess up.
- Use assertions to check preconditions and postconditions on parameters of protected and private access methods.
- Don't use assertions to check for software user errors. If you expect the user of your web-based online sales system to enter a 10-digit credit card number and she enters only 9 digits, don't use an assert. Instead, throw IllegalArgumentException. If you use assert, as soon as someone turns off assertions on your servlet container, the checking logic in your system would go away.

- Use assertions to check parameters and variables for conditions that shouldn't happen. For example, consider the following event handler method:

```
package oreilly.hcj.review;

public class Assertions {
  public void mouseClicked(final MouseEvent event) {
    Object source = event.getSource();
    assert(source != null);

    int hc = source.hashCode();
    // ...do code using source
  }
}
```

The virtual machine should never pass null as a source for a mouse event. However, just to be sure, the user asserts it. The granularity of assertions that you should use here is something of a judgment call. If you assert everything, you will have to write a lot more code; however, your code will be rock solid.

- Use assertions to check for invalid code branches. For example, consider the following GUI class:

```
package oreilly.hcj.review;

public class Assertions {
package oreilly.hcj.review;

import java.awt.event.ActionEvent;
import javax.swing.JButton;

public class SomeGuiPanel {

  private JButton cancelBtn;
  private JButton noBtn;
  private JButton yesBtn;

  public void actionPerformed(final ActionEvent event) {
    Object source = event.getSource();
    assert (source != null);

    if (source == yesBtn) {
      // ...do code
    } else if (source == noBtn) {
      // ...do code
    } else if (source == cancelBtn) {
      // ...do code
    } else {
      assert false : "Invalid Source " + source.toString();
    }
  }
}
```

In this class, the action handler expects the user to click on one of three buttons. The method doesn't expect there to be any other buttons to which the class is listening. However, if a developer added a new button but forgot to change the handler, there would be an extra button to deal with. On the final else clause, the method checks to make sure there aren't any other buttons by using assert. If the emphasized line is hit, the program will generate an assertion exception. In this case, using assert is much more elegant than using throw.

 Some may object that the program should always throw an irrecoverable error at this point regardless of whether assertions are enabled. This is a valid point. However, in a production environment, that is not always a good idea. The accountants using your software wouldn't know what an AssertionError is. Instead, when the program crashes, they are likely to give you an informative bug report such as, "It crashed while I was making my finance report." Its better to use assertions so the program can at least limp along if something weird happens. Let the developers and QA people deal with the assertion errors.

- Don't use an assertion to do any work. Assertions are developer-level errors and shouldn't be used to repair state in the program or perform complex logging. Also, don't forget that if a user runs the program without assertions, the code will be gone. If that code was critical to the functioning of the program, you could be in deep trouble.

- Don't bother internationalizing assertion error messages. Again, since assertions are developer-level issues, internationalizing them would be a waste of time.

- Use assertions to check post conditions. If you create a method and expect that it will never to return null to the user, you might write something like the following:

```
package oreilly.hcj.review;

public class SyntaxIssues {
  protected Object someHelperMethod() {
    Object result = null;
    //  ...do some code that sets result.
    assert (result != null); // check post condition.
    return result;
  }
}
```

In this code, the method checks the return value against a post-condition before returning the value. If the value is still null after all of the work, the assertion will toss an error.

Now that you have a good idea of when to use assert and when not to, apply what you have learned on an actual class:

```
package oreilly.hcj.review;

import java.awt.event.MouseEvent;
import java.util.Arrays;
```

```java
import java.util.Iterator;
import java.util.List;

public class Assertions {

    public static void main(final String[] args) {
        helperParseArgs(args);
        Iterator iter = System.getProperties()
                              .keySet()
                              .iterator();
        for (String key = null; iter.hasNext(); key = (String)iter.next()) {
            assert (key != null);
            System.out.println(key + "=" + System.getProperty(key));
        }
    }

    protected static void helperParseArgs(final String[] args) {
        assert (args != null);
        assert (!Arrays.asList(args)
                       .contains(null));
        // --
        List arglist = Arrays.asList(args);
        Iterator iter = arglist.iterator();
        for (String argument = null;
                iter.hasNext();
                argument = (String)iter.next()) {
            if (argument.startsWith("-D")) {
                if (argument.length() < 3) {
                    int idx = arglist.indexOf(argument);
                    throw new IllegalArgumentException("Argument" + idx
                                    + " is not a legal property argument.");
                }
                int valueIdx = argument.indexOf('=');
                System.setProperty(argument.substring(2, valueIdx),
                                    argument.substring(valueIdx + 1));
                assert (System.getProperty(
                        argument.substring(2, valueIdx))
                            .equals(argument.substring(valueIdx + 1)));
            }
        }
    }
}
```

In this code, you have a method that parses the arguments to the program and looks for system properties to set. If it encounters an argument such as -Dmy.property=5 on the command line, it will set the system property my.property to the value 5.

The method that does the actual work is a protected helper method that checks the arguments to the method for validity using assertions. You should also note that the second check to the method takes quite a bit of work to accomplish since the list has to go through and see whether there are any nulls in the argument list. At production time, however, this work will be removed by turning off assertions. Inside the for loop, the method doesn't use an assertion if the user gives a bad property name because this is an error made by the user of the program and not by the developers of the program.

Finally, the last assert statement checks that the system property was actually set properly. Notice that this assert does the exact same string manipulation work as the original setting of the system property. Some performance-minded developers may catch on to this fact and get the bright idea to store the key and value at each iteration of the loop, as shown here:

```
package oreilly.hcj.review;

public class Assertions {

for (String argument = null; iter.hasNext(); argument = (String)iter.next()) {
  if (argument.startsWith("-D")) {
    if (argument.length() < 3) {
      int idx = arglist.indexOf(argument);
      throw new IllegalArgumentException("Argument" + idx
                          + " is not a legal property argument.");
    }
    int valueIdx = argument.indexOf('=');
    String key = argument.substring(2, valueIdx);
    String value = argument.substring(valueIdx + 1);
    System.setProperty(key, value);
    assert (System.getProperty(key).equals(value));
  }
}
```

Although this will work, it is a bit wasteful. The extra allocations of the key and value variables are needed only if assertions are enabled. If assertions are disabled, then these variables will be used only once. Whether to use variables to store parts of an assertion is a judgment call. If the code that is creating the variable is very long, a variable may be the best bet. If the code is simple, you should just save yourself the extra allocations at production time.

Assertions and deployment

If you are developing an application using assertions, you should be aware that by default, assertions are not enabled in the virtual machine. To enable all assertions, you need to pass the argument -ea to your virtual machine. If you need to enable assertions on system classes, use the switch -esa. Additionally, there are facilities for enabling assertions on individual packages. You should consult your virtual machine documentation for information on how to do this.

When developing a product, you should always have assertions enabled, as they will help you catch bugs. Also, your QA testers *should* run a program with assertions enabled since it is their job to figure out how to break your code.

In a production release, the situation is a bit foggier. In the first days of a production product release, you may want to make sure the project runs with assertions enabled. Although you will loose some performance and incur a few crashes, you will be able to detect many errors caught by your assertions. When to turn off the assertions in a production environment is a judgment call that the project manager has to make. There will come a time when you think you have used the assertions enough to catch most of the errors, and performance and stability become the overriding need; after all, assertions *do* crash your program. At that point, it is time to update your shortcuts and batch files to turn off assertions. When releasing new features, you should employ a similar operating strategy. This will help you catch unexpected bugs.

Unfortunately, there is no way to turn assertions on and off in a running system; however, you can easily find out whether they are on by using the little assertion trick shown here:

```
boolean ASSERTIONS = false;
assert ASSERTIONS = true;
```

The assert expression here evaluates to true and will not throw an assertion error at any time. If assertions are enabled, then the code will run and `ASSERTIONS` will be set to true. If assertions are disabled, then the code won't be executed and `ASSERTIONS` will remain `false`.

Chaining Constructors

One of my personal pet-peeves is duplicated code. Unfortunately, you see a lot of it, especially in the creation of GUI widgets. The problem results from the way these widgets are built. Consider the button class shown in Example 1-6.

Example 1-6. Unchained constructors

```
package oreilly.hcj.review;
public class UnchainedConstructors extends JButton
  implements ActionListener {

  public UnchainedConstructors(final String text) {
    setText(text);
    String tooltip = new String("A button to show " + text);
    setToolTipText(tooltip);
  }

  public UnchainedConstructors(final String text, final String tooltip) {
    setText(text);
    setToolTipText(tooltip);
  }

  public UnchainedConstructors(final String text, final String tooltip,
                               final ActionListener listener) {
```

Example 1-6. Unchained constructors (continued)

```
    setText(text);
    setToolTipText(tooltip);
    addActionListener(listener);
  }
}
```

Although this code will work, it is wasteful and prone to errors. For example, if you change a line in the constructor that accepts three parameters and forget to make the same change in the other constructors, you would have a button that builds correctly under some circumstances, but fails to build correctly under others. This would lead to a debugging session that wouldn't be much fun. The symptom of the problem is in the thought, "If I change this in one constructor, I have to remember to change it in the others." Whenever you hear yourself thinking similar thoughts, you should realize that something is wrong. All of your code dependencies should be in the code, and not in your head. Inevitably, you will forget some of these dependencies during your project. Also, even if you have a photographic memory and perfect recall, the junior programmer working for you won't be privy to these details and could unintentionally bust the code you had so well thought out. To avoid having to remember these things, you can rewrite the class as shown in Example 1-7.

Example 1-7. Simple chained constructors

```
package oreilly.hcj.review;
public class ChainedConstructors extends JButton
  implements ActionListener {

  public ChainedConstructors(final String text) {
    this(text, new String("A button to show " + text), null);
  }

  public ChainedConstructors(final String text, final String tooltip) {
    this(text, tooltip, null);
  }

  public ChainedConstructors(final String text, final String tooltip,
                             final ActionListener listener) {
    setText(text);
    setToolTipText(tooltip);
    if (listener != null) {
      addActionListener(listener);
    }
  }
}
```

This code is much better; it chains the constructors so that each delegates to the constructor that takes all parameters. This constructor is referred to as the *primary constructor*. By using this technique, the code for the other constructors is limited only to what they do differently. This technique relieves you of having to remember to change each constructor if the common code is modified. You chain the constructors via the this( ) method. This special method allows you to call one constructor from another. It is analogous to using the super( ) method to construct base classes. The only remaining problem is that you have some rather ugly code as a result of chaining your constructors:

```
this(text, new String("A button to show " + text), null);
```

This code results from the fact that, just like super( ), you have to use the this( ) method as the first line in the constructor. I have yet to understand why this limitation is in Java, but it does indeed exist. As a result, some rather annoying problems are introduced. In this case, you were merely building a String object in the call to this( ). However, there are other cases where you will need to do a lot more work before calling the primary constructor. The secret to doing this without the ugliness is via helper methods:

```
package oreilly.hcj.review;
public class ChainedConstructors extends JButton
    implements ActionListener {

  public ChainedConstructors(final String text, final boolean showDate) {
    this(text, buildDateToolTip(text, showDate), null);
  }

  private static String buildDateToolTip(final String text,
                                         final boolean showDate) {
    final StringBuffer buf = new StringBuffer(250);
    buf.append("A panel to show ");
    buf.append(text);
    if (showDate) {
      buf.append(" created on ");
      DateFormat df = DateFormat.getInstance();
      buf.append(df.format(Calendar.getInstance().getTime()));
    }
    return buf.toString();
  }
}
```

Here, you create a new static method that manipulates the input to the constructor and returns the tool tip text. Then you use the resulting text as the input to the tooltip parameter of the primary constructor. This constructor helper technique makes your code much cleaner and allows you to chain constructors even when there is complex logic within the constructors. The resulting code is much more stable and easier to maintain.

When using helper methods, it is important that you keep in mind one restriction: the this pointer is not available to the virtual machine at the time of a this( ) or super( ) call. The result of this restriction is that you can't use any instance-scoped methods on the object being constructed. For example, the following code would be illegal:

```
public class ChainedConstructors extends JButton
    implements ActionListener {
```

```
public ChainedConstructors(final Class dataType) {
  this(buildClassText(dataType), dataType.getName( ), this);
}

protected String buildClassText(final Class dataType) {
  return dataType.getName().substring(dataType.getName( )
                       .lastIndexOf('.') + 1);
  }
}
```

In Java, a call such as buildClassText( ) is identical to the call this.buildClassText( ). The this reference is assumed unless you explicitly add some other kind of reference, such as an object or a class. In this case, the this pointer is not available yet, so you can't call instance-scoped methods on this object. In fact, even though the class ChainedConstructors implements ActionListener, you can't even use the this pointer to pass the object as a listener to itself. If you uncomment the above constructor in the code and try to compile it, you will get the following results:

```
>ant -Dexample=oreilly/hcj/review/ChainedConstructors.java compile_example
compile_example:
    [javac] Compiling 1 source file to C:\dev\hcj\bin
    [javac] C:\dev\hcj\src\oreilly\hcj\review\ChainedConstructors.java:43: cannot
reference this before supertype constructor has been called
    [javac]     this(buildClassText(dataType), dataType.getName( ), this);
    [javac]         ^
    [javac] C:\dev\hcj\src\oreilly\hcj\review\ChainedConstructors.java:43: cannot
reference this before supertype constructor has been called
    [javac]     this(buildClassText(dataType), dataType.getName( ), this);
    [javac]                                                         ^
    [javac] 2 errors
```

In short, the this pointer is off-limits to all constructor helper methods. Therefore, if you want to declare a helper method, you must make sure that the method is declared static. Since a static method doesn't have a this pointer and doesn't need one, the call will work properly. However, keep in mind that instance methods on objects already in scope are completely permissible, as shown here:

```
public ChainedConstructors(final Color color) {
  this(color.toString( ), "", null);
}
```

In this example, the instance method toString( ) on the color parameter passed to you is legal because it is already in scope.

While using chained constructors, you will come across situations in which you do not want to expose the primary constructor to the user of the class. The solution to this problem is to merely make the visibility of the primary constructor protected. That way, you get the best of both worlds. The constructors will be chained, and you won't reveal any more about the class than you want to. Although it is unusual to see a class with constructors that have various visibilities, it is quite legal.

Initialization

Initialization is the process of assigning values to variables prior to the execution of the constructor for a class. Initialization is used in many places, and is often poorly understood by developers. Many developers think of initialization as one topic, when, in fact, there are six types of initialization that you can use in your code. The simplest type of initialization is shown here:

```
package oreilly.hcj.review;
public class InitalizerDemo {
  public String description = "An initialized member";
}
```

The variable `description` in this class is assigned the value of `"An initialized member"` just prior to construction of each instance of the object. Therefore, even if the constructor does not explicitly set `description`, it will be guaranteed to contain the value set in the initializer.

This type of initialization is important for solidifying code because it allows you to pre-set instance attributes to default values before the constructor is called. In this manner, constructors can ignore these attributes if they wish. Although this type of initialization is useful, there are times when initializations need to be a bit more complex:

```
package oreilly.hcj.review;
public class InitalizerDemo {
  public long timestamp = System.currentTimeMillis();
}
```

In this initializer, you can call a method on the line of the initialization. This ability allows you to perform more complex initializations that would be impossible without a method. However, keep in mind that methods used in initializers are under the same restrictions as the helper methods for chained constructors that we discussed earlier—they should be `static` and can't use the `this` pointer.

In fact, you don't even need to define a helper method if you don't want to; an initializer can be a method itself:

```
package oreilly.hcj.review;
public class InitalizerDemo {

  private String xmlClasspath;
  {
    final StringBuffer buf = new StringBuffer(500);
    final String classPath = System.getProperty("java.class.path");
    StringTokenizer tok = new StringTokenizer(classPath,
                                  System.getProperty("path.separator"));
    buf.append("<classpath>\n");
    while (tok.hasMoreTokens()) {
      buf.append("  <pathelement location=\"");
      buf.append(tok.nextToken());
      buf.append("\"/>\n");
    }
```

```
    buf.append("</classpath>");
    xmlClasspath = buf.toString();
  }
}
```

In this code, you translate the classpath into an XML structure upon initialization of the object. This code will work fine, as you can see by running the oreilly.hcj. review.InitializerDemo class in the example code:

```
>ant -Dexample=oreilly.hcj.review.InitializerDemo run_example
run_example:
     [java] ------Dumping Contents-----------
     [java] --------------------------------
     [java] Initializer Demo
     [java] x86
     [java] C:\Documents and Settings\Robert
     [java] An initialized member
     [java] <classpath>
     [java]    <pathelement location="c:\j2sdk\\lib\tools.jar"/>
     [java]    <pathelement location="C:\j2sdk\addons\jakarta-ant-1.5\bin\\..\lib\xml-
apis.jar"/>
     [java]    <pathelement location="C:\j2sdk\addons\jakarta-ant-1.5\bin\\..\lib\
xercesImpl.jar"/>
     [java]    <pathelement location="C:\j2sdk\addons\jakarta-ant-1.5\bin\\..\lib\
optional.jar"/>
     [java]    <pathelement location="C:\j2sdk\addons\jakarta-ant-1.5\bin\\..\lib\ant.
jar"/>
     [java] </classpath>
     [java] --------------------------------
```

Although this initialization technique is useful, you shouldn't use it routinely. Instead, it should be saved for special circumstances, as it makes code a little cryptic to read. Use it only when you really need a special multiline initialization.

Instance attributes aren't the only kind of attributes in a class. Attributes declared with the static keyword are class-scoped. Class-scoped attributes can be initialized in a manner similar to instance-scoped attributes. Here is a simple case:

```
package oreilly.hcj.review;
public class InitalizerDemo {
  public static final String NAME = "Initializer Demo";
}
```

This code works exactly like the instance initializer, except that it is called when the class is loaded into the virtual machine by the ClassLoader. Another difference is that this attribute is final, so it cannot be changed after it is initialized.

Although I show final class-scoped attributes in the examples, keep in mind that the behavior of class-scoped attributes that are not final is identical to that of final class-scoped attributes.

Like instance initializers, you can call methods in static variable initialization:

```
package oreilly.hcj.review;
public class InitalizerDemo {
  public static final String ARCH = System.getProperty("os.arch");
}
```

You can also defer an initialization of a static variable to do something more complex:

```
package oreilly.hcj.review;
public class InitalizerDemo {
  public static final String USER_HOME;
}
```

In this code, you have created a constant without giving the constant a value. Perhaps the value you want requires more complex code than a simple assignment. This is where the special static{} method comes in. The ClassLoader automatically invokes all static{} initializer methods when the class is loaded into the virtual machine. It is in this method only that you can initialize final static variables that are not initialized on their declaration line. You can use this method in a similar manner as the method-based instance initializers:

```
package oreilly.hcj.review;
public class InitalizerDemo {
  public static final String USER_HOME;

  static {
    USER_HOME = System.getProperty("user.home");
  }
}
```

The variable USER_HOME will be filled with the string version of the user's home directory from the system properties. The value will then be final for the duration of the life of the virtual machine.

While using the static{} method, it is important to keep order in mind. Since static initializers are called in order of their declaration, you can get into a bit of trouble if you aren't careful:

```
public static class Values {
  public final static String VALUE_ONE = "Blue";

  static {
    System.out.println("static{} method for One");
    System.out.println(VALUE_ONE);
    System.out.println(VALUE_TWO);  // <= compiler error
  }

  public final static String VALUE_TWO = "Red";
}
```

In this code, the compiler cannot find VALUE_TWO because it has not been declared at the time when the static{} method was run. Since initializers are processed in order, you get a bug called an *illegal forward reference*. Get rid of the bug with a coding standard that declares all static variables first, and then declares static methods. This will keep you out of trouble with your compiler (although not necessarily with your programming logic).

While order is important, be aware that you cannot *depend* on the order of static initialization. Any methods that depend on ordering are likely to end up with some strange results. To make things a bit clearer, let's intentionally build an example of this problem. Example 1-8 shows the constructed bug.

Example 1-8. Erroneous dependence on static initializer order

```
package oreilly.hcj.review;
public class StaticOrderDemo {

  public StaticOrderDemo( ) {
  }

  public static final void main(final String[] args) {
  }

  public static class Ranges {
    public static final String[] RANGE_BLUE = { "Sky", "Navy" };

    public static final String[] RANGE_RED = { "Light", "Dark" };

    static {
      System.out.println("static{} method for Ranges");
      System.out.println(Arrays.asList(RANGE_BLUE));
      System.out.println(Values.VALUE_SPECIFIER);
      System.out.println(Arrays.asList(RANGE_RED));
    }
  }

  public static class Values {
    public static final String VALUE = "Blue";

    public static final String VALUE_SPECIFIER;

    static {
      System.out.println("static{} method for Values");
      System.out.println(VALUE);
      System.out.println(Ranges.RANGE_BLUE);
      VALUE_SPECIFIER = Ranges.RANGE_BLUE[1];
    }
  }
}
```

When the example is run, the static nested class Ranges is initialized first. As a result, you will see the following output:

```
>ant -Dexample=oreilly.hcj.review.StaticOrderDemo run_example
run_example:
```

```
[java] static{} method for Values
[java] Blue
[java] static{} method for Ranges
[java] [Sky, Navy]
[java] null
[java] [Light, Dark]
[java] [Ljava.lang.String;@1e3118a
[java] Class oreilly.hcj.review.StaticOrderDemo$Values Loaded
```

Note especially the null. Since Values.VALUE_SPECIFIER had not been initialized when it was used in the Ranges initializer, its value was null at the time of the System.out.println( ). Only microseconds later, when Values finishes initializing, it is no longer null. This kind of bug is very difficult to find because of its very transient life. The moral of this story is that you can never depend on the initialization order of static members.

 Although this example was specifically constructed for this book, I actually encountered this bug in production code several times. The first time resulted in an overnight programming frenzy to try to find and correct the bug.

To summarize, there are many kinds of initializers, which are all useful for setting values prior to object construction, but beware of the little gotchas with static initializers. In Example 1-9, all of the possible initializers are shown in one class.

Example 1-9. All the various initializers together

```java
package oreilly.hcj.review;
public class InitalizerDemo {
  /** Simple static initialization. */
  public static final String NAME = "Initializer Demo";

  /** Initialized static on one line. */
  public static final String ARCH = System.getProperty("os.arch");

  /** Static method based initialization. */
  public static final String USER_HOME;

  static {
    USER_HOME = System.getProperty("user.home");
  }

  /** Simple instance member initialization. */
  public String description = "An initialized member";

  /** Method call instance member initialization. */
  public long timestamp = System.currentTimeMillis();

  /** Complex instance member initialization. */
  private String xmlClasspath;
  {
```

Example 1-9. All the various initializers together (continued)

```
    final StringBuffer buf = new StringBuffer(500);
    final String classPath = System.getProperty("java.class.path");
    StringTokenizer tok =
      new StringTokenizer(classPath,
                            System.getProperty("path.separator"));
    buf.append("<classpath>\n");
    while (tok.hasMoreTokens()) {
      buf.append("  <pathelement location=\"");
      buf.append(tok.nextToken());
      buf.append("\"/>\n");
    }
    buf.append("</classpath>\n");
    xmlClasspath = buf.toString();
  }
}
```

One final thing to remember about all initializers is that you cannot throw any exceptions other than subclasses of RuntimeException within the initializer. All other exceptions will cause all sorts of compilation errors. Therefore, if you want to use methods that throw other types of exceptions, you will have to wrap up any possible exceptions in a try and catch block and then throw a RuntimeException; of course, you're caught up on chained exceptions by now, so this is no problem. With this arsenal of initializers at your command, you should be ready to tackle setting defaults for any type of class you can think of.

Access Issues

When you look through the many Java books that are available, they all talk about access restrictions. The words private, protected, and public are some of the first keywords that a newbie Java programmer learns. However, most of these books discuss access restrictions only with regards to the impact of restrictions on the code.

By now, you should know what a private method is and the difference between private and protected. Therefore, I won't bother rehashing this familiar territory. Instead, I would like to take your understanding of access restrictions to another level. Instead of focusing on what they do, I will focus on which to use in various situations.

Preferred Restrictions

While writing Java programs, many programmers fall into a definable pattern. All attributes are private, all interface methods are public, and all helper methods are private. Unfortunately, this causes a ton of problems in the real world. Consider the following common GUI code:

```java
package oreilly.hcj.review;

import java.awt.event.ActionEvent;
import java.awt.event.ActionListener;
import javax.swing.*;

public class SomeDialogApp extends JDialog implements ActionListener {

  private JButton okBtn = null;
  private JButton someBtn = null;

  // ...etc.

  public SomeDialogApp() {
    setJMenuBar(buildMenu());
    buildContents();
  }

  public void actionPerformed(final ActionEvent event) {
    Object source = event.getSource();
    if (source == this.okBtn) {
      handleOKBtn();
    } else if (source == this.someBtn) {
      handleSomeBtn();
    }

    // ...etc.
  }

  private void buildContents() {
    this.okBtn = new JButton("OK");
    this.okBtn.addActionListener(this);
    this.someBtn = new JButton("Something");
    this.someBtn.addActionListener(this);
    // ...etc.
  }

  private JMenuBar buildMenu() {
    JMenuBar result = new JMenuBar();

    // ...add items and menus
    return result;
  }

  private void handleOKBtn() {
    // handler code
  }

  private void handleSomeBtn() {
    // handler code
  }
}
```

In this code, the attributes are all private. There are also four private helper methods: handleSomeBtn( ), handleOKBtn( ), buildContents( ), and buildMenu( ). Everything in this class is okay until someone wants to modify the class. For example, what if I only want to change the functionality of the handleOKbtn( ) method and reuse the rest of the class? In this case, I would basically have to reimplement the entire dialog. Accessing the button instance itself is impossible, so I wouldn't be able to rebuild the actionPerfomed( ) method. Furthermore, since the helper method is private, I can't access that either. Time to reinvent the wheel.

On the other hand, if all those helper methods were protected instead of private, I would be able to simply redefine the meaning of the handleOKbtn( ) helper method and reuse the entire class.

When developing classes that others will use, you can never be sure what they will want to do to the class. But if your goal is to promote reuse, making the helper methods protected allows the users to extend the class. Also, since protected blocks users attempting to use the method directly, you won't be giving up any security on that front. On the other hand, those inheriting from your class will have access to these helper methods. However, the general assumption you should be making is that people extending the class generally know what they are doing. Even if they don't, the worst they can do is break their derived class.

I came hard up against this problem recently when trying to extend the Introspector class to perform some functionality. I merely wanted to redefine one method. However, because that method was private, and Introspector is implicitly final (which we will discuss in the next chapter), I couldn't do it.

In the end, you are better off using private for attributes—public for public methods, and protected for helper methods. This gives your class maximum reusability without breaking encapsulation.

Friends Allow Unrestricted Access

Most access permissions are clearly laid out in the class file. However, many Java programmers don't understand the access permissions as they are related to instances of the same class. I call these instances *friend instances*.

In real life, friends don't allow unrestricted access. You can rarely borrow a friend's car without asking. Java is much more friendly and trusting. In Java, instances of the same class are friends and give unrestricted access to all of their properties and methods. This unlimited access is a serious hazard that must be carefully avoided while making solid code. The class in Example 1-10 shows how friend instance access works.

Example 1-10. Demonstration of friend instance access

```
package oreilly.hcj.review;
public class FriendAccess {
  private int value;

  public FriendAccess(final int value) {
    setValue(value);
  }

  public void setValue(final int value) {
    this.value = value;
  }

  public int getValue( ) {
    return value;
  }

  public void someMethod(final FriendAccess obj) {
    if ((obj.value == 5) && (this.value == 5)) {
      obj.value = 25;  // <= Ouch, this works and bypasses the setter.
    }
  }
}
```

In someMethod, different instances of the same class have complete access to each other. This can become a problem when you modify the class a little bit. Hack on the class until you end up with this variation, which demonstrates the dangers of friend access:

```
package oreilly.hcj.review;
public class FriendAccess {
  private int value;

  public FriendAccess(final int value) {
    setValue(value);
  }

  public void setValue(final int value) {
    if (value > 10) {
      throw new IllegalArgumentException( );
    }
    this.value = value;
  }

  public int getValue( ) {
    return value;
  }

  public void someMethod(final FriendAccess obj) {
    if ((obj.value == 5) && (this.value == 5)) {
      obj.value = 25;
    }
  }
}
```

In this variation, the range-checking code that is emphasized in the setValue( ) method was added. Now, if you look back at someMethod( ), you see that the method body sets the property value of the instance passed and completely bypasses the setter. The problem is that you set value to something that the setter would have rejected as illegal. However, since you have access to the variables directly, you can make the change and get away with it. Later, when some other class uses the object, expecting its value to be less than or equal to 10, your code will explode. Fortunately, you can easily block this with another edit to the code:

```
package oreilly.hcj.review;
public class FriendAccess {
  private int value;

  public FriendAccess(final int value) {
    setValue(value);
  }

  public void setValue(final int value) {
    if (value > 10) {
      throw new IllegalArgumentException( );
    }
    this.value = value;
  }

  public int getValue( ) {
    return value;
  }

  public void someMethod(final FriendAccess obj) {
    if ((obj.value == 5) && (this.value == 5)) {
      obj.setValue(25); // <= IllegalArgumentException
    }
  }
}
```

If you write your class this way, you generate a lot of overhead due to the call to the setter. However, you also reap the benefits of having your setters work and your debugging time massively reduced. The bug in the above class should take any competent programmer about 10 seconds to fix once he sees the RuntimeException.

Directly setting member variables of a different instance is a problem waiting to happen and should be avoided. The compiler won't stop you from doing it—then again, a gun won't stop you from shooting yourself in the foot either.

In fact, I wouldn't even advise setting properties directly in the *same* instance. Properties that use setters and getters are special little creatures with their own needs. Many of the setters perform logic checks or do other tasks that you may miss if you set them directly in other utility methods. (See Example 1-11.)

Example 1-11. A bean that uses friendship to bypass setters

```
package oreilly.hcj.review;
public class FriendBean extends MutableObject {
  private int value;

  public FriendBean() {
    super();
  }

  public void setValue(final int value) {
    if (value > 10) {
      throw new IllegalArgumentException();
    }
    int oldValue = this.value;
    this.value = value;
    propertyChangeSupport.firePropertyChange("value", oldValue, value);
  }

  public int getValue() {
    return value;
  }

  public void someMethod() {
    if (Calendar.getInstance().get(Calendar.DAY_OF_WEEK) ==
        Calendar.THURSDAY) {
      this.value = 25;
    }
  }
}
```

One problem with this code is that someMethod() sets the property value directly while bypassing the setter and the property change event. If any GUI objects are registered as property change listeners, they won't know about the change and will display stale data. To fix this, you could potentially alter the method so that the method fires the property change event.

This will work, but, of course, you will have to replicate all of the other logic in the setter method whenever you set the value in a utility method. To make matters worse, whenever you add new logic to the setter, you must also remember to add the same logic to someMethod(). This would be extremely bad practice in object-oriented, or even procedural, software engineering. If you use the setter for the property, as the variation below shows, your life will be much easier:

```
package oreilly.hcj.review;
public class FriendBean extends MutableObject {
  private int value;

  public FriendBean() {
    super();
  }
```

```
public void setValue(final int value) {
  if (value > 10) {
    throw new IllegalArgumentException();
  }
  int oldValue = this.value;
  this.value = value;
  propertyChangeSupport.firePropertyChange("value", oldValue, value);
}

public int getValue() {
  return value;
}

public void someBetterMethod() {
  if (Calendar.getInstance().get(Calendar.DAY_OF_WEEK) ==
      Calendar.THURSDAY) {
    this.setValue(25);
  }
}
}
}
```

In this variation of your class, you reuse the functionality of the setter by calling the setter whenever you want to change the property's value. This approach is far easier to maintain and to change if the need arises; you have to change only the setter and not any other code. Overall, you should not be setting the value of properties, even in the same instance, without using the setters in the class. In fact, if a property has a setter, that setter should be the only thing that ever alters that property. In addition to preventing possible bugs, this technique implements proper encapsulation.

Common Mistakes

There are a certain group of mistakes in Java programming that are made over and over again at hundreds of companies throughout the world. Knowing how to avoid these mistakes will make you stand out from the crowd and look like you actually know what you are doing.

System Streams

The Java System streams represent the ability to write to the console or to read from it. When you invoke a method such as printStackTrace() with no arguments, its output is written to the default System stream, which is usually the console that started the program. However, these streams can cause problems in your code. Consider the following from a hypothetical GUI:

```
public void someMethod() {
  try {
    // do a whole bunch of stuff
  } (catch Exception ex) {
```

```
        ex.printStackTrace( );
        throw new MyApplicationException( );
    }
}
```

To debug this GUI, you print the stack trace if something goes wrong. The problem is that the code will print the stack trace to the console window, which may be hidden, or even running on another computer.

Printing to the console window is iffy, at best, in enterprise Java. In fact, there are times when you cannot use the console at all, such as when you write EJB code. At other times, you may be writing a library for others to use, and not have any idea of what the runtime environment is. Therefore, since one of your prime goals should be to promote reusability, you cannot count on the console always being around. The solution to the problem is to keep throwing those exceptions.

In JDK 1.4, there is a new facility that will tell you if one exception caused another. This is called the *Chained Exception Facility*. In short, if you throw an exception inside of a catch block, the virtual machine will note the exception that you are throwing, along with the exception and stack trace that caused you to enter the catch block in the first place. For more information on this facility, consult the JDK documentation at *http://java.sun.com/j2se/1.4.1/docs/relnotes/features.html#chained-exceptions*. The basics of using the chained exception facility are illustrated in this code block:

```
    public void someMethod( ) {
      try {
        // do a whole bunch of stuff
      } catch (IllegalAccessException ex) {
        throw new MyApplicationException( );
      }
    }
```

This version of the method takes advantage of chained exceptions by responding to the initial IllegalAccessException by throwing a new exception (MyApplicationException). The exceptions will keep propagating through the application until some code decides to catch them. When you finally do print the trace (presumably through a GUI, rather than a console window!), you will see that MyApplicationException was caused by IllegalAccessException, and the correct stack trace will be indicated.

Feel free to use the System streams in main( ) methods and in other classes in which you control their runtime environment. While you wouldn't want to use it in your application's data model classes, it may be acceptable for a GUI's frame window class.

When logging errors and debugging traces are inside a program or library, a much better solution is to use a logging package, which is much more robust. The Log4J package from Jakarta (*http://jakarta.apache.org/log4j/docs/index.html*) will allow you to print your exception messages in a configurable way, as shown in Example 1-12.

Example 1-12. Log4J as an alternative to the System streams

```
import org.apache.log4j.Logger

class SomeClass {

  /** Logger for this class. */
  private final static Logger LOGGER = Logger.getLogger(SomeClass.class);

  public void someMethod( ) {
    try {
      // do a whole bunch of stuff
    } catch( Exception ex) {
      LOGGER.error("Failure in SomeMethod", ex);
      throw new MyApplicationException( );
    }
  }
}
```

The benefit to the altered approach shown here is that you can route the output to whichever stream you desire. You can send the output to an XML file, relay it to another application via JMS, create an email to the system administrator, or even dump the information to *\/dev\/null* (though there's really no good reason to ever do this!). Using a logging package gives you far more flexibility than Java's System streams could ever provide.

Ultimately, using the System streams is okay only if you are writing a console-based application; for error handling, I wouldn't advise them at all. Also, tools and libraries should never write directly to System streams. Instead, they should pass errors and exceptions up to application-specific code that will do the logging for them.

System.exit( )

Every now and then you will encounter a third-party library that has code such as the following:

```
if (someSeriousErrorCondition) {
  System.exit(-1);
}
```

This code looks really benign, but watch out! It's a wolf in sheep's clothing. The problem here is that if you are a user of this library, you may not want the entire application to close because of this error. For example, if you are using this library as a part of a plug-in to another product, you should have only the plug-in crash and not the entire tool platform.

However, System.exit( ) crashes the entire application in an exceedingly brutal and bloody fashion. Just imagine the look of surprise, consternation, and growing anger on the face of your users when they try to run the plug-in, and their application simply exits without bothering to save two hours' worth of data. Although it sounds funny, it could lead to sore feet from looking for another job.

If you use System.exit( ) at all, your best bet is to use it *only* in the main method. If you ever write a library and embed System.exit( ) into it, you probably deserve any resulting physical violence.

 If you think this sort of thing doesn't happen in real life, you are in for a brutal surprise. While developing a scripting support plug-in for Eclipse, I found that the Jython libraries embed System.exit( ) in their code. This resulted in a very long debugging session in which I tried to figure out what the heck I did to get Eclipse to simply die. One more bug report filed; at least I'm an expert at Bugzilla now.

Default Execution

One common mistake I see developers make is shown in the following code:

```
if (source == yesBtn) {
   processYesBtn( );
} else if (source == noBtn) {
   processNoBtn( );
} else {
   processCancelBtn( );
}
```

In this code, the developer has three buttons in his panel. The if structure is designed to process the buttons if the user clicks on them. If the user clicks on yesBtn, then the first branch will be executed; if the user clicks on noBtn, then the second branch will be executed. Otherwise, the user *must* have clicked on cancelBtn.

However, there is one small problem. A junior programmer added a new button and registered the panel as an action listener. Unfortunately, he forgot to add handler code for the button. Now, when the user presses Load Favorites, the dialog simply doesn't work. The user subsequently files a bug report that reads something like, "When I try to load favorites, it doesn't work." However, your JUnit test works fine (because you don't depend on the action handling).

Now you get to spend 12 hours stepping through all 2,000 lines of code related to loading favorites. Eventually, you will detect the missing handler and feel an irresistible compulsion to toss your computer out the window.

Close that window and implement a coding standard instead. Change your if statements to look like the following:

```
if (source == yesBtn) {
   processYesBtn( );
} else if (source == noBtn) {
   processNoBtn( );
} else if (source == cancelBtn) {
```

```
    processCancelBtn( );
} else {
    assert false : source.toString( );
}
```

Those of you who studied the "assert" section probably saw this coming. The point I am trying to make here is to never use `else` clauses or `default` blocks in `switch` statements to perform specific tasks without checking your assumptions. If your `if-then-else` statement or `switch` statement is dealing with an enumerated set of values, go ahead and enumerate them; in your `default` or final `else` clause, throw an error.

CHAPTER 2

The Final Story

One fundamental principle of programming is that, generally, it is best to swap a logic error for a compiler error. Compiler errors tend to be found in seconds and are corrected just as fast. Syntax errors are a good example. A missing semicolon can make things confusing. If the compiler error is something particularly cryptic, the resolution may take as long as a couple of minutes to discover.

Logic errors, on the other hand, are the bane of all programmers. They hide and hate to reveal themselves. Logic errors seem to have minds of their own, constantly evading detection and dodging your efforts to pin down their cause. They can easily take a thousand times more effort to solve than the worst compiler errors. Worst of all, many logic errors are not found at all and occur only intermittently in sensitive places, which causes your customers to scream for a fix. Logic errors often require you to throw thousands of man-hours at them, only to finally discover that they are minor typos.

The Java keyword `final` can be instrumental in turning thousands of logic errors into compiler errors without too much effort. With some training in coding standards and some code retrofitting, you can save an enormous amount of man-hours that are better spent elsewhere. Also, you can save your support departments from having to deal with irate customers.

Final Constants

Final constants are a good place to start, since many of you are already familiar with the concept. Consider the code in Example 2-1.

Example 2-1. A class that doesn't use constants

```
package oreilly.hcj.finalstory;
public class FinalConstants {

  public static class CircleTools {
```

Example 2-1. A class that doesn't use constants (continued)

```
    public double getCircleArea(final double radius) {
      return (Math.pow(radius, 2) * 3.141);
    }

    public double getCircleCircumference(final double radius) {
      return ((radius * 2) * 3.141);
    }

    public double getCircleExtrudedVolume(final double radius,
                                          final double height) {
      return ((radius * 2 * height) * 3.141);
    }
  }
}
```

The problem with this code is that the developer has to change all three instances of the value 3.141, his estimate for π, in all three methods if he wants to make his calculations more precise. Seasoned developers will see the opportunity for a class-scoped constant, as seen in Example 2-2.

Example 2-2. Simple constants using final

```
package oreilly.hcj.finalstory;
public class FinalConstants {

  public static class CircleToolsBetter {
    /** A value for PI. **/
    public final static double PI = 3.141;

    public double getCircleArea(final double radius) {
      return (Math.pow(radius, 2) * PI);
    }

    public double getCircleCircumference(final double radius) {
      return ((radius * 2) * PI);
    }

    public double getCircleExtrudedVolume(final double radius,
                                          final double height) {
      return ((radius * 2 * height) * PI);
    }
  }
}
```

This code is much better. Now the developer can change the constant, and this one change will propagate throughout the class. The reason I am beating this particular dead horse is because there are some traps involving constants that trip up even experienced developers.

Public Primitives and Substitution

The first of these traps involves public primitive constants that are used by other code. Because primitive finals are substituted at compile time with their values, if you change a final that is used by other classes, you must remember to recompile those other classes or your change will not take effect. The same rule applies to constants of type java.lang.String. Although String is a constructed type, it is also substituted at compile time. All constructed types other than String, mutable or not, are not substituted at compile time. To understand how this works, look at Example 2-3.

Example 2-3. Various final variables

```
package oreilly.hcj.finalstory;
public class FinalReplacement {
  /** A string constant */
  public final static String A_STRING = "Hardcore Java";

  /** An int constant. */
  public final static int AN_INT = 5;

  /** A double constant. */
  public final static double A_DOUBLE = 102.55d;

  /** An array constant. */
  public final static int[] AN_ARRAY = new int[] {1, 2, 3, 6, 9, 18, 36};

  /** A color constant. */
  public final static Color A_COLOR = new Color(45, 0, 155);

  public void someMethod( ) {
    System.out.println(A_STRING);
    System.out.println(AN_INT);
    System.out.println(A_DOUBLE);
    System.out.println(AN_ARRAY);
    System.out.println(A_COLOR);
  }
}
```

Once the compiler sees code such as this, it starts substituting out the primitives and String objects. After the first pass of the compiler, the class will look something like this:

```
package oreilly.hcj.finalstory;
public class FinalReplacement {
  /** A string constant */
  public final static String A_STRING = "Hardcore Java";

  /** An int constant. */
  public final static int AN_INT = 5;

  /** A double constant. */
  public final static double A_DOUBLE = 102.55d;
```

```
/** An array constant. */
public final static int[] AN_ARRAY = new int[] {1, 2, 3, 6, 9, 18, 36};

/** A color constant. */
public final static Color A_COLOR = new Color(45, 0, 155);

public void someMethod( ) {
  System.out.println("Hardcore Java");
  System.out.println(5);
  System.out.println(102.55d);
  System.out.println(AN_ARRAY);
  System.out.println(A_COLOR);
  }
}
```

The compiler will concatenate consecutive String literals to form one literal. Therefore, the following two lines are identical from the point of view of the compiler:

```
public final static String A_STRING = "Hardcore Java";
public final static String A_STRING = "Hardcore"+ "Java";
```

Both of these lines would result in an identical declaration that is a string constant. Also, this optimization technique applies to where there are consecutive string literals in your code.

The primitive and String constants were substituted while the other constructed types were left as variables. Since this code is all in one class, if you change a constant, you have to recompile this class anyway. However, if another class (for example, ExternalUser) is using the constant A_STRING and you change it in FinalReplacement, you have a problem. ExternalUser will have to be recompiled to trigger a resubstitution using the new A_STRING value, but the Java compiler will not notice this dependency. Here's a simple version of ExternalUser:

```
package oreilly.hcj.finalstory;
public class ExternalUser {
  public static void main(String[] args) {
    System.out.println("The title of the book is: " +
                FinalReplacement.A_STRING + ".");
  }
}
```

This extremely simple class uses the A_STRING constant from the FinalReplacement class. If you run the main( ) method, the output will look like the following:

```
>ant -Dexample=oreilly.hcj.finalstory.ExternalUser run_example
run_example:
     [java] The title of the book is: Hardcore Java.
```

Now change the value of A_STRING to "Java Hardcore" in the FinalReplacement class:

```
/** A string constant */
  public final static String A_STRING = "Java Hardcore";
```

Recompile `FinalReplacement` using the following command:

```
>ant -Dexample=oreilly/hcj/finalstory/FinalReplacement.java compile_example
compile_example:
    [javac] Compiling 1 source file to C:\dev\hcj\bin
```

Now run the `ExternalUser` example again:

```
>ant -Dexample=oreilly.hcj.finalstory.ExternalUser run_example
run_example:
    [java] The title of the book is: Hardcore Java.
```

There is no change despite the change in the `A_STRING` constant. To fix this problem, recompile the `ExternalUser` class:

```
>ant -Dexample=oreilly/hcj/finalstory/ExternalUser.java compile_example
compile_example:
    [javac] Compiling 1 source file to C:\dev\hcj\bin
```

Running the example once more gives you the output you were seeking when you changed `A_STRING` in `FinalReplacement`:

```
>ant -Dexample=oreilly.hcj.finalstory.ExternalUser run_example
run_example:
    [java] The title of the book is: Java Hardcore.
```

The Java compiler doesn't automatically notice the dependency between the `String` and primitive constants and their users. Some build environments recognize this dependency automatically but don't depend on it.

In fact, whenever you change a public primitive constant, it's a good idea to simply rebuild the whole project, just to be safe. If your code is also being used by other projects, make sure you put the change in your release notes so that others will know to recompile their projects.

 During a project for the aerospace industry, my consulting company changed a primitive public constant and forgot to change the release notes. We promptly broke a customer's code and only hours later did we figure out that they needed to rebuild all 400 of their classes to get it working.

Excessive Constants

The overuse of class-scoped constants is another common trap that can clutter up otherwise well-built code. For example, consider a situation in which there are many constants in a mathematically oriented class, as shown in Example 2-4.

Example 2-4. Excessive use of private constants

```
package oreilly.hcj.finalstory;
public class FinalConstants {
```

Example 2-4. Excessive use of private constants (continued)

```java
public class SomeClass {
  /** Contains the constant for the first equation. */
  private static final double K1 = 3.141;

  /** Contains the offset for the first equation. */
  private static final double X1 = 15.0;

  /** Contains the constant for the second equation. */
  private static final double K2 = 1.414;

  /** Contains the offset for the second equation. */
  private static final double X2 = 45.0;

  /** Contains a constant for both equations. */
  private static final double M = 9.3;

  public double equation1(final double inputValue) {
    return (((Math.pow(inputValue, 2.0d) / K1) + X1) / M);
  }

  public double equation2(final double inputValue) {
    return (((Math.pow(inputValue, 3.0d) * K2) + X2) * M);
  }
 }
}
```

Although there is nothing technically wrong with this code, it is a rather nasty mess. If your equations become large, with multiple constants and numerous terms, the situation turns into something more appropriate for a horror movie. To avoid this trap, rewrite this disaster:

```java
package oreilly.hcj.finalstory;
public class FinalConstants {

  public class SomeClassBetter {
    /** Contains a constant for both equations. */
    private static final double M = 9.3;

    public double equation1(final double inputValue) {
      final double K = 3.141;
      final double X = 15.0;

      return (((Math.pow(inputValue, 2.0d) / K) + X) / M);
    }

    public double equation2(final double inputValue) {
      final double K = 1.414;
      final double X = 45.0;

      return (((Math.pow(inputValue, 3.0d) * K) + X) * M);
    }
  }
 }
```

Although the method-scoped `final` variables may look strange, they are quite legal and useful. For the compiler, the semantics for method-scoped constants are the same as those for class-scoped constants. The compiler will replace primitive and `String` constant variables with the value of the variable at compile time.

In fact, since the constants in Example 2-4 are private, you know that they cannot be accessed outside of the class, so there is no reason to leave them in the scope of the class. In the process of making your code easier to read and understand, you removed the need for those silly 1s and 2s in your constant names. Since the constants are used only in those methods, it is appropriate to restrict them to the methods in which they are used.

Take Advantage of Warning Options in Good Development Tools

Good tools can really help you to identify private variables and mistakes associates with them. For example, my IDE is configured to warn me if a private member of a class is not used in that class. Not only does this help me find private constants that should have been declared public, it also helps me clean up code that has been developed for a while and may have accumulated some lint throughout the process. Eclipse, for example, has many of these options; you should turn on all of them to warning level. Using these warnings can save you a lot of debugging time down the road.

To summarize, if you have a `private final static` that is used only in one method, you should probably move it into that method. On the other hand, if the constants are being used in more than one method, you should leave them as class-scoped. The constant `M` was not moved because it was being used by two of the methods.

Final Variables

While we are on the subject of scoped `final` variables, you should keep in mind that these variables don't have to be primitives to be useful. Final variables that are scoped and constructed can be used as a powerful tool to solidify code in methods.

Method-Scoped final Variables

Although `final` variables that appear within methods are a little strange to some people at first, they become quite addictive once you get used to reading them. See Example 2-5.

Example 2-5. Catching mistakes with method-scoped final variables

```
package oreilly.hcj.finalstory;
public class FinalVariables {
```

```
    public static String someMethod(final String environmentKey) {
      final String key = "env." + environmentKey;
      System.out.println("Key is: " + key);
      return (System.getProperty(key));
    }
}
```

In this class, you build a scoped `final` variable that adds a prefix to the parameter `environmentKey`. In this case, the `final` variable is final only within the *execution scope*, which is different at each execution of the method. Each time the method is entered, the `final` is reconstructed. As soon as it is constructed, it cannot be changed during the scope of the method execution. This allows you to fix a variable in a method for the duration of the method. To see how this works, use the test program in Example 2-6.

Example 2-6. Testing final variables

```
package oreilly.hcj.finalstory;
public class FinalVariables {

  public final static void main(final String[] args) {
    System.out.println("Note how the key variable is changed.");
    someMethod("JAVA_HOME");
    someMethod("ANT_HOME");
  }
}
```

Running this test program results in the following:

```
>ant -Dexample=oreilly.hcj.finalstory.FinalVariables run_example
run_example:
    [java] Note how the key variable is changed.
    [java] Key is: env.JAVA_HOME
    [java] Key is: env.ANT_HOME
```

Each time the method is entered, the passed-in `environmentKey` parameter is appended to the constant prefix and then frozen for the duration of the method call. So why make the variable final? Because once this variable is set in the body of the method, it cannot be changed. Consider what would happen if you made a mistake like the one shown in Example 2-7.

Example 2-7. A coding mistake caught by a final variable

```
package oreilly.hcj.finalstory;
public class FinalVariables {

  public static String someBuggedMethod(final String environmentKey) {
    final String key = "env." + environmentKey;
    System.out.println("Key is: " + key);
```

Example 2-7. A coding mistake caught by a final variable (continued)

```
    key = new String("someValue"); // <= compiler error.
    return (System.getProperty(key));
  }
}
```

When you try to compile this code, it will give the following result:

```
>ant -Dexample=oreilly/hcj/finalstory/FinalVariables.java compile_example
compile_example:
    [javac] Compiling 1 source file to C:\dev\hcj\bin
    [javac] C:\dev\hcj\src\oreilly\hcj\finalstory\FinalVariables.java:53: cannot
assign a value to final variable key
    [javac]     key = new String("someValue"); // <= compiler error.
    [javac]     ^
    [javac] 1 error
```

> In the example code, I commented out the compiler error; you will
> have to uncomment it to run this test. I use a similar procedure for all
> compiler errors throughout the book.

In this example, the mistake was made of trying to reassign key to a different value. This type of mistake simply happens; however, since you are a savvy programmer, and you used the final keyword, the compiler tells you that an error was made. This is a great example of trading a logic error for a compiler error.

The technique of fixing variables with final is extremely handy for long or complicated methods that have many local variables. When alerted by the compiler, repairing this mistake takes a matter of seconds. If you don't use final to fix your variables now, you run the risk of spending long hours to find logic bugs, only to discover that someone reset your variable halfway through the method because of a typo.

Deferred Initialization

If you want to, you can defer the initialization of a final variable within the method. Hold onto your hat because Example 2-8 is going to look a little weird at first.

Example 2-8. Method-scoped final variables with deferred initialization

```
package oreilly.hcj.finalstory;
public class FinalVariables {

  public void buildGUIDialog (final String name) {
    final String instanceName;
    if (name == null) {
      // no problem here.
      instanceName = getClass().getName() + hashCode();
    } else {
```

```
        // no problem here as well.
        instanceName = getClass().getName() + name;
    }

    JDialog dialog = new JDialog();

    // .. Do a bunch of layout and component building.

    dialog.setTitle(instanceName);

    // .. Do dialog assembly

    instanceName = "hello";  // <= compiler error
  }

}
```

In this case, you declare a final variable at the start of the method without giving it a value, since the contents of that variable depend on whether the user passed you null. During the if statement, check for null and then assign the variable appropriately. Once you assign the variable a value, it can't be assigned a value again. However, you could have gone through half the method before assigning the variable its value. This coding technique allows you to make single-shot, assign-and-freeze variables. After assignment, these variables behave like constants for the rest of the method.

 Method-scoped final variables aren't the same as constants, although they behave like constants at times. The difference is that method-scoped final variables are *variable*. Each time the method is entered, their values are changed based on the needs of that particular execution. However, method-scoped constants always have the same values regardless of the circumstances under which the method is run. Also, primitive and String method-scoped final variables are not substituted at compile time like primitive and String method-scoped constants.

In addition to deferring the initialization of method variables, you can defer the initialization of instance-scoped variables and class-scoped variables. Instance-scoped variables must be initialized in a constructor, and class-scoped variables must be initialized in the static{} method or you will receive compiler errors stating that the variable has not been initialized.

Chained deferred initialization

One interesting trick you can employ with deferred initialization is to chain the initialization of multiple final variables together. For example, consider the following code, which chains instance-scoped final variable initialization:

```
package oreilly.hcj.finalstory;
public class ChainingFinals {
  public final String name;
  public final int nameLength = this.name.length;
  // public final String anotherValue = name;  // <== Won't compile

  public ChainingFinals(final String name) {
    this.name = name;
  }
}
```

In this code, the emphasized line will work properly because the final variable name must be initialized in the constructor to the class. Therefore, the final variable nameLength can take advantage of name when the instance is initialized. However, make sure that you use the this keyword in front of the variable name. If you don't, it won't compile.

```
package oreilly.hcj.finalstory;
public class ChainingFinals {
  public final String name;
  public final int nameLength = name.length; // <== Won't compile

  public ChainingFinals(final String name) {
    this.name = name;
  }
}
```

In this slightly revised example, I left off the keyword this when using name. As a result, the line won't compile but will instead tell me that name is not declared. The compiler requires that you use the this reference when chaining finals in this manner.

Chaining final initialization can be a great tool for precaching data or initializing final members that are dependent on other final members. It also has the benefit of giving you insight into how object instantiation is managed in the virtual machine. As a result of this process, the constructor to the class is run before the initializers.

Final Parameters

Just when you think it's safe to hit Compile, you can go even further with finals. To illustrate, suppose you hire a new developer and, while adding a new feature, he decides to make a little change to the equation2() method from Example 2-4. The changes he makes are shown in Example 2-9.

Example 2-9. Danger of nonfinal parameters

```java
package oreilly.hcj.finalstory;
public class FinalParameters {

  public double equation2(double inputValue) {
    final double K = 1.414;
    final double X = 45.0;

    double result = (((Math.pow(inputValue, 3.0d) * K) + X) * M);

    double powInputValue = 0;
    if (result > 360) {
      powInputValue = X * Math.sin(result);
    } else {
      inputValue = K * Math.sin(result);
    }

    result = Math.pow(result, powInputValue);
    if (result > 360) {
      result = result / inputValue;
    }

    return result;
  }

}
```

The problem is that the new guy changed the value of the parameter passed in to the method. During the first `if` statement, the developer made one little mistake—he typed `inputValue` instead of `powInputValue`. This caused errors in the subsequent calculations in the method. The user of the function expects certain output and doesn't get it; however, the compiler says that everything in the code is okay. Now it's time to put on another pot of coffee and hope your spouse remembers who you are after you figure out this rather annoying problem.

Little bugs like this are often the most difficult to locate. By Murphy's Law, you can absolutely guarantee that this code will be in the middle of a huge piece of your project, and the error reports won't directly lead you here. What's more, you probably won't notice the impact of the bug until it goes into production and users are screaming for a fix.

You cannot afford to forget that once you write code, the story is not over. People will make changes, additions, and errors in your code. You will have to look through the code and fix everything that was messed up. To prevent this problem from occurring, do the following:

```java
package oreilly.hcj.finalstory;
public class FinalParameters {
```

```
    public double equation2Better(final double inputValue) {
      final double K = 1.414;
      final double X = 45.0;

      double result = (((Math.pow(inputValue, 3.0d) * K) + X) * M);

      double powInputValue = 0;
      if (result > 360) {
        powInputValue = X * Math.sin(result);
      } else {
        inputValue = K * Math.sin(result);    // <= Compiler error
      }

      result = Math.pow(result, powInputValue);
      if (result > 360) {
        result = result / inputValue;
      }


      return result;
    }
```

When you state that the parameter inputValue is final, the compiler will catch any attempts to assign another value to that parameter and give you an error message with the line number and reason for the problem. The benefit of this little trick (which takes about two seconds to implement) becomes even more obvious when you consider the hypothetical Java bean shown in Example 2-10.

Example 2-10. A bean with a bug

```
public class Person {
  private String name = null;
  public void setName(String name) throws PropertyVetoException {
    String oldName = this.name;
    vetoableChangeSupport.fireVetoableChange("name", oldName, name);
    name = name;
    propertyChangeSupport.firePropertyChange("name", oldName, name);
  }
}
```

On the emphasized line, the programmer forgot to use the prefix this on the left-hand side of the assignment; the line should have read:

```
    this.name = name;
```

Instead, the assignment does absolutely nothing. In a data model with 212 objects and over 1,000 attributes, bugs like this are extremely difficult to detect. However, if you have a policy to always label method parameters as final, such an assignment will cause a compiler error. The final parameter version is shown here:

```
    public class Person {
      private String name = null;
```

```
    public void setName(final String name) throws PropertyVetoException {
        String oldName = this.name;
        vetoableChangeSupport.fireVetoableChange("name", oldName, name);
        name = name; // <= Compiler error
        propertyChangeSupport.firePropertyChange("name", oldName, name);
    }
}
```

When compiling this code, the programmer immediately gets a compiler error on the (erroneous) assignment line. The programmer looks back at the code, spots the bug in about two seconds, fixes it, gets another soda, and continues work without even thinking about how much trouble he just avoided. The coding standard here saved him hours of work.

Final Collections

Periodically, while programming, you may want to make constant sets and store them in final variables for public use. This desire can lead to all sorts of problems. Consider the code in Example 2-11.

Example 2-11. A collection in a final static member

```
package oreilly.hcj.finalstory;
public class FinalCollections {

  public static class Rainbow {

    public final static Set VALID_COLORS;

    static {
      VALID_COLORS = new HashSet( );
      VALID_COLORS.add(Color.red);
      VALID_COLORS.add(Color.orange);
      VALID_COLORS.add(Color.yellow);
      VALID_COLORS.add(Color.green);
      VALID_COLORS.add(Color.blue);
      VALID_COLORS.add(Color.decode("#4B0082")); // indigo
      VALID_COLORS.add(Color.decode("#8A2BE2")); // violet
    }
  }
}
```

The goal of this code is to declare a class with a Set of final and static Colors representing the colors of the rainbow. You want to be able to use this Set without concerning yourself with the possibility of accidentally changing it. The problem is that the Set isn't final at all! Break it with Example 2-12.

Example 2-12. A defect caused by a nonimmutable set

```
package oreilly.hcj.finalstory;
public final static void someMethod( ) {
```

Example 2-12. A defect caused by a nonimmutable set (continued)

```
   Set colors = Rainbow.VALID_COLORS;
   colors.add(Color.black); // <= logic error but allowed by compiler
   System.out.println(colors);
}
```

The reference to the Set is final, but the Set itself is mutable. In short, your constant variable isn't very constant. The point is that final is *not the same* as immutable.

You can firm up this code in the same way you locked down returned collections from a bean in Chapter 1:

```
package oreilly.hcj.finalstory;
public static class RainbowBetter {

    public final static Set VALID_COLORS;

    static {
      Set temp = new HashSet();
      temp.add(Color.red);
      temp.add(Color.orange);
      temp.add(Color.yellow);
      temp.add(Color.green);
      temp.add(Color.blue);
      temp.add(Color.decode("#4B0082")); // indigo
      temp.add(Color.decode("#8A2BE2")); // violet
      VALID_COLORS = Collections.unmodifiableSet(temp);
    }
  }
}
```

This version of the class is much better. Your Set of Colors cannot be modified because you have turned it into an immutable object. The reference to the Set is final, and the contents of the collection are locked down.

In the static{} initializer, note how you have to use a temporary set to store the colors. This is because you can set a final variable only once, even in the initializer. If you try to set it more than once or change the variable in the initializer, your compiler will give an error message stating that you cannot change the final variable. Remember that deferred finals are a one-shot deal. Once set (no pun intended), they can't be changed.

Now that you have a strategy to lock down your Set, let's revisit the old logic bug that we discussed in Example 2-12:

```
package oreilly.hcj.finalstory;
public final static void someMethod() {
   Set colors = RainbowBetter.VALID_COLORS;
   colors.add(Color.black); // <= exception here
   System.out.println(colors);
}
```

Now that you have the Set locked down, this code results in an exception. Specifically, the method will throw an UnsupportedOperationException whenever the user tries to use any write methods on VALID_COLORS, as it is now immutable. In this case, you haven't been able to trade a logic bug for a compiler bug, but you have been able to trade a logic bug for an exception. Although this trade isn't as good, it's still definitely worthwhile. Always use the java.util.Collections class to get unmodifiable collections and maps when creating final collections and maps.

As far as unmodifiable sets go, the performance hit is negligible. As it turns out, the JDK implements unmodifiable collections in a performance-conscious way. If you look into the JDK source, you will see the static nested classes UnmodifiableSet and UnmodifableCollection. The code in Example 2-13* is pasted directly from the JDK source. All I did was change the spacing to conform to O'Reilly standards and remove the Javadoc for brevity's sake.

Example 2-13. Implementation of unmodifiable collections

```
package oreilly.hcj.finalstory;
public static Collection unmodifiableCollection(Collection c) {
  return new UnmodifiableCollection(c);
}

static class UnmodifiableCollection implements Collection, Serializable {
  // use serialVersionUID from JDK 1.2.2 for interoperability
  private static final long serialVersionUID = 1820017752578914078L;

  Collection c;

  UnmodifiableCollection(Collection c) {
    if (c==null)
      throw new NullPointerException();
    this.c = c;
  }

  public int size()      {return c.size();}
  public boolean isEmpty()     {return c.isEmpty();}
  public boolean contains(Object o)   {return c.contains(o);}
  public Object[] toArray()     {return c.toArray();}
  public Object[] toArray(Object[] a) {return c.toArray(a);}
  public String toString()        {return c.toString();}

  public Iterator iterator() {
    return new Iterator() {
      Iterator i = c.iterator();

      public boolean hasNext() {return i.hasNext();}
      public Object next() {return i.next();}
```

* From JDK source Java.util.Collections.

Example 2-13. Implementation of unmodifiable collections (continued)

```java
    public void remove( ) {
       throw new UnsupportedOperationException( );
     }
  };
}

public boolean add(Object o){
  throw new UnsupportedOperationException( );
}

public boolean remove(Object o) {
  throw new UnsupportedOperationException( );
}

public boolean containsAll(Collection coll) {
  return c.containsAll(coll);
}

public boolean addAll(Collection coll) {
  throw new UnsupportedOperationException( );
}

public boolean removeAll(Collection coll) {
  throw new UnsupportedOperationException( );
}

public boolean retainAll(Collection coll) {
  throw new UnsupportedOperationException( );
}

public void clear( ) {
  throw new UnsupportedOperationException( );
}
}
public static Set unmodifiableSet(Set s) {
  return new UnmodifiableSet(s);
}
```

When you call `Collections.unmodifiableSet( )`, the class creates a new instance of
this static nested class and sets the source collection as the delegate object. As you
can see in the example code from the JDK, the class `UnmodifiableSet` implements
`java.util.Set` and inherits from `UnmodifiableCollection`, which in turn implements `java.util.Collection`. Together, they form a delegate structure. Any read
call to the `UnmodifiableCollection` is forwarded to the delegate collection. However, if the user tries to access a write operation, the class throws an instance of
`UnsupportedOperationException`. Therefore, the additional overhead of the
`UnmodifiableSet` is only a single method call.

This delegate structure also plugs another big hole: if the UnmodifiableSet class inherited from HashSet, then the user could just cast the instances back to HashSet to gain access to write methods. The delegate structure in the JDK quite elegantly blocks this, ensuring that an UnmodifiableSet truly is unmodifiable, even when placed in the hands of a clever and sneaky programmer.

All of the other collection classes work similarly to UnmodifiableSet. You should use these heavily in your code. Regrettably, there is no similar way to lock down final array objects, so be careful when using them.

Instance-Scoped Variables

Another type of final class member that can be very useful is instance-scoped final attributes. Consider the code in Example 2-14.

Example 2-14. A creation date property

```
package oreilly.hcj.finalstory;
public class FinalMembers {
  /** Holds the creation date-time of the instance. */
  private Date creationDate =
    Calendar.getInstance(TimeZone.getTimeZone("GMT")).getTime( );

  /**
   * Get the Date-Time when the object was created.
   *
   * @return The creation date of the object.
   */
  public Date getCreationDate( ) {
    return this.creationDate;
  }
}
```

The job of the property creationDate is to hold the date and time of the instance's creation. This property represents a read-only property that is set once; after all, an object can be created only once. However, there is a problem with this property: it leaves a massive potential bug lurking in your code. To illustrate this, lets look at another part of the same class in Example 2-15.

Example 2-15. A modification date property

```
package oreilly.hcj.finalstory;
public class FinalMembers {
  /** Holds the modification date-time of the instance. */
  public Date modificationDate = creationDate;

  public void setModificationDate(Date modificationDate) {
    if (modificationDate == null) {
      throw new NullPointerException( );
    }
```

Example 2-15. A modification date property (continued)

```
    this.creationDate = modificationDate;
  }

  public Date getModificationDate( ) {
    return this.modificationDate;
  }
}
```

Here, you have a neat and cryptic little logic bug. If you didn't see the bug instantly, that only reinforces my point. The problem is that the writer of the setModificationDate( ) method is obviously setting the wrong parameter. Due to a simple typo, instead of setting modificationDate, this method sets creationDate. No one ever intends to write bugs like this, but it happens. Fortunately, there is a way you can block this problem with a coding standard:

```
package oreilly.hcj.finalstory;
public class FinalMembers {

  private final Date creationDate2 =
    Calendar.getInstance(TimeZone.getTimeZone("GMT")).getTime( );

  public Date getCreationDate2( ) {
    return this.creationDate2;
  }

  public void setModificationDate2(Date modificationDate) {
    if (modificationDate == null) {
      throw new NullPointerException( );
    }
    this.creationDate2 = modificationDate; // <= Compiler error.
  }
}
```

Now that the creationDate2 is final, any attempts to write to it after it is initialized will cause a compiler error.

Instance-scoped final variables have a similar morphology to method-scoped final variables. They are constructed once at each instantiation of the class and then are frozen for the life of the instance. They are ideal for read-only attributes set only at instantiation.

This technique gives you yet another coding standard that can save your skin. What used to be a difficult-to-find logic bug is magically transformed by the keyword final into a minor compile-time bug. Finding the logic bug could potentially take hours of painstaking work with a debugger. The compile-time bug you replaced it with would be fixed by a programmer in only a few seconds. It's unlikely the programmer would even notice the repair!

You can take this concept even further. When writing classes, you can create instance-scoped attributes that are final and are not initialized. The class in Example 2-16 shows how this deferred initialization works.

Example 2-16. Deferring final initialization to the constructor

```
package oreilly.hcj.finalstory;
public class FinalMembers {

  /** Holds the creation date-time of the instance. */
  private final Date creationDate3;

  /**
   * Constructor
   *
   * @param creationDate The creation date.
   * @param modificationDate The last modification date.
   */
  public FinalMembers(final Date creationDate,
                      final Date modificationDate) {
    if (modificationDate.compareTo(creationDate) < 0) {
      throw new IllegalArgumentException("modificationDate");
    }
    this.creationDate3 = creationDate;
    // do a bunch of date calculations.
    this.creationDate3 = modificationDate;  // <= compiler error
  }

  /**
   * Second constructor.  Use current date for creation date.
   *
   * @param modificationDate The last modification date.
   */
  public FinalMembers(final Date modificationDate) {
    this.modificationDate = modificationDate;
    // <= compiler error: 'creationDate may not have been initialized'
  }
}
```

In this example, you create a member variable named creationDate3 and set it as final, but don't initialize it. Upon construction, the user passes a date to the class and creationDate3 is set. As before, once it is set, it cannot be changed. This ability to defer an initialization to a constructor gives you a lot of flexibility and safety in object initialization.

In the first constructor, you accidentally try to set creationDate3 twice: once with the creationDate parameter and once with the modificationDate parameter. Obviously, the author of this file mistyped the variable name and meant to type **this.modificationDate** in the second instance. However, since you are being vigilant with the final keyword, you catch the error at compile time and correct it.

As a bonus, if you forget to set the variable, as in the second constructor in Example 2-16, you get a compiler error telling you that the variable hasn't been initialized:

```
>ant -Dexample=oreilly/hcj/finalstory/FinalMembers.java compile_example
compile_example:
    [javac] Compiling 1 source file to C:\dev\hcj\bin
    [javac] C:\dev\hcj\src\oreilly\hcj\finalstory\FinalMembers.java:69: variable
creationDate3 might not have been initialized
    [javac]    public FinalMembers(final Date modificationDate) {
    [javac]                                                     ^
    [javac] 1 error
```

The reason you get this compiler error is because Java requires that all instance-scoped final variables and members must be set before the end of the constructor. In a similar manner, all class-scoped members must be set by the end of the static initialization of the class they are declared in, and all method-scoped finals must be set by the end of the method in which they are declared in.

In the case of Example 2-16, your coding standard has given you two layers of security for the price of one. This is a bargain that no programmer could pass up!

Final Classes

A final class is a class that does not allow itself to be inherited by another class. Final classes mark endpoints in the inheritance tree.

There are two ways to make a class final. The first is to use the keyword final in the class declaration:

```
public final class SomeClass {
   // ...Class contents
}
```

The second way to make a class final is to declare all of its constructors as private:

```
public class SomeClass {
   public final static SOME_INSTANCE = new SomeClass(5);

   private SomeClass(final int value) {
   }
}
```

When you give all constructors private visibility, you are *implicitly* declaring the class as final; often, this is not the intended result. In fact, it is the omission of the keyword final on the class declaration that should alert you to the fact that something is wrong. The class above may very well need to be final, in which case you should always specifically use the keyword final in the class declaration. If you don't follow this rule, you could end up causing some devious problems.

To find an example of these problems, you need to look no further than the JDK itself. In the `java.beans` package, you will find a class called `Introspector` (see Chapter 8). Take a look at its single constructor in Example 2-17.*

Example 2-17. The java.beans.Introspector source snippets

```
public class Introspector {
  // ...snip...
  private Introspector(Class beanClass, Class stopClass, int flags)
    throws IntrospectionException {
    // ...snip...
  }
}
```

The constructor for the `Introspector` class is private. I noticed this while studying this class. My goal was to extend the `Introspector` and create a class that is more feature-rich than `Introspector` itself. Unfortunately, since the only constructor of the class is private, it is impossible to extend this class. In the case of the `Introspector` class, there is no reason that the class should be final. The `Introspector` class is a good example of how implicit `final` classes can cause problems.

Most singleton classes shouldn't be declared as `final`. You never know what other features your class's user will dream up. However, since singleton classes need to be protected from external instantiation, you can't make the constructor public. The solution to the problem is a protected constructor, as shown in Example 2-18.

Example 2-18. An extensible singleton

```
package oreilly.hcj.finalstory;
public class Singleton {
  private static final Logger LOGGER = Logger.getLogger(Singleton.class);
  public static Singleton instance = null;
  private final String[] params;

  public static void init(final String[] params) {
    // ...do some initialization...
    instance = new Singleton(params);
  }

  protected Singleton(final String[] params) {
    this.params = params;
    if (LOGGER.isDebugEnabled()) {
      LOGGER.debug(Arrays.asList(this.params).toString());
    }
  }
}
```

* J2SDK source code. © 2002 by Sun Microsystems.

Since this singleton class has a protected constructor instead of a private constructor, you can extend its functionality while protecting it against construction by the user. This will allow you to extend the singleton, as shown in Example 2-19.

Example 2-19. An extension of a singleton

```
package oreilly.hcj.finalstory;
public class ExtendedSingleton extends Singleton {
  private final static int DEFAULT_VALUE = 5;
  private final int value;

  public static void init(final String[] params) {
    instance = new ExtendedSingleton(params, DEFAULT_VALUE);
  }

  public static void init(final String[] params, final int value) {
    instance = new ExtendedSingleton(params, value);
  }

  protected ExtendedSingleton(final String[] params, final int value) {
    super(params);
    this.value = value;
  }
}
```

The protected constructor technique is not limited to classes with instance variables and methods. A protected constructor should be declared for classes that are entirely static in nature. Although these classes have no other instance members, it would be possible, if a bit pointless, to instantiate them. Preventing this instantiation while providing extensibility is definitely an asset to the development process.

There are rare circumstances when a class should be made final. One example is the concept of the constant object class, which we will discuss in Chapter 5. However, making classes *implicitly* final is never a good thing; if you want to make a class final, come right out a declare it with the class declaration.

Final Methods

Final methods are an interesting feature of Java. They allow you to make a class partially final without preventing its inheritance by another class. To make a method final, use the `final` keyword on the declaration, as shown in Example 2-20.

Example 2-20. A final method

```
package oreilly.hcj.finalstory;
public class FinalMethod {
  public final void someMethod( ) {
  }
}
```

This declaration is the antithesis of the abstract keyword. Whereas the abstract keyword declares that subclasses *must* override the method, the final keyword guarantees that the method can *never* be overridden by subclasses. Subclasses can inherit from the FinalMethod class and can override any method other than someMethod( ).

You should never make a method final unless it *must* be final. When in doubt, leave the final keyword off a method. After all, you never know the kinds of variations the users of your class may come up with.

One example of a situation in which making a method final *is* the proper route to take is when a read-only property is used. Example 2-21 shows an example of such a property.

Example 2-21. A final property

```
package oreilly.hcj.finalstory;
public class FinalMethod {
  /** A demo property. */
  private final String name;

  protected FinalMethod(final String name) {
    this.name = name;
  }

  public final String getName() {
    return this.name;
  }
}
```

In this example, the name property is set at construction time and can never be changed. Also, you have defined that you never want a subclass to hide this property (which it could by declaring its own name property if getName( ) wasn't final). This is a good reason to make a method final. By making getName( ) a final method, you can guarantee that the user of subclasses of this object will always call this method when she executes getName( ). In the JDK, the method getClass( ) in java.lang. Object is final for this very reason.

Conditional Compilation

Conditional compilation is a technique in which lines of code are not compiled into the class file based on a particular condition. This can be used to remove tons of debugging code in a production build. To understand the power of conditional compilation, consider Example 2-22, which demonstrates a method that does a complex transaction and logs it using Log4J.

Example 2-22. A method with traces

```
package oreilly.hcj.finalstory;
import org.apache.log4j.Logger;
```

Example 2-22. A method with traces (continued)

```java
public class ConditionalCompile {
  private static final Logger LOGGER =
    Logger.getLogger(ConditionalCompile.class);

  public static void someMethod() {
    // Do some set up code.
    LOGGER.debug("Set up complete, beginning phases.");
    // do first part.
    LOGGER.debug("phase1 complete");
    // do second part.
    LOGGER.debug("phase2 complete");
    // do third part.
    LOGGER.debug("phase3 complete");
    // do finalization part.
    LOGGER.debug("phase4 complete");
    // Operation Completed
    LOGGER.debug("All phases completed successfully");
  }
}
```

If you assume that there is a lot of code in each phase of the method, the logging shown in this example could be essential to finding business logic errors. However, when you deploy this application in a production environment, you have to go back through the code and eliminate all the logging, or this method will run like a three-legged dog in quicksand. Even if Log4j is set to a higher error level, every logging statement requires a call to another method, a lookup in a configuration table, and so on.

Leaving extensive logging in your program is just not a viable option. I remember going to a new company and working on some code written by biologists. I fired up the GUI, which was one of those "typical slow Java GUIs," and immediately noticed something odd. In my console window, there was so much stuff being written that the word "spam" hardly does it justice. In just initializing the application, the program wrote in the neighborhood of 6,000 lines of tracing information. "No wonder this GUI is slow," I thought. Writing out traces is an extremely CPU-expensive activity, and you should avoid it in a production system whenever possible.

To reduce the overhead, you could try to turn off the logging using a variable:

```java
package oreilly.hcj.finalstory;
import org.apache.log4j.Logger;

public class ConditionalCompile {
  private static final Logger LOGGER =
    Logger.getLogger(ConditionalCompile.class);

  private static boolean doLogging = false;
```

```
public static void someMethodBetter() {
  // Do some set up code.
  if (doLogging) {
    LOGGER.debug("Set up complete, beginning phases.");
  }

  // do first part.
  if (doLogging) {
    LOGGER.debug("phase1 complete");
  }

  // do second part.
  if (doLogging) {
    LOGGER.debug("phase2 complete");
  }

  // do third part.
  if (doLogging) {
    LOGGER.debug("phase3 complete");
  }

  // do finalization part.
  if (doLogging) {
    LOGGER.debug("phase4 complete");
  }

  // Operation Completed
  if (doLogging) {
    LOGGER.debug("All phases completed successfully");
  }
  }
}
```

In this code, you used the doLogging variable to shut off the logging information at runtime. Using if statements such as this improves your runtime performance and allows you to turn the logging on and off whenever you want. When doLogging is true, you get all of the logging along with the performance hit. When doLogging is false, you get no logging, and somewhat less of a performance hit.

This may be a good idea in some cases. However, if your logging is printing out extensive information, this technique will still slow things down. When the variable is false, instead of printing out the debugging information, the CPU performs one comparison each time it hits a logging statement.

 When using the isDebugEnabled() method in Log4J, the cost is much more than one comparison per if statement.

Also, you can't afford to forget that in a method run thousands of times, a few comparisons per method can add up quickly.

You need the ability to compile conditionally, depending on your build paradigm. In development mode, you want all of the debugging code. In deployment mode, you don't. C++ refugees will undoubtedly recognize this ability in the #ifdef directive. Although Java doesn't have this directive, the final keyword can be used to accomplish similar results:

```
package oreilly.hcj.finalstory;
import org.apache.log4j.Logger;

public class ConditionalCompile {
  private static final Logger LOGGER =
    Logger.getLogger(ConditionalCompile.class);

  private final static boolean doLogging = false;

  public static void someMethodBetter() {
    // Do some set up code.
    if (doLogging) {
      LOGGER.debug("Set up complete, beginning phases.");
    }

    // do first part.
    if (doLogging) {
      LOGGER.debug("phase1 complete");
    }

    // do second part.
    if (doLogging) {
      LOGGER.debug("phase2 complete");
    }

    // do third part.
    if (doLogging) {
      LOGGER.debug("phase3 complete");
    }

    // do finalization part.
    if (doLogging) {
      LOGGER.debug("phase4 complete");
    }

    // Operation Completed
    if (doLogging) {
      LOGGER.debug("All phases completed successfully");
    }
  }
}
```

By converting the doLogging attribute into a final attribute, you have told the compiler that whenever it sees doLogging, it should replace it with false as per the compile-time substitution rules from earlier in the chapter. The first pass of the compiler changes the code to something like this:

```
package oreilly.hcj.finalstory;
import org.apache.log4j.Logger;

public class ConditionalCompile {
  private static final Logger LOGGER =
    Logger.getLogger(ConditionalCompile.class);

  private static boolean doLogging = false;

  public static void someMethodBetter() {
    // Do some set up code.
    if (false) {
      LOGGER.debug("Set up complete, beginning phases.");
    }

    // do first part.
    if (false) {
      LOGGER.debug("phase1 complete");
    }

    // do second part.
    if (false) {
      LOGGER.debug("phase2 complete");
    }

    // do third part.
    if (false) {
      LOGGER.debug("phase3 complete");
    }

    // do finalization part.
    if (false) {
      LOGGER.debug("phase4 complete");
    }

    // Operation Completed
    if (false) {
      LOGGER.debug("All phases completed successfully");
    }
  }
}
```

Once this is done, the compiler takes another look at it and sees that there are unreachable statements in the code. Since you are working with a top-quality compiler, it doesn't like all those unreachable byte codes. So it removes them, and you end up with this:

```
package oreilly.hcj.finalstory;
import org.apache.log4j.Logger;
```

```
public class ConditionalCompile {
  private static final Logger LOGGER =
    Logger.getLogger(ConditionalCompile.class);

  private static boolean doLogging = false;

  public static void someMethodBetter() {
    // Do some set up code.
    // do first part.
    // do second part.
    // do third part.
    // do finalization part.
    // Operation Completed
  }
}
```

This is perfect! By setting the value of the doLogging to true or false and recompiling the class, you can turn on and off inclusion of code in your program. When you build for development, you alter the code to set doLogging to true. When you build a production release, set it to false. You now have the best of both worlds.

 Remember that if you change a primitive final static logging variable, you'll have to change the class that contains that variable and recompile all the classes that reference it.

Conditional Compilation Variable Location

When implementing conditional compilation, the question of where to put these compilation variables always comes up. There are many potential solutions to the problem, but you need to watch out for a couple of pitfalls.

First of all, putting a variable in the top-level package of your product is probably not a good idea. The problem is that there may be other classes in this package as well. Since all classes will be referencing this package, you could accidentally create circular package dependencies.

 Circular dependencies arise when Package A depends on Package B, which in turn depends on Package A. Circular dependencies make it very difficult to separate code into components, and circular references make code fragile by allowing bugs to migrate across the dependencies into other packages.

Your best bet is to create a new package in each of your major products. If you are an employee of a Sun, for example, each major product would be defined by the package directly under com.sun. I like to create a package named _development under the major packages of my clients' products. The leading underscore helps me remember that this package is not part of the product base but is instead a container for things such as these variables. Inside this new package, place a class named DevelopmentMode.

In this class, install one variable for each package in your product. Then you can simply import the class and access the appropriate variable. For the *Hardcore Java* example code, the class would look something like the following.

```java
package oreilly.hcj._development;

public final class DevelopmentMode {
  /** Development mode constant for package oreilly.hcj.bankdata. */
  public static final boolean hcj_bankdata = true;

  /** Development mode constant for package oreilly.hcj.bankdata. */
  public static final boolean hcj_collections = true;

  /** Development mode constant for package oreilly.hcj.bankdata. */
  public static final boolean hcj_constants = true;

  /** Development mode constant for package oreilly.hcj.bankdata. */
  public static final boolean hcj_datamodeling = true;

  /** Development mode constant for package oreilly.hcj.bankdata. */
  public static final boolean hcj_exceptions = true;

  /** Development mode constant for package oreilly.hcj.bankdata. */
  public static final boolean hcj_finalstory = true;

  /** Development mode constant for package oreilly.hcj.bankdata. */
  public static final boolean hcj_immutable = true;

  /** Development mode constant for package oreilly.hcj.bankdata. */
  public static final boolean hcj_nested = true;

  /** Development mode constant for package oreilly.hcj.bankdata. */
  public static final boolean hcj_proxies = true;

  /** Development mode constant for package oreilly.hcj.bankdata. */
  public static final boolean hcj_references = true;

  /** Development mode constant for package oreilly.hcj.bankdata. */
  public static final boolean hcj_review = true;

  private DevelopmentMode() {
    assert false: "DevelopmentMode is a Singleton.";
  }
}
```

In this class, you don't specify the oreilly package because it would be a bit redundant, since all the code you would be writing for your company would be in that package. However, the variable naming here is a matter of taste. The important fact is that all packages can be turned from development to deployment mode in one place. Using the constant is easy:

```
package oreilly.hcj.finalstory;

import oreilly.hcj._development.DevelopmentMode;

public class ConditionalCompile {

  public void projectVariables() {
    if (DevelopmentMode.hcj_finalstory) {
      // ...do conditional code.
    }
  }
}
```

You merely use the constant in the same way it was used in the last section. This allows you to take advantage of conditional compilation in a maintainable manner. However, be careful not to place any malfunctioning code into the _development package (or whatever you named your package), or you may create circular package dependencies. The _development package shouldn't depend on anything other than third-party libraries and the JDK itself.

Using final as a Coding Standard

I imagine that many of you never thought you would see an entire chapter written on a single keyword. However, this particular keyword is quite useful. I strongly advise that you spread final all over your code. You should use it so much that not seeing it becomes a rare, if not completely unknown, occurrence.

This coding standard may take a little getting used to but it will really pay off in the long term. The best way to get started is to force yourself to use final heavily whenever you write or edit code. Also, you should force the junior developers working for you to adopt the use of final as a coding standard. They may grumble and balk for a bit, but the coding standard will quickly become so automatic that the developers won't consciously think about it.

Like good Javadoc habits, this one is much easier to implement if you do it while you are coding. Having to go back through old code to implement the standard is a real pain. For this reason, I suggest you make it a coding standard starting today. If you have tools that allow you to edit the code templates, edit them to introduce final everywhere you can. Also, when you edit someone else's code, introduce the final variable liberally. Doing so helps to guarantee that no one can mess up your code without actually trying to do so.

CHAPTER 3
Immutable Types

The source of one of the most persistent problems encountered in Java is the fact that variables for constructed types are *always* references, and these references are passed by value. Essentially, this allows anyone with a reference to the object to change the object. Although this may not be bad in some circumstances, it would be disastrous in others. If one part of the program is expecting data to be in an object, and another part of the program alters that data to be `null`, the program would crash with `NullPointerExceptions`. Since the part of the program that changed the data object is different from the part that generated the exceptions, the bug could be very difficult to locate.

One approach to this problem is to make the data object an instance of a class that cannot be changed after construction; these types are referred to as *immutable types*. Instances of immutable types are called *immutable objects*. If your data object is an immutable object, the other classes using the object simply have no way to change the data in the object. This is the main advantage of immutable objects; you can pass their references all over the place without having to worry about breaking encapsulation or thread safety.

Although immutable objects exist in many languages, they take on a more serious role in Java. Like virtual shoelaces, they tie together the language of Java without getting much credit. However, the conscious and correct usage of immutable types is often the mark of a Java guru.

Fundamentals

Immutable types are not as simple as they appear at first. In fact, there are devious pitfalls with immutable types that can ensnare even the best developers. However, as long as you know where these traps lie, evading them is an easy matter. Let's start the journey by trying to create an immutable type.

Creating Immutable Types

Creating an immutable type is a simple process that takes just a minute to learn. You merely have to create a class that has no write methods; this includes property set methods as well as other methods that alter the state of the instance. See Example 3-1.

Example 3-1. An immutable person

```
package oreilly.hcj.immutable;

public class ImmutablePerson {
  private String firstName;
  private String lastName;
  private int age;

  public ImmutablePerson(final String firstName, final String lastName,
                         final int age) {
    if (firstName == null) {
      throw new NullPointerException("firstName");
    }
    if (lastName == null) {
      throw new NullPointerException("lastName");
    }
    this.age = age;
    this.firstName = firstName;
    this.lastName = lastName;
  }

  public int getAge() {
    return age;
  }

  public String getFirstName() {
    return firstName;
  }

  public String getLastName() {
    return lastName;
  }
}
```

In the ImmutablePerson class, you allow the user to pass in all arguments to the constructor and then simply don't declare any write methods to the attributes. Once the person is constructed, it looks like it can't be changed. However, unfortunately, it can be changed. This type is immutable by all appearances, but there is actually a hole.

Cracked Immutables

Using reflection, a Java developer can remove the access protection on the class and then change variable values. It is true that this wouldn't be a very smart thing to do; however, I have seen far stranger things in my career.

 At this point, don't worry about how the access permission can be removed. We will beat that subject to death in Chapter 9, which covers this trick as well as many other reflection techniques.

In fact, you don't even need to use reflection to make ImmutablePerson suddenly go mutable. The attributes in the ImmutablePerson class are immutable only with respect to outside classes. This doesn't prevent an eager-to-please junior developer from writing a method into the class that ends up changing firstName to null and crashing the whole GUI code base with NullPointerExceptions. Afterwards, you will probably end up spending several hours debugging the code before it finally occurs to you that your immutable type isn't so immutable.

Fortunately, there is a way you can block both of these misguided developers in one move. Using your old friend final, you can rewrite your immutable object, as shown in the following code:

```
package oreilly.hcj.immutable;

public class ImmutablePerson {
  private final String firstName;
  private final String lastName;
  private final int age;

  public ImmutablePerson(final String firstName, final String lastName,
                         final int age) {
    if (firstName == null) {
      throw new NullPointerException("firstName");
    }
    if (lastName == null) {
      throw new NullPointerException("lastName");
    }
    this.age = age;
    this.firstName = firstName;
    this.lastName = lastName;
  }

  public int getAge() {
    return age;
  }

  public String getFirstName() {
    return firstName;
  }
```

```
    public String getLastName( ) {
      return lastName;
    }
  }
```

In the new version of ImmutablePerson, each of the attributes of the class has been declared final. This will prevent even the most enterprising developer or reflection guru from changing the attributes once they are set at construction time. Whenever you create immutable types, you should freeze the immutable variables using this technique.

False Immutable Types

Often you will encounter types that look immutable but really aren't. These objects are deceiving because they have no write methods but have the ability to change anyway. Here's an example:

```
package oreilly.hcj.immutable;

import java.awt.Point;

public class SomeData {

  private final Point value;

  public SomeData (final Point value) {
    this.value = value;
  }

  public Point getValue( ) {
    return value;
  }
}
```

Although this class looks like a normal immutable type, it suffers from two gaping holes.

The first hole occurs in the constructor. Since variables that contain constructed objects in Java are actually reference variables, this.value points to the same object the caller passed in. Therefore, the caller actually still has a reference to the object held in the internal variable this.value. This can be a problem if the caller has code that looks like the following:

```
package oreilly.hcj.immutable;

import java.awt.Point;

public class SomeClass {

  public final static void main(final String[] args) {
    Point position = new Point(25, 3);
    SomeData data = new SomeData(position);
```

```
        position.x = 22;
        System.out.println(data.getValue());
    }
}
```

If you run this demo program, you will see the following results:

```
>ant -Dexample=oreilly.hcj.immutable.SomeClass run_example
```

```
run_example:
    [java] java.awt.Point[x=22,y=3]
```

Since the method constructing SomeData has the reference to the Point object that it passes to the constructor, it can still alter the data long after the object is constructed. The getter method suffers from a similar problem: when the Point is returned from the get method, the caller will get a reference to the same instance as the one contained in your supposedly immutable type. Also, the final keyword doesn't protect you because it will only block someone from changing the Point to which the variable position points; even as a final, the contents of the Point object stored in the position variable are changeable.

The solution to this problem is to make copies of mutable objects when creating new instances of classes. Your SomeData class would be better written as:

```
package oreilly.hcj.immutable;

import java.awt.Point;

public class SomeBetterData {
  /** Holds the value */
  private final Point value;

  public SomeBetterData(final Point value) {
    this.value = new Point(value);
  }

  public Point getValue() {
    return new Point(value);
  }
}
```

In this version of SomeData, the Point being passed to the constructor of the class is copied, and then the copy is set as the data member. This means that the caller or the constructor can change the point all they want, and the actual value in SomeBetterData won't change. With the getter, the story is similar. Whenever a user calls you to get the value, copy the Point and send back the copy. What the caller does with the copy is of no concern.

Also, don't forget methods you call inside your immutable types as well. If at some point you call a method such as the following, you could have problems:

```
SomeClass.someMethod(this.value);
```

This call has the same problem as your old getter. However, the problem is slightly different: in this case, you are calling another method in another class from within the immutable object. The problem is that you are passing the reference to the internal variable to the remote method. This is dangerous because you don't know what the remote method will do with the object. In this situation, you should make a copy, just like you did for the getter:

```
SomeClass.someMethod(new Point(this.value));
```

Whenever you are creating immutable types with parameters that are not immutable, make sure that you copy all of the mutable parameters. However, if the parameters are immutable themselves, you can afford to simply store the reference to the object; since neither the class nor the caller can change the value, the object is safe.

In fact, the "copy all mutable objects rule" should be applied even to types that *are* mutable. Whenever you allow a user of your class to have references to the objects that are internal to your class, all of your encapsulation work flies out the window. Save yourself some headaches and just copy like a demon:

```
package oreilly.hcj.immutable;
import java.awt.Point;

public class SomeDataObject {
  private Point coordinate = new Point( );

  public void setCoordinate(final Point coordinate) {
    if (coordinate == null) {
      throw new NullPointerException("coordinate");
    }
    if ((coordinate.x < 0 ) || (coordinate.y < 0)) {
      throw new IllegalArgumentException( );
    }
    this.coordinate = new Point(coordinate);
  }

  public Point getCoordinate( ) {
    return new Point(coordinate);
  }
}
```

 Encapsulation is the process of exposing only the interface of a class to the users of that class, the idea being not to show any implementation details of the class.

This data object class is safely encapsulated because whenever the user calls the setCoordinate( ) method, the incoming Point object is copied before it is stored. Similarly, whenever coordinate is returned by the getCoordinate( ) method, it is copied. There is no way that the developer can break your encapsulation because he can never get a reference to the internal object.

Immutable Problems

Although immutable objects are extremely useful in creating solid code, they can cause problems if you aren't paying attention. The most important thing to remember about immutable objects is that whenever you try to change them, you actually end up creating new objects that are themselves immutable. This can result in some extremely slow code. The String trap is one of the most prevalent examples of this problem.

The String Trap

The most commonly used immutable type in the Java language is java.lang.String. However, many good developers don't know that String is immutable. They are fooled by all of the "operations" that can be done to a String. They often say, "How can String be immutable? I can concatenate strings and replace values." However, these well-meaning developers are wrong!

Whenever you perform an operation on a string, you are actually creating copies of the string that are modified to accommodate your request. This applies to concatenation as well as to operations such as splitting and replacing strings. However, the fact that this nuance of Java is not well-known is the cause of many common programming problems.

For example, consider the following code used to concatenate strings in a sentence:

```
public void buildSentence (String[] words) {
  String sentence = new String( );
  for (int idx = 0; idx < words.length; idx++) {
    sentence += " " + words[idx];
  }
}
```

The problem with this code is that at each and every iteration of the for loop, the virtual machine allocates an entirely new String object; this new object contains the characters in the sentence variable concatenated with the word being added. Since the String object is immutable, a new String object must be created to reflect each modification. Assuming that 234,565 words are being added, you may want to take a long lunch.

If that isn't bad enough, remember that all of those intermediary String objects that this code created are not purged from memory until garbage collection is run, at which point the program will hit another speed bump the size of Mt. Everest. So, on top of a slow program, you have a program that eats memory like candy.

This problem is not unique to String objects. Every immutable type suffers from the fact that the compiler must allocate an entirely new object to change the object. The solution to the allocation problem in the previous example is to use `java.lang.StringBuffer`:

```
public void buildSentence (String[] words) {
    final StringBuffer sentence = new StringBuffer(1000);
    for (int idx = 0; idx < words.length; idx++) {
        sentence.append(" ");
        sentence.append(words[idx]);
    }
}
```

This version of the method from Example 1-7 is much improved. The `StringBuffer` is a mutable object, so it can be changed without memory reallocation. The compiler will allocate a new object only when the `StringBuffer` exceeds its capacity.

> You can even tune the buffer instance to your needs to optimize these allocations. For concatenations that aren't very long, such as dynamic SQL, you can get away with 500 or 1,000 as the buffer size. For those that are extremely long, you can put in bigger initial sizes and increments:
>
> ```
> final StringBuffer moreSpace = new StringBuffer(2500);
> ```

Your previously slow program now runs like a Ferrari, and takes up only a fraction of the memory it did before.

Buffering Bad Performance

Now that you have the concept of immutable types firmly in mind, you know that you should use `StringBuffer` objects when trying to concatenate `Strings`. On top of that, you have mastered the `StringBuffer` class and are now ready to use it in your `toString()` methods. However, before you get too excited, let's examine a couple of common `StringBuffer` pitfalls:

```
package oreilly.hcj.immutable;
public final static String dumpArray(int[] array) {
    final StringBuffer buf = new StringBuffer(500);
    buf.append("{");
    for (int idx = 0; idx < array.length; idx++) {
        buf.append("[" + idx + "] " + array[idx]);
    }
    buf.append("}");
    return buf.toString();
}
```

The problem with this code is that it is a performance hog. Referring to the Javadoc documentation on the `StringBuffer` class, you will find that whenever you concatenate `Strings` using the + operator, the virtual machine creates a new `StringBuffer` object to do the concatenation. Since you already have a `StringBuffer`, this is wasteful; why not reuse the buffer you already created? In the previous method, you created not just one `StringBuffer`, but an additional one for each iteration in the loop.

Each time this method runs, it allocates (words.length + 1) StringBuffer objects. Since allocation within a loop should be avoided, rewrite this method to decrease processor time and memory usage:

```
package oreilly.hcj.immutable;
public final static String dumpArrayBetter(int[] array) {
  final StringBuffer buf = new StringBuffer(500);
  buf.append("{");
  for (int idx = 0; idx < array.length; idx++) {
    buf.append("[");
    buf.append(idx);
    buf.append("] ");
    buf.append(array[idx]);
  }
  buf.append("}");
  return buf.toString();
}
```

In this revised method, you create only one StringBuffer instance and append to that buffer in each iteration. The method contains more lines, but it is now lightning quick.

If you're not convinced of the impact of these changes, run the oreilly.hcj.review. BufferingBadPerformance class in this book's example code. But beware: the micro program may appear to hang because of this allocation snippet:

```
public static final void dumpArrayReallyBad(int[] array) {
  String result = new String("}");
  for (int idx = 0; idx < (array.length); idx++) {
    result += "[" + idx + "] " + array[idx];
  }
  result += "}";
}
```

This method uses String allocations and is horribly slow. It can literally take minutes to run with values that the other methods crunch in seconds. If you want to try the test with high values, I suggest you either comment the execution of this method out or get a small book to read, perhaps *War and Peace*. A sample run of the program is shown here:

```
>ant oreilly.hcj.review.BufferingBadPerformance run_example
run_example:
    [java] Building 10000 element Fibbonacci Number array took 0 millis
    [java] Using dumpArray took 150 millis
    [java] Using dumpArrayBetter took 40 millis
    [java] Using dumpArrayReallyBad took 88347 millis
```

The dumpArrayBetter( ) method was significantly faster than the dumpArray( ) method. However, the output shows that dumpArrayReallyBad( ), which uses string allocations, took more than 88 seconds to run! If you choose values bigger than 10,000, your virtual machine will probably run out of memory before dumpArrayReallyBad( ) is done.

When you run the examples, your times may vary depending on the speed of your computer and other programs you are running, but the ratios should consistently represent the claims of improved performance achieved by using a single buffer.

Although small improvements in speed, such as the difference between dumpArray( ) and dumpArrayBetter( ), may not seem very important, they will add up quickly if the affected method is run thousands of times. Consider a method run 20,000 times in the course of a batch processing call. If you shave just 15 milliseconds off each iteration loop, you save 15 × 20,000, or 300,000 milliseconds. A call that took five minutes before now runs in the blink of an eye.

Immutable or Not

There are good reasons to make things immutable, but there are also good reasons to make them mutable. Although you should make each decision on a case-by-case basis, the following factors should help:

- If the object is supposed to be a constant, it should always be immutable.
- If the object will be changed frequently, it should be a mutable object. For example, a class such as StringBuffer is changed frequently, so it wouldn't make much sense as an immutable object.
- If the object is very large, be careful if you opt for immutability. Large immutable objects need to be copied in order to be changed; this copying can slow down a program significantly.
- Sets and other collections returned from a method should be immutable to preserve encapsulation.

CHAPTER 4
Collections

The single most common type of question encountered on Sun's Java Developer Connection forums has to do with the usage of collection classes in the `java.util` package. Since there are many Java developers out there that have migrated from other professions, this is not surprising. Those who haven't taken university-level data structures courses may find the collections to be a bit confusing.

However, the proper use of collections is one of the cornerstones of quality Java programming. Therefore, this chapter will explore them in detail. We will cover the architecture of the collections framework and the usage and concepts behind each collection type. However, we won't cover many of the actual methods in the collections, since these are easily understood by studying the Javadoc. The goal of this discussion is to help you decide which collection to use and why it is the best for a specific job.

Collection Concepts

During the early days of object-oriented programming, one of its main deficiencies was its inability to manage collections of objects. For years, C++ suffered because the collections management that was available was not standardized. To attack this problem, various vendors designed packages of collection classes that could be purchased and implemented. However, even these packages did not solve the portability problem among cooperating vendors. For example, if my company had bought Rogue Wave Tools.h++, all of your business partners would have needed to make a similar purchase to extend your software.

To fix this fundamental deficiency, Sun introduced standard collection classes in the earliest version of the JDK. This decision, along with the other common class libraries in the JDK, contributed to the rapid rise of Java technology. Now, instead of my partner companies having to make a separate and often expensive purchase, they can simply use the collections in the JDK.

An Interface-Based Approach

The JDK collection classes can be found in the java.util package. They are structured using an interface-implementation model. For each type of collection, there is one interface and various implementations. For example, the List interface is implemented by the AbstractList, ArrayList, LinkedList, and Vector classes.

 Don't worry about these implementation classes for now; we will discuss them later in the chapter.

Interfaces are a special approach to object-oriented engineering. While classes implement the concept, the interface defines the concept. For example, an ArrayList and a LinkedList are both conceptually lists.

The interfaces of the java.util package are the only components that should be exposed to the users of your classes, unless you have no other choice. This follows from the idea of encapsulation, which dictates that the programmer should not expose implementation details to the user of a class, but only the interface to that class. For example, the following code is an example of a good interface-based technique:

```
public class SomeClass {
   HashSet someSet = new HashSet( );

   protected Set someMethod( ) {
     return this.someSet;
   }
}
```

In this example, the programmer exposes only the interface of someSet to the users and does not let them know which implementation is being used. Code programmed in this manner is very flexible and bug-resistant. For example, if you decide that HashSet does not perform well enough, you can always change the implementation without affecting the users of the class. By contrast, consider the following code, which does not use interfaces:

```
public class SomeClass {
   HashSet someSet = new HashSet( );

   protected HashSet someBadMethod( ) {
     return this.someSet;
   }
}
```

In this example, if you found a bug that occurred because you were using a HashSet, you could not easily change the implementation used for the set. If you did, you would then have to change all of the code that is using your class. This could echo around your code base for quite a while as you chase bugs.

You should expose the underlying collection implementation in your code only when you have no other choice, such as when the users of your code need access to a specific functionality of the implementation. In fact, this is a good policy to follow within classes as well. The example would have been much better written as:

```
public class SomeClass {
  Set someOtherSet = new HashSet();

  protected Set someOtherMethod() {
    return this.someOtherSet;
  }
}
```

In the revised class, you leverage the usage of interfaces for the instance variable type and for external communication. This gives you even more protection from migrating bugs that may result from an implementation change. If another method in the class uses someOtherSet as a Set and not a HashSet, then you can easily change to another Set implementation as the need arises.

Collection Types

Now that you have mastered the interface approach, you should examine the actual interfaces in the java.util package and the differences between them.

There are two types of general collections that form the basis of all collection classes:

`java.util.Map`

> This interface represents collection types that store values in a lookup table. Each value is stored by using a key that can later fetch that value from the map. Maps can take many forms; one recognizable form is a dictionary. A dictionary class stores words and their definitions. The `java.util.Map` classes work the same way.

`java.util.Collection`

> This interface represents generic collections other than those that store values in a key-based lookup table. These collections have a variety of access mechanisms.

These two interfaces form the conceptual base for the entire `java.util` package. Other collections that extend the conceptual basis are derived from these interfaces.

Maps

The `java.util.Map` class defines a map that is unsorted and iterated in a fairly unpredictable manner. In fact, one of the warnings for the `Map` class in the Javadoc is that the iteration order is *not* predictable. This is not a problem in many situations, such as storing event listeners that listen for specific events. In this case, the key could be the event type and the value store could be a set of listeners; since the map would never be iterated in order, having a defined iteration order is not needed.

However, there may be times when you want more control over the iteration order of a `Map`. For example, if you are creating a tree control to show the files on a user's computer, you may want to display these objects in alphabetical order for easy reading and interaction. For this purpose, you would need a specialized kind of map:

`java.util.SortedMap`

> This interface extends a map to specify the iteration order of the keys in the map. This map has a restriction: it can only use keys that it can sort. You must give the class a `Comparator`, which is an implementation of the `java.util.Comparator` to implement the sorting, or you must use keys that implement the `java.lang.Comparable` interfaces.

Other than the difference in iteration order, the main difference between `SortedMaps` and `Maps` is that `SortedMaps` are generally slower when it comes to inserting and removing items because the map must rearrange itself to accommodate new values. Regular `Maps` don't have to worry about these issues. For this reason, you should use only a `SortedMap` if you must have a fixed iteration order.

One thing that `Maps` and `SortedMaps` have in common is that they are unable to contain the same key more than once. Each key has a defined and assigned value. If you add a new element to a map with a key that the map is already using, the map implementation will simply replace the old value with the new one.

Collections

The Collection interface has several variants that are used to extend the Collection functionality. The Collection class itself defines only collections of objects and says nothing about their iteration order, method of access, or ability to contain duplicates. However, it is fairly uncommon for developers to directly use a Collection to store anything. Usually, you need to be more specific about the constraints of your Collection. For this purpose, the JDK provides you with three types of Collections:

java.util.Set

> Sets are collections that do not guarantee the order in which they will be iterated. However, they do guarantee that no duplicates will be found inside the set.

java.util.List

> Lists are collections that are in a specific order and can be accessed through a numerical index. They can also contain duplicate elements. Note that just because the elements are arrayed in an order doesn't necessarily mean they are *sorted*. The elements in a list are usually in the same order in which they were inserted. They may or may not be sorted, depending on the programmer's needs.

java.util.SortedSet

> Sorted sets maintain the order of the objects within the set, depending on one of two criteria. Either the objects are sorted according to their natural sorting order, as defined by their implementation of Comparable, or they are sorted using a supplied comparator. We will discuss the specifics of both procedures later in the chapter.

Now that you have all of the nifty features of these subtypes, the question becomes, "What good is the Collection interface?" The first reason it exists is because it provides a conceptual basis for all collections. The second reason is to give the collections an easy way to convert from one type of collection to another. In this manner, you can copy lists to sets, and so on.

Implementations

Now that you have the various types of collections in mind, it is time to turn your attention to the implementation of these collections. A List, for example, can be implemented a number of ways, each with advantages and disadvantages. However, before you can understand the various implementations of Lists and other collections, you need to understand how collections and maps determine equality and order.

Determining Equality and Order

Until now, we have been discussing equality and order quite a bit, but without explaining how these conditions are actually discovered by the collections. For example, how does a Map decide if two keys are the same, and how does a SortedSet determine the order used to sort the objects? To answer these questions, you have to tackle the basic principles of object equality: identity and comparability.

Equality versus identity

For many collections to do their job, they need to know which objects are equal. For example, a Set can't exclude duplicate entries if it doesn't know how to check to see whether supplied objects are equal. These collections take advantage of the fact that all objects in Java descend from the common class java.lang.Object.

Since all objects descend from Object, the Set implementations can call the method equals( ) on all objects. This allows the set to compare objects. However, there is one catch: for this to be effective, the object must define (or inherit) a valid implementation of equals( ).

The default implementation of equals( ) compares two objects to see whether they are the same object in the virtual machine by *identity*, not by *equality*. Suppose you create two Address objects that define the addresses of employees. Both address objects can contain the same street name, number, country, postal code, and other data. However, these objects are two different instances (and therefore reside at two different memory addresses). In this case, the Address objects are equivalent, but they are not the same object—i.e., they are not identical. If you use the default implementation of the equals( ) method, you would always get a result of false despite the fact that the objects are equal. To solve this problem, you need to override the definition of equals( ) to compare the actual data in the class. While creating your new equals method, you need to keep the following requirements in mind:

- The method must consistently return the same value for any single comparison of objects x and y no matter how many times the comparison is run, assuming that no data changes in x and y.

- The method should be symmetric so that x.equals(y) returns the same result as y.equals(x).

- The method should be transitive so that if x.equals(y) and y.equals(z) returns true, then z.equals(x) also returns true.

- Whenever the comparison is against a null value, the method should always return false—i.e., (x.equals(null) == false) should be true for all types of x.

- The method should be reflexive so that x.equals(x) is always true.

 Don't forget to override the implementation of hashCode( ) when you override equals( ). There is a contract between these two methods that says that any objects evaluating as equivalent must also return the same hash code. For more information on this contract, see the Javadoc for java.lang.Object.equals( ).

The overridden equals( ) method ensures that collections that are not supposed to contain duplicates do indeed prevent them. It also illustrates an important concept in programming. Two objects are said to be equal in *identity* if they are the same object instance, whereas two objects are said to have *equality* if they contain the same data.

Comparing objects

The problem of sorting in collections is solved by defining a way to compare two objects. This can be accomplished using two different techniques. The first technique is to have the objects implement java.lang.Comparable. The Comparable interface contains a single method defined by the following signature:

```
public interface Comparable {
  public int compareTo(Object o);
}
```

The compareTo( ) method returns an integer indicating the comparison of the this object to the target object. If compareTo( ) returns a negative integer, then the this object is said to be less than the object given in the parameter o. If the returned integer is positive, then the this object is greater than the given object. If the integer is 0, the object is comparatively the same as the this object. Generally, implementations will ignore anything other than whether the return value is positive, negative, or 0. Therefore, it is useless to worry about defining how much less than the given object the return value is. For example, a returned value of -8 would be treated the same as a returned value of -1.

One important factor to remember about this comparison is that it does *not* compare equality. Two objects that are not equivalent may result in a compareTo( ) result of 0. This occurs often when objects try to sort on only one or two fields in the class. For example, if you consider a Person object, you would want to sort on first name and last name but not necessarily on the other fields, such as age and tax identification number. In this case, compareTo( ) would return a value of 0 for two people named Paul Henry despite the fact that one is a senior executive and the other is an infant.

The compareTo( ) method has a number of requirements similar to the equals( ) method:

- Like the equals( ) method, the compareTo( ) method must return the same value for any single comparison of objects x and y no matter how many times the comparison is run, assuming that no data changes in x and y.

- The method should be transitive—i.e., if object x is comparatively greater than object y, and object y is comparatively greater than object z, object x should be greater than object z. This is generally written using the following mathematical notation:

    If x > y and y > z then x > z

- The method must ensure that the comparison is consistent. For example, if x. compareTo(y) yields -1, then y.compareTo(x) should yield 1.

- The method should be reflexive so that x.compareTo(x) always returns 0.

- It is *recommended* that objects that are comparatively 0, but are not necessarily equals( ), indicate this in the documentation to the class.

It is always a good idea to implement the Comparable interface for objects that may be stored inside ordered collections. This implementation defines what is known as the *natural ordering* of instances. However, there are some situations in which a developer may want to sort the objects in a collection based on a value other than the natural ordering. The java.util.Comparator interface is used for this purpose.

Suppose you have a set of data objects that contain a variety of information, and you want to be able to sort that information to achieve something other than the natural ordering. For example, if you have a set of Person objects, you may want to sort them by age or occupation instead of name. To accomplish this, create a new implementation of the Comparator interface that will sort the objects. Example 4-1 shows a Comparator that sorts Person objects based on their tax identification number.

Example 4-1. An age Comparator

```
package oreilly.hcj.collections;

import java.util.Comparator;
import oreilly.hcj.bankdata.Person;

public class TaxIdComparator implements Comparator {
  public int compare(final Object x, final Object y) {
    return ((Person)x).getTaxID( )
           .compareTo(((Person)y).getTaxID( ));
  }
}
```

In this example, you take advantage of the compareTo( ) method built into java.lang. String to compare the two people based on the values of their taxID property. Now that you have a new Comparator implementation, you can sort the people by passing this comparator to sorting collections:

```
public class SomeClass {
  protected void demoComparator( ) {
    SortedSet people = new TreeSet(new TaxIdComparator( ));

    // ...add people to the set.
  }
}
```

Once you have created the sorted set and assigned the comparator, you can be sure that the people inserted into the set will always be sorted in order of taxID. You can also implement more complicated comparators that are configurable.

Big O Notation

Implementing collections in programming languages has been a topic of computer science since the first days of structured languages. This topic was born out of the desire to efficiently store and analyze information in computer systems. It is a true science with theories, mathematics, and concepts. One of the most important pieces of mathematics necessary to understanding collections is the concept of *Big O Notation*. Big O Notation is a mathematical term used to express the efficiency of an algorithm depending on the number of elements the algorithm must work on. The notation is called Big O Notation because of the conspicuous usage of the letter O in the formulas. The O stands for *orders of magnitude*. The general idea is that the lower the orders of magnitude, the faster the algorithm is.

Consider a list of people stored in a random order. Big O Notation will tell you how long, on average, it will take you to find any one person in the list by name. If you think about the worst-case scenario, you will realize that you may look through all of the elements in a list, only to find that your target person is the last element on the list. As the list grows in size, your worst-case scenario gets…worse. If you have 100 people in your list, your worst-case scenario would involve performing 99 checks to find a person. If your list is 100,000 people, then you would have to do 99,999 checks before you find the person. This is described in Big O Notation with the formula $O(n)$. This shorthand is read as "the orders of magnitude grows in proportion to n."

By contrast, if you store people that are sorted by name in an ordered list, you can use a binary search algorithm to find the target person, called x, by name. This algorithm compares the person at the halfway point in the list, y, to the target person. If the person x evaluates as equal to person y, then the person is found, and the algorithm stops. However, if the person x evaluates as greater than person y, then the algorithm uses the upper half of the list for the search. If person x evaluates as less than person y, the algorithm uses the lower half of the list. The algorithm then splits up the targeted half and repeats the splitting process until it finds the person or narrows the list to one person that isn't the target person.

The binary search algorithm has an order of magnitude of $O(\log2(n))$. This means that the worst-case scenario to find a person in a list of size n is the result of $\log2(n)$. In the case of your 100,000-person list, the result of this equation is roughly 16.609 operations. In other words, the worst-case scenario is that you would need 17 compares to find the target person.

 Most calculators have only a $\log10(n)$ function. To find $\log2(n)$ on these calculators, you can employ the simple formula $\log2(n) - \log10(n)/\log10(2)$.

The most common orders of magnitude that you will encounter are the following. They are listed in order of most efficient to least efficient.

O(1)

Constant time. No matter how big the list, the time to find the target is always the same.

O(log2(n))

This notation is often abbreviated O(log(n)). For 100,000 people, the value would be 17 compares.

O(n)

For 100,000 people, you would need 99,999 compares.

O(n × log(n))

For 100,000 people, you would need 1,700,000 compares!

O(n²)

My computer couldn't compute this result for 100,000 entries; however, for 100 entries, it is 10,000. This number increases very rapidly.

O(n!)

The factorial is the series of integers from 1 to n multiplied together. For example, if n = 10, the factorial is 10 × 9 × 8 × 7 × 6 × 5 × 4 × 3 × 2 × 1 = 3628800. If you write an algorithm with this order of magnitude, you will definitely have problems.

Big O Notation is not limited to calculating search time in a collection. In fact, it can be applied to any computer algorithm as a measure of efficiency. Generally, algorithms higher than O(n) are not feasible as solutions to practical problems.

Lists

Now that you have an understanding of the basic concepts, you are ready to study various types of collections. Once you have decided that you need a List, the next step is to decide exactly which List you need to use. To make a good decision, you need to have a good understanding of the three standard implementations of List.

 Although anyone can implement the collection interfaces in their code, we will stick to the classes defined in the java.util package. Personally, I like to augment this with the collections classes from Jakarta Commons, available at *http://jakarta.apache.org/*.

java.util.Vector

The Vector class has been with the JDK for quite a long time. If you look at the @since tag in the Javadoc for this class, you will see that it was introduced in JDK 1.0.

A Vector is essentially a dynamic resizing array. You create a vector by specifying its initial size and the size of the chunk you want to use to resize the Vector should it exceed its storage capacity. The following code creates a Vector that starts with 100 elements and grows by 100 elements (when needed):

```
Vector v = new Vector(100, 100);
```

There are other constructors to vectors that use default values for sizes and increments. Additionally, there is an extra constructor for Vector that copies a collection into a Vector and uses the default value for incrementation.

Since Vector is an implementation of the List interface, instances of Vector also allow the user to access each element in a similar manner to that of an array. Therefore, you can think of Vectors as something of a resizable array.

In fact, inside the Vector class, the data is stored as an array of objects. When you initialize the Vector, this array is allocated according to the initial size that you specify in the constructor. As the capacity of the Vector is exceeded, a new array is allocated that is equal to the size of the old array plus the capacityIncrement you specified in the constructor. If you didn't specify either of these values, the class uses its default sizes.

When the Vector class has to resize, it copies the old array into the new array using the System.arraycopy( ) method. Although this method uses fast native code to copy the array, copying is still quite slow and will get slower as the size of the Vector grows. This is why it is important to assign values to capacity and capacityIncrement that minimize the number of resize operations without wasting too much memory.

Using an array to store the data inside a Vector has one other major disadvantage. When inserting an element into a Vector at a specific position, the Vector must use System.arraycopy( ) to move the data to accommodate the insertion, as Figure 4-1 demonstrates.

Figure 4-1 shows the result of inserting a String element at index 2 into the Vector. Since there was already an element at index 2, the Vector had to use System. arraycopy( ) to push the elements further down into the array. If you remove elements at an index, the same process has to be performed to compress the array.

What this all adds up to is that Vector is not very good at inserts and removals of items. However, the array storage paradigm makes Vector very good at accessing elements quickly. Therefore, Vector is a good choice for a list whose prime function is to access the data in the list rapidly, and a poor choice if the data in the list will be modified frequently.

However, the Vector class has one major problem: since Vector was designed to be thread-safe, it is replete with synchronized blocks in the code. This allows multiple

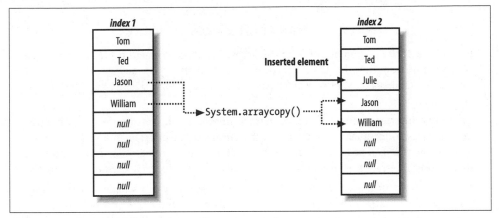

Figure 4-1. Inserting an element into a Vector at an index

threads to use a Vector safely, but significantly slows down its performance. The semantics of synchronized code are outside the scope of this book; however, I can tell you that the process of synchronization is a costly one.

 If you are interested in learning more about synchronization and thread programming, check out *Java Threads* by Scott Oaks and Henry Wong (O'Reilly).

In situations in which data structures will not be accessed by multiple threads or in which the synchronization can be provided outside of the list, using Vector is a sad waste of performance. However, if you will be tossing your list around various threads, you should stick with Vector.

java.util.ArrayList

The ArrayList class is JDK 1.2's answer to the synchronization problem in the Vector class. This class does essentially the same job as the Vector class but without synchronization. The lack of thread safety within the ArrayList class makes it much faster than Vector. However, it still suffers from the same performance problems as Vector when resizing, adding, or removing elements.

If you need a class that has all of the features of Vector but not the internal synchronization, you should choose a list class.

java.util.LinkedList

The LinkedList class also implements the List interface and allows you to store objects in a defined order. However, it implements this ability in a very different way than Vector or ArrayList.

Whereas Vector and ArrayList hold their data in an array of objects, LinkedList uses a special node structure to connect the objects. Each object is stored in a node that contains three attributes: one to contain the data in the node, one to be used as a reference to the next node, and one to be used as a reference to the previous node. The start of the chain of references is usually referred to as the *head* of the list, and is the only node actually stored in the class variable. The structure of a LinkedList is shown in Figure 4-2.

This node-based structure makes it easy to insert or remove elements in the LinkedList. All that the list needs to do is create a node and rewire the references to the previous and next objects. There is (thankfully) no need to copy references or perform any other costly actions.

On the other hand, the structure of a LinkedList makes finding any particular element in the list a costly exercise. Since the LinkedList class has to step through the nodes one by one from the head of the list until the element is found, the search will be slow.

Some of the data structure purists out there may have noticed that LinkedList is, in fact, not a normal linked list at all. In fact, a normal linked list has only a reference to the next object and not a reference to the previous object. The LinkedList class in the java.util package is actually a *doubly linked list*.

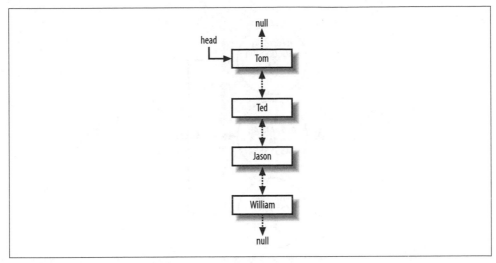

Figure 4-2. Structure of a LinkedList

For these reasons, LinkedList is a great class for manipulating data and shuffling it around. It is ideal for tasks such as sorting and performing frequent insertions and removals. However, it is really bad at accessing data quickly. You should use LinkedList if the primary function of your list is to manipulate data in the list.

Maps and SortedMaps

Maps are useful structures for storing things such as key/value pairs. The Map interface and its descendant SortedMap have many implementations. Once you have decided that you need to use a map as your collection, you will then need to decide exactly which map to use.

java.util.HashTable

The Hashtable class is one of the two grandfathers of Java collections, the other being Vector. The Hashtable class stores a series of keyed values in a structure that uses the hash code of the object to store things quickly. To understand how a Hashtable works, it is important that you understand the hash system.

When a Hashtable is constructed, it creates a table to hold the data of the collection. This table is an array of arrays. Each of the subarrays represents a bucket in which the class can store a set of values. All of the buckets are the same size.

As you insert new items into the table, the hash code of the object is used to determine which bucket the object should go into. Once the correct bucket is found, the object is inserted into that bucket. The structure of the class is shown in Figure 4-3.

Each bucket holds data within a particular range of hash codes. As you add items to the table, the hash code of the key is computed and the correct bucket is chosen.

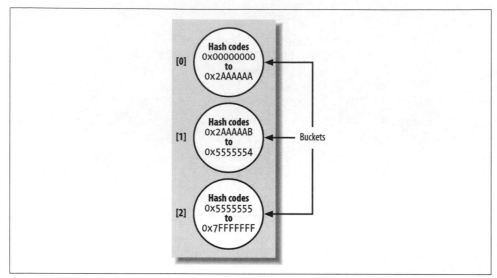

Figure 4-3. Hash-based storage

One of the advantages of this structure is that it can hold very large data sets without impeding performance. As the map grows, the number of buckets grows, and the range of hash codes allowed in each bucket gets smaller. The result is that the map can find any object, taking, on average, the same amount of time as it does to find any other object. In Big O Notation, this is referred to as 0(1). This is the best-case scenario for algorithm efficiency.

As the map grows, it fills up until its load reaches a certain percentage. This loadFactor can be given to the class at construction time, or the user can choose to use the default value of 0.75f. When using the default, as soon as the map becomes 75% full, the class will increase the size of the map, usually by creating more buckets and narrowing the range. Once the new map is ready, the class will *rehash* the map by computing the hash codes of each object in the map and filing them in their proper buckets. This is a fairly slow process, so you don't want to do it often. On the other hand, since hash-based data structures take up a lot of memory, you wouldn't want to allocate maps with huge initial capacities either. Finding the optimal performance for a hash-based data structure is often dependent on how the class will be used in the program. If the data size in the map is fairly constant, you can use higher load factors. However, if the data is constantly changing size and memory is tight, you may want to use lower load factors. The default size of 0.75 provides this good balance in most situations.

The Hashtable class is indeed useful. However, it is internally synchronized, which makes it thread-safe but much slower than other alternatives.

java.util.HashMap

Essentially, a HashMap is an implementation of the Hashtable class without internal synchronization. It sacrifices thread safety for higher performance. Other than this difference, they are conceptually the same. If you don't need to pass your map around in a threaded environment, or if thread safety can be provided externally to the map, then you should use a HashMap.

java.util.LinkedHashMap

A LinkedHashMap is an implementation of the SortedMap interface that allows you to guarantee that the iteration of the keys is in a predictable order. It uses the same technique as the HashMap and HashTable classes to store the data. However, LinkedHashMap also maintains a running LinkedList that contains all of the keys in the map in a sorted order.

Although keeping the keys in a sorted order is advantageous when it comes to iterating through the map, maintaining the extra linked list causes LinkedHashMap to be slower than HashMap. Use it with caution.

java.util.IdentityHashMap

An IdentityHashMap is the same as a HashMap, except that objects are compared based on identity, not equality.

In this map, key objects evaluate as equal only if they are the same instance in the virtual machine. This differs from other collections that evaluate for equality based on the result of calling the equals( ) method.

Since this map doesn't compare based on equality, you can insert multiple keys into the map even when they evaluate as equals according to the equals( ) method; they only need to be different instances. For example, the following two instances could be placed in the same IdentityhashMap:

```
String x = new String("tom");
String y = new String("tom");  // <== Different instance!
IdentityHashMap ihm = new IdentityHashMap( );
ihm.put(x, new Integer(15));
ihm.put(y, new Integer(8));
```

If you try this with a normal HashMap, the value for the key tom would be replaced on the second line. With an IdentityHashMap, both values are inserted. However, just because you can do this doesn't mean you should; I don't recommend inserting duplicate keys into an IdentityHashMap because it can result in some very confusing code.

All other operations on an IdentityHashMap work the same way as they do on a HashMap. The following code takes up where the last snippet left off:

```
String z = new String("tom");
Integer obj = ihm.get(z);
```

In this code, the variable element will contain the value null. This is because z is not the same instance as x or y even though they contain the same value. When working with IdentityHashMaps, you should keep these gotchas in mind.

java.util.WeakHashMap

A WeakHashMap is just like a HashMap, except that the keys used in the map are stored in weak references. We will cover weak references in Chapter 10.

java.util.TreeMap

A TreeMap is the other implementation of the SortedSet interface. However, unlike LinkedHashMap, the TreeMap class doesn't store its elements in a hash-based data structure. Instead, it stores its elements, unsurprisingly, in a tree.

Specifically, the TreeMap class uses a structure called a binary tree. Figure 4-4 shows how this structure looks in memory.

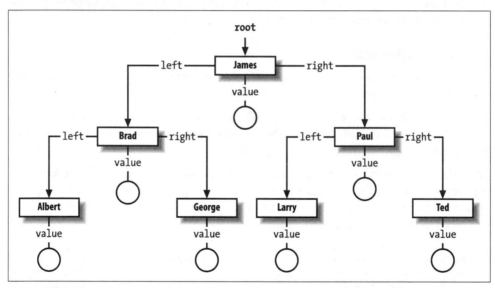

Figure 4-4. Binary tree storage of a TreeMap

Inside TreeMap is a variable called root, which stores the root of the tree. Each node in the tree stores a key and a value, and each element stores a left and a right element. When a new element is inserted, the key is evaluated against the root. If the key is the same, then the root value in the root entry will be replaced with the new value. However, if the key evaluates as less than the root (compareTo( ) returns -1), the TreeMap will use the left member of the root to navigate to the next element. If the key evaluates as greater than the root (compareTo( ) returns 1), the TreeMap will use the right member to navigate to the next element. This process of evaluation continues until the key is found or the TreeMap hits a leaf node, which is a node without a left or right member. If the TreeMap hits a leaf node, it will add a new entry containing the key and value and tack it on to the leaf node.

Keep in mind that determining whether a node is a leaf is dependent on which side, left or right, to which the TreeMap wants to surf. A particular node could be a leaf node with respect to left but not to right, as right may have a reference to another entry.

Every now and then, the tree will become lopsided—that is, it has more elements on one side of root than on the other. When this occurs, the tree is rebalanced by using the middle key in the sorted keys as the new root entry. The other entries are then copied into the new tree using the algorithm for adding new entries. This rebalancing process is slow.

The process of adding or removing a key from a TreeMap has a $O(log2(n))$ efficiency. It isn't as good as a LinkedHashMap with its $O(1)$ efficiency, but a LinkedHashMap has to store two data structures for the elements in the map—one to accomplish the actual storage and another to keep a list of the keys in a sorted order. For this reason, TreeMaps are better at storing large sets of data. Since $log2(n)$ grows very slowly as n increases, this size trade-off is often worth the cost.

If you are morbidly curious, where n is 100,000,000, $log2(n)$ is only 26.5754247590989. This means that if you have a map that contains a hundred million entries, a TreeMap will be able to find any arbitrary key using a maximum of 27 compares. That is usually good enough in most situations. On the other hand, storing references to all 100,000,000 entries *twice* would take up too much memory.

Sets and SortedSets

If you have opted to use a set as your collection, you will first need to decide whether the data needs to maintain a sorting order. This question is more complex than it appears.

For example, a set of contacts in an address book doesn't necessarily need to maintain sorting order even though the items may be displayed in a sorted order in the interface. In fact, the sorting order may be invalid if you built the list to sort based on last name, and the user wants it sorted based on email address. However, a set that holds the instructions to make a certain part in a factory must be kept in a specific sorted order to ensure that they are followed correctly.

The question you should ask yourself is, "Do my objects need to be in a sorted order for presentation only, or is there some other underlying logical reason for the sorting?" If they only need to be *presented* in sorted order, then you can easily copy them to a list or SortedSet in the GUI and sort them at presentation time. However, if there is another underlying logical reason to sort them in one predefined order, then you should opt for a SortedSet. Try to avoid sorting your sets. Sorting sets introduces significant overhead in the insertion and deletion of items in a set and can impede performance.

java.util.HashSet

A HashSet is an implementation of the Set interface that stores its contents using a hash system. This system works the same way as a HashMap. In fact, one interesting piece of Java trivia is that the HashSet class is implemented using only the key set of the HashMap class. The HashSet class merely inserts a dummy value for each key in the map and hides the fact that it is using a map from the user.

java.util.LinkedSet

A LinkedSet is an implementation of the Set interface that guarantees a predictable iteration order. It does this by maintaining a LinkedList of the objects in the set, which can significantly decrease the amount of memory.

Note that just because the order is predictable does not mean that the order is sorted. In fact, the only real benefit of a LinkedHashSet over a regular HashSet is that the iteration of the set remains constant over time and isn't as random as HashSet. However, I have never seen a programming situation in which this is enough of a concern to balance the significantly larger memory consumption.

java.util.TreeSet

A TreeSet is implemented the same way HashSet is. However, instead of using a HashMap as a backing store, it uses TreeMap. Therefore, the TreeSet class inherits the same benefits and limitations as the TreeMap class.

Choosing a Collection Type

When faced with such a wide variety of collections, it is often difficult to decide which collection type you should use. The general rule is that you should use the collection type that is the most restrictive and still accomplishes your needs. The reason for this is that collections tend to slow down as their abilities increase.

First, you should decide whether you need values that can be looked up by a key. If so, then you are restricted to a Map type. If not, then you can use a more general Collection type. If you decide to use a Collection type, the next thing you need to ask is whether you need duplicates in your collection. If so, then you will need to use a List; otherwise, a Set should suffice.

After you have made these decisions, you should decide whether you need the objects to be sorted. This decision is much hazier than the other decisions. Almost all collections will need to be sorted at one time or another by a user. However, there are other ways of doing this sorting, such as copying the collection and sorting it in a list. You should opt for SortedSets or SortedMaps only if there is a reason why the collection should always be sorted in a specific manner. Sorted collections and maps must maintain the sorting order, so they tend to be significantly slower than other collections and take up more memory. You should incur this performance hit only if you need the functionality.

As for choosing the implementations, you need to consider the merits of each type of implementation before determining which is the best. Figure 4-5 should help you make that decision.

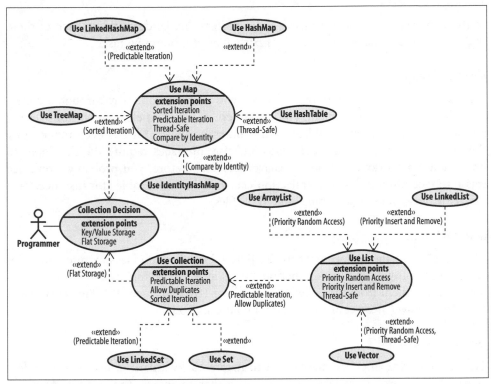

Figure 4-5. Choosing the right collection

In this book, we deal only with the JDK standard collection types. However, the Apache Jakarta Commons project has a library of other collection types that broadens the selection scope significantly. I highly encourage developers to seek out this project at *http://jakarta.apache.org/commons/collections.html* and take a look at other options.

Iterating Collections

Now that you have the fundamentals of collections firmly in mind, you need a way to iterate through collections. You can accomplish this using three types of iterator interfaces.

The java.util.Enumeration, java.util.Iterator, and java.util.ListIterator interfaces are used to iterate through data objects in a collection. The collections themselves are responsible for implementing these interfaces and for providing the iterator for the caller. They do this using inner classes.

Three Iterators

In the JDK, there are three principle types of iterators. Understanding each of them will help you pick the best one for your particular programming task.

java.util.Enumeration

This is the oldest of the iterators. It allows you to iterate one way through a collection. Once you pass an element, you cannot go back to that element without getting a new enumeration. One problem with enumeration is that it has been replaced by the Iterator interface. The Collection and Map interfaces require the developer to implement an Iterator but not an Enumeration. Therefore, you probably won't use this interface often unless the collection classes are not available (for instance, during J2ME programming on some limited profiles).

java.util.Iterator

This interface is the replacement in the JDK 1.2+ collection class architecture. Not only does it provide the same functionality as an Enumeration, but it allows you to remove an element from the collection by calling Iterator.remove( ). However, using Iterator.remove( ) can cause some rather confusing code.

java.util.ListIterator

The ListIterator interface allows you to iterate backwards in a list as well as forwards. This iterator is available only on classes that implement the List interface.

Fail-Fast Iterators

Many collections provide a *fail-fast iterator*. Essentially, this means that the iterator is designed to fail if the user modifies the list during iteration. For example, consider the following code:

```
package oreilly.hcj.collections;
public class SomeClass {

  protected void markPreferredCustomer(final String someCustomer) {
    Set set = new HashSet( );
    // ...add items to the set.
    String element = null;
    Iterator iter = set.iterator( );
    while (iter.hasNext( )) {
      element = (String) iter.next( );
```

```
      // ...perform some logic
      if (element.equals(someCustomer)) {
        set.add(new String("p->" + element));
        set.remove(element);
      }
    }
  }
}
```

With the emphasized lines, the developer tries to modify the set while the iteration is still ongoing. The result of such an attempt will be a ConcurrentModificationException. When you are iterating through a collection, you must use the iterator methods to manipulate the list. Also, the Iterator class allows you only to remove an item. This makes sense because iterators can iterate over many kinds of collections that often have different semantics for adding new elements.

In the end, you are better off not using Iterator.remove( ). Instead, you should save the changes you want to make and execute them after iterating through the collection. Also, if your collection can be accessed by multiple threads, you should surround the whole process with a synchronized block to prevent one thread from attempting modifications while another is iterating.

Collection Gotchas

Collections provide you with a powerful tool for storing and traversing data. However, they have their share of gotchas that the savvy developer needs to beware of.

Storage by Reference

One of the most prevalent gotchas has to do with how collections store data. Collections store data by making references to that data, *not* by copying the actual data. This is important to remember because the collection holding the data is not necessarily the only object that can access the underlying value of that data. Since the variables for all constructed types in Java are references, and these reverences are passed by value, another part of your program could have a reference to a data object in your collection.

Failure to Override hashCode( )

When placing collections in a hash-based data set, the collections will place objects with similar hash codes in the same bucket. This can be a problem if you forget to override the hashCode( ) method in your collected objects.

If you don't override hashCode( ), the collections will use the default implementation in the java.lang.Object class. This implementation needs the memory location of the object to compute the hash code. However, if you create a lot of objects, it is likely that they will be close to each other within the memory. The result would be a HashMap with most of the objects in the first bucket and few, if any, in the other buckets. Such an unbalanced HashMap would behave poorly; in extreme conditions, it could degrade from O(1) to O(n) efficiency.

The solution to this problem is to make sure you override the hashCode( ) method to give your data an even distribution inside the buckets of the hash-based collection. Instead of calculating based on location, you should calculate based on the data in the object. However, don't forget to override equals( ) if you override hashCode( ).

 The Jakarta Commons Lang library contains utilities that make creating high-quality hash codes easy. I highly recommend you check it out at *http://jakarta.apache.org/*.

Lack of Type Safety

One of the most persistent problems with the Java collection classes is the lack of type safety. Since the collection classes store Object instances, a user can insert anything into a collection. This could easily lead to multiple ClassCastException instances being thrown. It also introduces problems with quality data validation, which we will discuss in Chapter 6.

In JDK 1.5, Sun plans to introduce the concept of parameterized types, which will provide this type safety. However, the subject of parameterized types is far outside the scope of this chapter; we will cover them in Chapter 12.

However, until JDK 1.5 hits the market, you need to realize that just because you think the collection contains only one type doesn't necessarily mean there isn't a rogue object in the collection. The only solution to this quandary is vigilance and good code management through exhaustive testing and checking.

Collecting Problems

There are many things that you can do with Java collections. However, like any power tool, you can do a great deal of harm if you aren't careful. See Example 4-2.

Example 4-2. A bean with a collection hole

```
package oreilly.hcj.review;
public class Customer extends Object implements Serializable {

  private Set purchases;

  public void setPurchases(final Set purchases)
    throws PropertyVetoException {
    final Set oldPurchases = this.purchases;
    vetoableChangeSupport.fireVetoableChange("purchases", oldPurchases,
                                    this.purchases);
```

Example 4-2. A bean with a collection hole (continued)

```
    this.purchases = purchases;
    propertyChangeSupport.firePropertyChange("purchases", oldPurchases,
                                            this.purchases);
  }

  public Set getPurchases() {
    return this.purchases;
  }
}
```

This is almost exactly how my IDE generated my bean property. The only thing I did was add the keyword `final` to the parameter declaration and to the `oldPurchases` variable. The class looks pretty good, but it has a huge, gaping hole.

The getter returns a reference to the Set when someone asks for it. The problem with returning this reference is shown in the usage of your property:

```
    package oreilly.hcj.review;
    public class BeanCollections {
      public static void someFunction(final Customer customer) {
        if (customer == null) {
          throw new NullPointerException();
        }
        Set purchs = customer.getPurchases();
        Set names = new HashSet();  // going to use to store customer names.
        names.add(new String("Jason"));
        purchs.add(new String("Fred"));  // typo; he meant names, not purchs.
      }
    }
```

In the above code, a `String` was added to a `Set` that isn't meant to contain `String` objects. After this code runs, a `String` object will be inside the purchases `Set` that is meant to contain only `Purchase` objects. Since adding the `String` to the purchases `Set` bypasses the setter, the internals of the `Customer` object were changed while all type-checking code was being bypassed! The defective `Set` is not detected, and the code compiles, deploys, and still doesn't break. Down the line, more code is written for your system:

```
    public void makeCustomerReport() {
      Set purchases = someObject.getCustomer(12345).getPurchases();
      for (Iterator iter = purchases.iterator();; iter.hasNext();) {
        Purchase purchase = (Purchase)iter.next(); // ClassCastException
        reportingObject.add(purchase);
      }
    }
```

Because there is a `String` object in a `Set` that is supposed to contain only `Purchase` objects, a `ClassCastException` is in this piece of code. This is one of those mysterious bugs that can baffle you for two hours and then make you want to break something when you figure it out. Worse, if this bug occurs only intermittently, you have an evil problem to deal with. However, you can prevent this headache before it even starts:

```
package oreilly.hcj.review;
public class Customer extends Object implements Serializable {

  public void setPurchases2(final Set purchases2)
      throws PropertyVetoException {
    final Set newPurchases2;
    if (purchases2 != null) {
      newPurchases2 = Collections.unmodifiableSet(purchases2);
    } else {
      newPurchases2 = null;
    }

    final Set oldpurchases2 = this.getPurchases2();
    vetoableChangeSupport.fireVetoableChange("purchases2", oldpurchases2,
                                    newPurchases2);
    this.purchases2 = new HashSet(purchases2);
    propertyChangeSupport.firePropertyChange("purchases2", oldpurchases2,
                                    getPurchases2());
  }

  public Set getPurchases2() {
    if (this.purchases2 == null) {
      return null;
    }
    return Collections.unmodifiableSet(this.purchases2);
  }
}
```

The new version of the Customer class can encapsulate much more efficiently. When setting the purchases property, instead of copying the reference, you actually copy the Set itself. When getting the purchases property, you give the caller an unmodifiable set. The end result is a minor performance hit but superior code from a debugging and maintenance perspective. With this technique, if the user tries to add a String object to the returned Set, he will get an UnsupportedOperationException at the line where he tries to add the String object:

```
purchs.add(new String("Fred"));  // <= UnsupportedOperationException
```

This prevents the user of the Customer class from changing the internals of the Customer object without going through the setter. More importantly, no one can bypass the property veto listeners and checking code in the Customer class. You have traded a few clock cycles for several man-hours. If this technique adopted as a general policy in your office, the savings could be measured in thousands of man-hours.

One of the ugly aspects of the setPurchases2() method is all of the checks have to account for null sets. Every time you call the getter of the purchases property, you have to check for null. These checks can become a real hassle and make the code difficult to read. However, with a coding standard, you can avoid all of this unpleasantness. Example 4-3 shows the optimal code for your Customer class.

Example 4-3. Optimal structure for collection-based properties

```
package oreilly.hcj.review;
public class Customer extends Object implements Serializable {

  private Set purchases3 = new HashSet();

  public void setPurchases3(final Set purchases3)
        throws PropertyVetoException {
    if (purchases3 == null) {
      throw new NullPointerException();
    }
    final Set oldPurchases3 = this.getPurchases3();
    final Set newPurchases3 = Collections.unmodifiableSet(purchases3);
    vetoableChangeSupport.fireVetoableChange("purchases3", oldPurchases3,
                                      newPurchases3);
    this.purchases3 = new HashSet(purchases3);
    propertyChangeSupport.firePropertyChange("purchases3", oldPurchases3,
                                      getPurchases3());
  }

  public Set getPurchases3() {
    return Collections.unmodifiableSet(this.purchases3);
  }
}
```

In the optimal version of your Customer class, the property purchases3 can never be null. You have implemented a coding standard in which the property will always be a Set. It can be an empty Set if there are no purchases for a particular customer, but it will always be an initialized object. This makes your life a lot easier and your code much cleaner. To illustrate, see Example 4-4, which operates on a data model that allows nulls in Sets.

Example 4-4. Dealing with collection properties that can be null

```
package oreilly.hcj.review;
public static void makeGroupReport(final Set customers) {
  if (customers == null) {
    throw new NullPointerException();
  }
  Iterator purchaseIter = null;
  Iterator customerIter = null;
  Set purchases = null;
  Customer customer = null;
  Purchase purch = null;

  customerIter = customers.iterator();
  while (customerIter.hasNext()) {
    customer = (Customer)customerIter.next();
```

```
    System.out.println("Purchases for " + customer.getName());
    purchases = customer.getPurchases3();
    if (purchases != null) {
      purchaseIter = purchases.iterator();
      while (purchaseIter.hasNext()) {
        purch = (Purchase)purchaseIter.next();
        System.out.println(purch.getItemName() + "\t" + purch.getPrice());
      }
    }
    System.out.print("Total Purchases = ");
    if (purchases != null) {
      System.out.println(purchases.size());
    } else {
      System.out.println(0);
    }
    System.out.println();
  }
}
```

The emphasized lines show the number of checks for `null` you have to make. Let's compare this to the code in Example 4-5, which does the same job with a data model that does not allow sets to be `null`.

Example 4-5. Dealing with collection properties that cannot be null

```
package oreilly.hcj.review;
public static void makeGroupReportBetter(final Set customers) {
  if (customers == null) {
    throw new NullPointerException();
  }
  Iterator purchaseIter = null;
  Iterator customerIter = null;
  Set purchases = null;
  Customer customer = null;
  Purchase purch = null;

  customerIter = customers.iterator();
  while (customerIter.hasNext()) {
    customer = (Customer)customerIter.next();
    System.out.println("Purchases for " + customer.getName());
    purchases = customer.getPurchases3();
    purchaseIter = purchases.iterator();
    while (purchaseIter.hasNext()) {
      purch = (Purchase)purchaseIter.next();
      System.out.println(purch.getItemName() + "\t" + purch.getPrice());
    }
    System.out.println("Total Purchases = " + purchases.size());
    System.out.println();
  }
}
```

This code is much cleaner and shorter. Since you never have to test for null, you can simply grab an Iterator directly. If a customer has no purchases, the inner while loop will merely exit when the call to purchaseIter.hasNext( ) returns false. Example 4-5 is far superior to Example 4-4 in terms of code maintenance, readability, and speed.

The benefits of non-null sets also extend to other data structures. Collections, maps, and arrays should never be null, but they should be empty if they don't have data.

CHAPTER 5
Exceptional Code

The common attribute of all exceptional code is, not surprisingly, the proper use of exceptions. Exceptions can give your code immense debugging power and provide a base for indicating user errors. At one time, using exceptions for business logic errors was considered to be bad form. Instead of throwing an exception, the programmer was encouraged to use deeply nested if statements to catch user errors. Java has changed this perspective somewhat through the use of two types of exceptions, both of which are covered extensively in this chapter.

Two Types of Exceptions

Java started out by borrowing the C++ exception mechanism. However, early in the development of the JDK, Sun made some important modifications. Instead of only one category of exception, Java has two. Today, Java differentiates between an Exception and a RuntimeException. To understand how this differentiation is advantageous, you must first understand these two types of exceptions.

The Exception Subclasses

When a method can throw an Exception, the exception must be caught in the body of the method or declared in the throws clause of the method declaration:

```
public void someDatabaseMethod () throws SQLException {
  // Do some JDBC Work.
}
```

In this code, the method someDatabaseMethod() can throw a SQLException if there is a problem with the database. Since SQLException is a descendant of the Exception class, someDatabaseMethod() must either handle the exception with a try-catch block or declare that the method throws the SQLException. Since someDatabaseMethod() declares that it throws SQLException, any method calling someDatabaseMethod() is required to catch the exception or declare that it also throws the exception. This process of passing the responsibility to callers must be propagated down the call stack until the exception is actually handled. This mechanism allows code to clearly show the problems that may occur within a method and require the user of that method to handle them.

Superfluous exceptions

The problem with declaring a method in the `throws` clause is that these exceptions can become lengthy and superfluous. If you have ever encountered a method that threw five or six exceptions, you know exactly what I mean. Since you have to catch exceptions or rethrow them, using third-party libraries that throw a lot of exceptions can become a pain. In fact, there are instances when throwing even one exception is an annoyance. Consider the basic JDBC program in Example 5-1 to get a good idea of what I mean.

Example 5-1. Throwing superfluous exceptions

```
package oreilly.hcj.exceptions;
public class SuperfluousExceptions {

  public void prepareJDBCDriver() throws ClassNotFoundException {
    Class.forName("com.mysql.jdbc.Driver");
  }

}
```

In a JDBC program, the first thing you need to do is load the database driver into the virtual machine by using the `Class.forName()` call with the name of the database driver class as the parameter. This will call the static initializers of the driver class. However, it is possible that the named class does not exist in the classpath. If the virtual machine cannot find the class, the call `Class.forName()` throws a `ClassNotFoundException`. This type of error becomes a problem only if it happens *routinely*. In fact, it should occur only if the user has a classpath problem; proper usage of the method will *never* result in an exception being thrown. Yet this exception will still often need to be caught or declared that it is thrown by your method.

Luckily, in Example 5-1, you have only one superfluous exception that you have to catch. However, once you use reflection (see Chapter 8), you will find that there are several exceptions that can complicate your code. Example 5-2 shows a problematic method using reflection.

Example 5-2. Catching multiple superfluous exceptions

```
package oreilly.hcj.finalstory;
public class SuperfluousExceptions {

  public void reflectionMethod()
    throws NoSuchMethodException, IllegalAccessException,
           InvocationTargetException, ClassNotFoundException,
           MyCustomException {
```

Example 5-2. Catching multiple superfluous exceptions (continued)

```
      Class.forName("oreilly.hcj.bankdata.Gender");
      // ...some code
      Method meth = Gender.class.getDeclaredMethod("getName", null);
      meth.invoke(Gender.MALE, null);
      // ...other code working with result that may
      // throw a program exception
  }
}
```

This code shows how things can become problematic with multiple exception types in a throws clause. In Example 5-2, the only exception that is particularly important is MyCustomException, which indicates a violation of a business rule. If any other exceptions are thrown, it would indicate a configuration or programming error that shouldn't happen routinely. However, since all of the other exceptions listed could occur and are direct descendants of Exception, you must either declare them or handle them. This makes the code bulky, hard to read, and generally annoying.

Furthermore, declaring your method to throw Exception or Throwable (the parent exception) isn't a good solution, either. The problem with declaring that a method throws Exception or Throwable is that you cloud the dynamics of your method by complicating the problems that can occur in that method. For example, if reflectionMethod( ) was declared with throws Exception, and you called it from another method, you could end up with something like the following:

```
    public void someMethod( ) throws Exception {
      try {
        // .. some code that starts a purchase transaction..
        reflectionMethod( );
      } catch (final Exception ex) {
        if (ex instanceof MyCustomException) {
          if (((MyCustomException)ex).getType( ) ==
                        MyCustomException.CREDIT_CARD_DECLINED) {
          // check if customer has other cards,
          //  if not throw a billing error.
          throw new MyCustomException(MyCustomException.BILLING_ERROR);
          }
        } else {
          throw ex;
        }
      }
    }
```

In this code, the only exception that someMethod( ) is interested in catching is the MyCustomException with a CREDIT_CARD declined type. If it catches this exception, someMethod( ) will then try to use other credit cards that the customer has; if it doesn't, then it will transform the exception type into a BILLING_ERROR.

The main problem with this method is that since any kind of Exception can be thrown in the try block, the method must rethrow these exceptions or deal with them. Therefore, someMethod( ) also has to declare a throws clause for Exception. This problem quickly propagates in your code until practically every method is declared with throws Exception. Furthermore, this code masks any exceptions that may be legitimate within someMethod( ), such as a NullPointerException.

To avoid this situation, you need to filter your exceptions so that you don't have to declare them in the throws clause, but still maintain differentiated exceptions that can propagate down the call stack. This is why there is a second type of exception, the RuntimeException subclasses.

The RuntimeException Subclasses

RuntimeException and its subclasses are treated differently than Exception and its direct subclasses by the compiler and virtual machine. Unlike Exceptions, RuntimeExceptions are not required to be declared in the throws clause of the method. These types of exceptions indicate a problem that should *not* routinely happen. NullPointerException and IllegalArgumentException are good examples of RuntimeException subclasses that indicate that something unexpected happened in the code, and that the problem is unrelated to business logic or user error. Both of these exception types indicate a programming error and not something that would normally happen in the course of the program.

Interestingly, RuntimeException inherits directly from the Exception class, and it is ignored in a throws clause, a feature that is built into the Java virtual machine and compiler.

RuntimeExceptions allow you to clean up the method in Example 5-2 and turn it into something more manageable:

```
package oreilly.hcj.finalstory;
public class SuperfluousExceptions {

  public void reflectionMethod2( ) throws MyCustomException {
    try {
      Class.forName("oreilly.hcj.bankdata.Gender");
      // ...some code
      Method meth = Gender.class.getDeclaredMethod("getName", null);
      meth.invoke(Gender.MALE, null);
      // ...other code working with result that may
      // throw a program exception
    } catch (final NoSuchMethodException ex) {
      throw new RuntimeException(ex);
    } catch (final IllegalAccessException ex) {
      throw new RuntimeException(ex);
    } catch (final InvocationTargetException ex) {
      throw new RuntimeException(ex);
```

```
      } catch (final ClassNotFoundException ex) {
        throw new RuntimeException(ex);
      }
    }


  }
```

In reflectionMethod2(), you use RuntimeException with the chained exception facility from Chapter 1. This allows you to filter the exceptions that would indicate configuration or programming problems and pass them on without declaring them in the throws clause; you can declare only MyCustomException in the throws clause without causing any problems. Implement the filter by catching each exception that would indicate a programming error and rethrow it inside of a RuntimeException.

Masking exceptions

Although filtering exceptions is a powerful technique, there is a danger to filtering exceptions that trips up many unaware developers:

```
package oreilly.hcj.finalstory;
public class SuperfluousExceptions {

  public void reflectionMethod3() throws MyCustomException {
    try {
      Class.forName("oreilly.hcj.bankdata.Gender");
      // ...some code
      Method meth = Gender.class.getDeclaredMethod("getName", null);
      meth.invoke(Gender.MALE, null);
      // ...other code working with result that may
      // throw a program exception
    } catch (final Exception ex) {
      if (ex instanceof MyCustomException) {
        throw (MyCustomException)ex;
      }
      throw new RuntimeException(ex);
    }
  }


}
```

Although this code looks fine from a superficial point of view, it is horrendous from a maintenance point of view. The first problem is that this method effectively masks the throwing of all exception types except for your custom exception. This may seem like a good idea; however, you may have code in the method that throws a java.text.ParseException. This exception may indicate that the user typed an unreadable date format in a field. This is a business logic exception that *should* be declared on the method line so that callers will be aware of the possible error and account for it. However, since you globally mask all exception types, you unintentionally turn this business logic exception into a RuntimeException. As a result, the compiler doesn't warn you that you haven't declared the exception, developers don't account for it, and you end up having to perform repairs throughout your entire program six weeks later.

Ignoring exceptions

If masking exceptions bothers you, you should find this next example downright disturbing:

```java
package oreilly.hcj.finalstory;
public class SuperfluousExceptions {

  public void reflectionMethod3() throws MyCustomException {
    try {
      Class.forName("oreilly.hcj.bankdata.Gender");
      // ...some code
      Method meth = Gender.class.getDeclaredMethod("getName", null);
      meth.invoke(Gender.MALE, null);
      // ...other code working with result that may
      // throw a program exception
    } catch (final Exception ex) {
      if (ex instanceof MyCustomException) {
        throw (MyCustomException)ex;
      }
    }
  }
}
```

If group masking of exceptions is bad, then ignoring exceptions is absolutely evil. In this code, the exceptions aren't even rethrown as RuntimeExceptions; they are dumped and disappear altogether. There are *very few* examples of situations in which it is okay to completely ignore exceptions. Even these few examples don't allow the user to ignore exceptions in a large block of code. When you ignore exceptions, you are pretending that the exception isn't an error. This should be done only if you are certain that it isn't an error. One of these rare examples is shown in Example 5-3.

Example 5-3. An example of exceptions that can be legitimately ignored

```java
package oreilly.hcj.finalstory;
public class SuperfluousExceptions {

  public void reflectionMethod5(final String[] packageList)
    throws MyCustomException {
    try {
      Class.forName("oreilly.hcj.bankdata.Gender");
      // ...Reflection based code
      // ...other code working with result that may
      // throw a program exception
      // try to load a class by searching through some packages.
      for (int idx = 0; idx < packageList.length; idx++) {
        try {
          Class.forName(packageList[idx] + "MyClass");
```

Example 5-3. An example of exceptions that can be legitimately ignored (continued)

```
      } catch (final ClassNotFoundException ex) {
        // not an error.
      }
    }
  } catch (final NoSuchMethodException ex) {
    throw new RuntimeException(ex);
  } catch (final IllegalAccessException ex) {
    throw new RuntimeException(ex);
  } catch (final InvocationTargetException ex) {
    throw new RuntimeException(ex);
  } catch (final ClassNotFoundException ex) {
    throw new RuntimeException(ex);
  }
}

}
```

In reflectionMethod5( ), the ClassNotFoundException is ignored during the for loop. The goal of the emphasized block of code is to look through a search path of packages and load a class that may be in one of these packages. In this case, a ClassNotFoundException in an iteration of the loop is definitely not an error, but a legitimate potential outcome. This is one example of a situation in which it is legitimate to ignore exceptions. However, note that even in this case, the try-catch block contains only the single line of code that attempts to load the class. You should also note that only the specific exception that is known to be an error is caught and ignored. Finally, later in the method, notice that any other ClassNotFoundException exceptions that may be thrown are filtered. Unlike the ClassNotFoundException instances that could be thrown in the for loop, instances thrown outside of the for loop indicate an error and should be propagated.

While filtering exceptions, you should always watch for unintentional side effects, such as masking and ignoring exceptions. For this reason, it's best to be as explicit as possible in your code. Using multiple catches to catch specific exceptions will make your code a bit longer, but the advantages far outweigh the costs.

Exception or RuntimeException

Now that you have the concepts of Exception and RuntimeException types clearly in mind, the only decision left is to figure out when to make a class a subclass of Exception and when to make it a subclass of RuntimeException. Generally, this depends on the circumstances and the nature of the exception. If you consider NullPointerException, you know that this exception always indicates a programming error. However, with IllegalAccessException, the case is less clear. In some circumstances, such as during authorization control, it is a legitimate logic error. In other circumstances, such as in reflectionMethod( ), it indicates a programmer error.

Although whether to make an exception a `RuntimeException` or an `Exception` is something of a judgment call, the following guidelines should help:

- If an exception is always the result of a programming error, make it a direct descendant of `RuntimeException`.

- If an exception represents a user's failure to enter data properly, you may be able to get away with using `RuntimeException`. This will allow you to propagate the `RuntimeException` in business logic classes without having to declare it. However, the GUI or other interface to the program should always watch for these kinds of errors. We will discuss one of these types of exceptions in Chapter 6.

- If the exception is always the result of a business logic error, make it a direct descendant of `Exception` and use exception filtering when appropriate.

When to Use Exceptions

Two of the biggest problems in most Java software are using exceptions (of either variety) improperly, or not using them at all. The failure to use exceptions properly accounts for more logic errors in production systems than any other single issue. The errors often result from forgetting to use exceptions or from declaring excessive custom exception types.

Forgetting Exceptions

When using the `Exception` classes, a common mistake made by many software engineers is to neglect the exceptions already provided in the JDK. When writing methods, the savvy developer often uses `NullPointerException`, `IllegalArgumentException`, and the other built-in exception types. This allows the developer to precheck parameters to avoid corrupting data. The Java bean shown in Example 5-4 shows how forgetting to use these exceptions can be dangerous.

Example 5-4. Forgetting to use built-in exceptions

```
package oreilly.hcj.finalstory;
public class ExceptionUsage {

  /** Storage for a customer name (Required). */
  private String customerName;

  public void setCustomerName(final String customerName) {
    this.customerName = customerName;
  }

  public String getCustomerName() {
    return this.customerName;
  }

}
```

Although everything looks okay here, there is a glaring omission. Note how the customer name is said to be required; however, the setter does not check the name coming in. If the user of this bean passes null or a zero-length string for customerName, the property would be in a corrupted state. You can prevent problems like this by checking every single parameter for data validity. The RuntimeException classes can help:

```
package oreilly.hcj.finalstory;
public class ExceptionUsage {

    public void setCustomerName(final String customerName) {
      if (customerName == null) {
        throw new NullPointerException();
      }
      if (customerName.length() == 0) {
        throw new IllegalArgumentException();
      }
      this.customerName = customerName;
    }
}
```

This example is much better. You check the parameter customerName for all possible problems before you even worry about the body of the method. As an added bonus, with RuntimeException types, you do not have to declare these exceptions in a throws clause. Now, if the programmer passes invalid parameters to the method, the method will trigger an exception. This will generate a stack trace that will allow the programmer to resolve the issue during development instead of letting it sneak into production. Such extensive use of exceptions can be the difference between solid code and Swiss cheese.

Too Many Exceptions

On the other hand, it's possible to go a bit crazy with exceptions. Some developers declare all sorts of exception classes:

```
package oreilly.hcj.finalstory;
public class GUIErrorException extends Exception {
}

public class CreditCardDeclinedException extends Exception {
}

public class BillingException extends Exception {
}

public class NoReservationException extends Exception {
}
```

Although there is nothing technically wrong with these classes, they are a bit excessive. If you were to continue this paradigm, you would have hundreds of exception classes in a real system, each with no content. Whenever you write a class that has

---

no content, there should be a good reason to do so. In this case, there is no good reason—you could easily get a similar result with exception type constants and one exception class, as shown in Example 5-5.

Example 5-5. An exception class with type IDs

```java
package oreilly.hcj.finalstory;
public class MyCustomException extends Exception {

  public static final int GUI_ERROR = 0;
  public static final int NO_RESERVATION = 1;
  public static final int TRANSACTION_ERROR = 2;
  public static final int BILLING_ERROR = 3;
  public static final int CREDIT_CARD_DECLINED = 4;

  final int type;

  public MyCustomException(final int type) {
    if ((type != GUI_ERROR)
        && (type != NO_RESERVATION)
        && (type != TRANSACTION_ERROR)
        && (type != BILLING_ERROR)
        && (type != CREDIT_CARD_DECLINED)) {
      throw new IllegalArgumentException();
    }
    this.type = type;
  }

  public int getType() {
    return this.type;
  }
}
```

If you declare a new exception class, make sure that the exception is fundamentally different than the other exceptions. Also, make sure that there isn't already an exception for the type of exception you need. For example, you shouldn't declare a business logic exception type for `null` pointers, but use `NullPointerException` instead.

> In a contract for a telecommunications company, I saw a lot of empty exception classes. For practically every type of error, it had a specific exception class. I spent the next week refactoring and converting them to one exception class with type IDs that could be used to differentiate the problems. As a result, I reduced the code base by nearly 350 lines.

Using the new composite exception class is quite easy. Instead of throwing different types of exceptions, you merely pass a constant to the constructor of the composite exception class:

```java
public void billCard2(String cardNumber, Date expiration, Float amount)
  throws MyCustomException {
```

```
// verify card type and expiration...
if (!validCard) {
  throw new MyCustomException(MyCustomException.BILLING_ERROR);
}

// checking code...
if (!approved) {
  System.err.println(cardNumber + "\t" + expiration + "\t" + amount);
  throw new MyCustomException(MyCustomException.CREDIT_CARD_DECLINED);
}
}
```

In fact, it is easier to use the composite class than the various empty exception classes. When using individual exception classes, you have to declare all of the thrown exceptions in a throws clause:

```
public void billCard(String cardNumber, Date expiration, Float amount)
    throws BillingException, CreditCardDeclinedException {
  // verify card type and expiration...
  if (!validCard) {
    throw new BillingException( );
  }

  // checking code...
  if (!approved) {
    System.err.println(cardNumber + "\t" + expiration + "\t" + amount);
    throw new CreditCardDeclinedException( );
  }
}
```

Of course, if you change the business logic of the billCard( ) method in a way that introduces a new potential error, you will have to change the signature of the method to throw the new exception type. This means you may have to change all of the code that uses this method to account for the new method signature. Not only is this a time-consuming task, it is also frequently not possible. For example, if your product is a library used by your customers, such a change would break all of the software that your customers have written using the library.

For these reasons, you should make sure that you create new exceptions only for fundamentally different things. For most business applications, one business logic exception class should suffice.

Finally for Closure

In the try-catch-finally triad, is the finally clause is often neglected. This clause allows you to write code that will run regardless of the outcome of the method. Whether the code within a try block throws an exception or not, code in a finally block will be executed by the compiler. The JDBC program in Example 5-6 shows how finally is used.

Example 5-6. Closing database resources with finally

```
package oreilly.hcj.finalstory;
public class FinallyForClosure {

  public int getValue(final Connection conn, final String sql)
    throws SQLException {
    int result = 0;
    Statement stmt = null;
    ResultSet rs = null;
    try {
      stmt = conn.createStatement();
      rs = stmt.executeQuery(sql);
      if (rs.next()) {
        result = rs.getInt(1);
      }
    } catch (final SQLException ex) {
      throw ex;
    } finally {
      if (rs != null) {
        rs.close();
      }
      if (stmt != null) {
        stmt.close();
      }
    }
    return result;
  }

}
```

In this code, even if a SQLException is thrown, the method will attempt to close the ResultSet and Statement and thus release the resources they were consuming. In this manner, you can ensure that the database resources are closed no matter what happens. It is good practice to use finally blocks whenever you seize external resources inside of a try block.

Although there is nothing technically wrong with the code in Example 5-6, you can make it even better. To understand how, consider the catch clause:

```
    } catch (final SQLException ex) {
      throw ex;
    } finally {
```

The catch clause is this example is superfluous. To use a finally block, you do not have to catch any thrown exceptions; you can merely ignore them and let them be thrown by the method. When you reconsider the getValue() method, it becomes obvious that not catching the exceptions is a good idea.

The getValue() method may throw a SQLException during the course of the method. Whatever happens, you need to close the database resources used in the call to prevent a resource leak. However, the attempted closure of these resources could generate SQLException instances as well. For this reason, you must declare that the method throws SQLException. The classic solution to this problem is to catch the exception from the try block and rethrow it, as shown in Example 5-6. However, a better approach is to use the finally block without catching the exceptions at all:

```
package oreilly.hcj.finalstory;
public class FinallyForClosure {

  public int getValue2(final Connection conn, final String sql)
    throws SQLException {
    int result = 0;
    Statement stmt = null;
    ResultSet rs = null;
    try {
      stmt = conn.createStatement();
      rs = stmt.executeQuery(sql);
      if (rs.next()) {
        result = rs.getInt(1);
      }
    } finally {
      if (rs != null) {
        rs.close();
      }
      if (stmt != null) {
        stmt.close();
      }
    }
    return result;
  }

}
```

Because this try block contains a finally block but no catch block, any exceptions thrown in the code will be merrily shot out of the method call, and the finally block will still be executed. This results in a much cleaner piece of code.

Exceptional Traps

Exceptions give you substantial power in your debugging and error-handling capabilities. However, they can lead to elusive corruption bugs, which can take hours to eradicate. See Example 5-7.

Example 5-7. A data table model with a problem

```
package oreilly.hcj.finalstory;
public class ExceptionalTraps implements TableModel {

  /** Cache of the data fetched. */
  private ArrayList data;

  /** Holds the sql used to fetch the data. */
  private String sql;
```

Example 5-7. A data table model with a problem (continued)

```
/**
 * Gets data from the the database and caches it for the table model.
 *
 * @param conn The database connection to use.
 * @param sql The SQL to use.
 *
 * @return The result value.
 *
 * @throws SQLException If there is a SQL error.
 */
public int loadData(final Connection conn, final String sql)
  throws SQLException {
  int result = 0;
  Statement stmt = null;
  ResultSet rs = null;
  Object[] record = null;
  this.data = new ArrayList();
  try {
    this.sql = sql;
    stmt = conn.createStatement();
    rs = stmt.executeQuery(sql);
    int idx = 0;
    int columnCount = rs.getMetaData().getColumnCount();
    while (rs.next()) {
      record = new Object[columnCount];
      for (idx = 0; idx < columnCount; idx++) {
        record[idx] = rs.getObject(idx);
      }
      data.add(record);
    }
  } finally {
    if (rs != null) {
      rs.close();
    }
    if (stmt != null) {
      stmt.close();
    }
  }
  return result;
}

public void refresh(final Connection conn) throws SQLException {
  loadData(conn, this.sql);
}
}
```

This snippet is from a JDBC-powered GUI. The code is supposed to provide a table model for a set of data from a database. When the user calls loadData( ), the given SQL is run against the database, and the data is stored in a cache, which will be used by the GUI. This SQL is also stored in a local data member so that the user can periodically refresh the data in the table model.

Unfortunately, if this code throws an exception, it stops working in a catastrophic way. Suppose there is a transaction issue that causes the method to throw an exception. To understand what would happen, pretend you are the computer on which the method is being executed:

```
public int loadData(final Connection conn, final String sql)
    throws SQLException {
    int result = 0;
    Statement stmt = null;
    ResultSet rs = null;
    Object[] record = null;
```

Up to this point, you have set things up and initialized variables. The next thing you do is clear the old cache of data to prepare for the new records:

```
this.data = new ArrayList();
```

Now that you have a sparkling clean cache, you can change the sql member of the class to store the SQL that you will use in the upcoming database call:

```
try {
  this.sql = sql;
```

Finally, you are ready to connect to the database and start loading the data into the table model:

```
stmt = conn.createStatement();
rs = stmt.executeQuery(sql);
int idx = 0;
int columnCount = rs.getMetaData().getColumnCount();
while (rs.next()) {
  record = new Object[columnCount];
  for (idx = 0; idx < columnCount; idx++) {
    record[idx] = rs.getObject(idx);
```

After the seventh iteration of the loop, a transaction exception occurs, which causes this call to fail and subsequently throw a SQLException. The flow will now pass to the finally block:

```
} finally {
  if (rs != null) {
    rs.close();
  }
  if (stmt != null) {
    stmt.close();
  }
}
return result;
}
```

Now that you are done with the method call, let's examine the results. Hitting the exception on the rs.getObject(idx) call caused the method to end prematurely, and the data wasn't loaded completely. However, the sql member of the class now contains the SQL of the *failed* call. What's worse is that the data in the table is now partially loaded.

The contents of the object are totally scrambled. Other objects that do not expect the data to be scrambled, such as listeners, will probably also throw exceptions. The result could be a chain reaction of hundreds of exceptions that eventually crash the program. The user, not knowing anything about databases or exceptions, fills out a bug report that says, "Using the 'Find My Data' menu item sometimes causes the client to crash."

Once you receive this bug report, you first try to replicate the error to figure out what is wrong with the method. However, you don't get the transaction problem the user did, so you can't reproduce the bug. You now have a transient bug that will be extremely difficult to find. There could be thousands of lines of code between the invocation of the menu item and this method. The phrase "needle in a haystack" was invented for times like this!

The problem is not with the actual SQLException but with the programmer's use of exceptions within the method. In this case, the data in the method is hopelessly scrambled because the programmer did things in a problematic order. By setting instance members *prior* to the possible occurrence of exceptions in the class, he introduced the possibility of scrambled data. The good news is that you can block this problem with a coding standard. Here is another look at the method, rewritten to prevent corruption:

```
package oreilly.hcj.exceptions;
public class ExceptionalTraps implements TableModel {

  public int loadData2(final Connection conn, final String sql)
    throws SQLException {
    int result = 0;
    Statement stmt = null;
    ResultSet rs = null;
    Object[] record = null;
    ArrayList temp = new ArrayList();
    try {
      stmt = conn.createStatement();
      rs = stmt.executeQuery(sql);
      int idx = 0;
      int columnCount = rs.getMetaData().getColumnCount();
      while (rs.next()) {
        record = new Object[columnCount];
        for (idx = 0; idx < columnCount; idx++) {
          record[idx] = rs.getObject(idx);
        }
        temp.add(record);
      }
    } finally {
      if (rs != null) {
        rs.close();
      }
      if (stmt != null) {
        stmt.close();
      }
    }
```

```
      this.data = temp;
      this.sql = sql;
      return result;
   }
}
```

In the new version of the loadData( ) method, you first try to do all of the operations that could cause an exception *prior* to setting the instance variables. To accomplish this, create a temporary list to hold the data and then add the records to that list. Once all the data is loaded and the connections are cleaned up, set the instance members of the class appropriately. The SQL is copied and the temporary list becomes the new data cache. This technique guarantees that the data can never become corrupted. If an exception is thrown in the method body, the virtual machine will execute the finally block and exit the method, and the instance members won't be set.

Revisiting the example of a transaction problem, an error in processing the client's request results in old data being shown in the GUI table. Not bothering to look at the log showing the transaction exception, the user merely clicks the menu item again, and goes about his business.

In the data table example, the effects of corruption are a rather minor GUI problem. In other cases, they can be much more critical. For example, a customer's order may not be completely processed, while the customer's account indicates that it has. This would result in an angry and potentially lost customer. In any application, remember that data is sacred, and data corruption is the devil.

Being vigilant for signs of data corruption is not always easy because this particular devil likes to hide from you and attack when least expected. Try to flush out this devil in Example 5-8.

Example 5-8. A sneaky corruption issue

```
package oreilly.hcj.exceptions;
public class ExceptionalTraps implements TableModel {

  public void processOrder(final Object order, final Customer customer) {
    this.processedOrders.add(order);
    doOrderProcessing( );
    billCreditCard(customer);
  }
}
```

This example seems harmless enough. In reality, it's about as harmless as explosives attached to a ticking clock. The problem is that although the method does not declare any exceptions to be thrown, it isn't certain that the two called methods won't throw runtime exceptions. To illustrate, look at the billCreditCard( ) method, which is called by the processOrder( ) method:

```
    package oreilly.hcj.exceptions;
    public class ExceptionalTraps implements TableModel {
```

```
    public void billCreditCard(final Customer customer) {
        if (customer == null) {
            throw new NullPointerException();
        }
        System.err.println(customer);
    }
}
```

Since runtime exceptions aren't required to be declared in the method declaration, they could be lurking in these methods and you wouldn't know it. In this case, if the customer is null, a NullPointerException will be thrown. If these exceptions do occur, then the system would think you have processed the order because you have already added it to the processedOrders member, but you have actually failed to process the order.

The best way to avoid this problem, and the main rule you should establish for all of your code, is, whenever possible, to make the setting of instance variables the last thing you do in any method. You can rewrite the method in Example 5-8 to reflect this policy:

```
    public void processOrder(final Object order, final Customer customer) {
        doOrderProcessing();
        billCreditCard(customer);
        this.processedOrders.add(order);
    }
```

In the revised method, the order will be added to processedOrders only after all other operations have succeeded. In this manner, you can be sure that an order is processed properly and is not in a corrupted state.

One example of where it isn't possible to set instance variables in the method after everything else has been completed is demonstrated by the a bound property of a Java bean:

```
    public void setSomeProperty(final String someProperty) {
        final String oldSomeProperty = this.someProperty;
        this.someProperty = someProperty;
        propertyChangeSupport.firePropertyChange("someProperty",
                                                 oldSomeProperty,
                                                 someProperty);
    }
```

In this case, the bound property has to actually change *before* the listeners are informed of the property change events. If you mix up the steps, then any class getting the event and reading the new values would actually be reading old data. The fact that you have no choice but to put the event-firing after the setting of the instance variable is the only excuse for setting instance variables before performing any dangerous work.

However, there is still a problem with your exceptions. The fact that the firePropertyChange() and the methods called after it can cause runtime exceptions leaves you with a hole in your logic. For example, consider a GUI in which the event fired causes data to be reloaded and then other panels to be refreshed. In this case, the firePropertyChange() is the entry point in potentially hundreds of consecutive method calls, any of which could throw runtime exceptions and corrupt the object. This problem can be solved by using exception firewalls.

The idea behind exception firewalls stems from the fact that the listeners of an object are passive in nature. The object firing the events is notifying the listeners of an event, but it couldn't care less if the listeners actually react because of the event. In this case, you could build a shield around the exceptions that allow your program to continue:

```
public void setSomeProperty2(final String someProperty) {
  final String oldSomeProperty = this.someProperty;
  this.someProperty = someProperty;
  try {
    propertyChangeSupport.firePropertyChange("someProperty",
                                             oldSomeProperty,
                                             someProperty);
  } catch (final Exception ex) {
    LOGGER.error("Exception in Listener", ex);
  }
}
```

In the revised version of your setter, the exceptions that occur as a result of notifying the listener of the event are caught and routed to a logging device and will not propagate through the setter. Not only does this technique protect the bean object from corruption, it also allows the actual position of the exception to be found much more efficiently. If your event had caused another event, which in turn had caused another event, the exception could have propagated through several methods before it was reported.

Naturally, since this code is specific to the actual firing of the events and not the beans, the exception firewall code would be better off in the listener support classes, such as PropertyListenerSupport.

Note that this technique is appropriate only for passive listeners. In the case of a PropertyVetoListener, this technique would not be appropriate because the setter has to abort the change if the change is vetoed.

In all other cases, you should wait until the last lines of the method to set values of instance members. By using temporary variables to hold intermediate results in long methods, this is easily accomplished.

CHAPTER 6

Nested Classes

One aspect of the Java language that is not widely understood is the concept of nested classes. These classes allow you to constrain an entire class within a limited scope of another class or method. The concept of nesting a class within another class or method presents unique issues not found elsewhere in object-oriented programming. Not all types of nested classes should be used routinely, so you will likely encounter most of them in other people's code. Therefore, it is important that you understand how the various nested classes function.

Nested classes fall into one of three basic categories:

- Inner classes
- Limited-scope inner classes
- Static nested classes

Each of these categories has its own access rules and usage.

Inner Classes

Inner classes are fairly common within the JDK, especially in collections. Example 6-1 shows a class-scoped inner class.

Example 6-1. A class-scoped inner class

```
package oreilly.hcj.nested;
public class InnerClassDemo extends JDialog {

  public InnerClassDemo(final int beepCount) {
    super( );
    setTitle("Anonymous Demo");
    contentPane = getContentPane( );
    contentPane.setLayout(new BorderLayout( ));

    JLabel logoLabel = new JLabel(LOGO);
    contentPane.add(BorderLayout.NORTH, logoLabel);
```

Example 6-1. A class-scoped inner class (continued)

```
    JButton btn = new BeepButton("Beep");
    contentPane.add(BorderLayout.SOUTH, btn);
    pack();
    this.beepCount = beepCount;
  }

  private class BeepButton extends JButton implements ActionListener {

    public BeepButton(final String text) {
      super(text);
      addActionListener(this);
    }

    public void actionPerformed(final ActionEvent event) {
      try {
        for (int count = 0; count < beepCount; count++) {
          Toolkit.getDefaultToolkit().beep();
          Thread.sleep(100);  // wait for the old beep to finish.
        }
      } catch (final InterruptedException ex) {
        throw new RuntimeException(ex);
      }
    }
  }
}
```

This code shows how inner classes are used in a GUI dialog. To create a special kind of button that beeps when you click on it, the `javax.swing.JButton` class has been extended and the appropriate action listener has been added. In the constructor, another of these special buttons is instantiated and added to the dialog. Although this seems pretty simple, there are a couple of interesting points worthy of study.

First of all, you may notice that the variable `beepCount`, used in the `for` statement, is in scope inside the action listener, even though it was not declared in the `actionPerformed()` method. This is because inner classes can access all members of the declaring class, even private members. In fact, the inner class itself is said to be a member of the class; therefore, following the rules of object-oriented engineering, it should have access to all members of the class.

The other interesting point is the visibility keyword on the class declaration line:

```
    private class BeepButton extends JButton implements ActionListener {
```

Because this class is declared as private, other classes can't instantiate this class. This restriction behaves as public, protected, and private visibility keywords behave for any other member of the enclosing class.

Using public visibility with inner classes leads to some rather strange syntax. To demonstrate, let's create an example of a public inner class and then use it. The inner class is shown here:

```
// From oreilly.hcj.nested.MonitorScreen
public class MonitorScreen {

  public class PixelPoint {
    private int x;
    private int y;

    public PixelPoint(final int x, final int y) {
      this.x = x;
      this.y = y;
    }

    public int getX() {
      return x;
    }

    public int getY() {
      return y;
    }
  }
}
```

In this example, an inner class represents a pixel on your screen. Since the inner class is public, you can create an instance of PixelPoint outside of the enclosing class. Your first attempt may look something like the following:

```
package oreilly.hcj.nested;
public class PublicInnerClassAccess {
  public static final void main(final String[] args) {
    MonitorScreen.PixelPoint obj =
        new MonitorScreen.PixelPoint(); // <= Compiler error.
  }
}
```

The problem here is that the scope of the inner class is restricted only to an instance of the enclosing class. For this reason, such a static declaration won't work. You need an instance of the class to complete the construction. This can be accomplished with the following code:

```
package oreilly.hcj.nested;
public class PublicInnerClassAccess {
  public static final void main(final String[] args) {
    MonitorScreen screen = new MonitorScreen();
    MonitorScreen.PixelPoint pixel = screen.new PixelPoint(25, 40);
    System.out.println(pixel.getX());
    System.out.println(pixel.getY());
  }
}
```

In this version, you create a new instance of `MonitorScreen` and use it to create a new instance of `PixelPoint` with the following code:

```
screen.new PixelPoint(25, 40);
```

The syntax of the creation looks strange, but it really does work, as you can see in this book's sample code. That being said, I don't recommend you use this sort of syntax routinely, as it is confusing to read and violates the object-oriented engineering principles behind inner classes.

Inner classes are best used to represent composition relationships in an object model. Therefore, the enclosing instances should always have total control over the enclosed instances. In this case, a `PixelPoint` cannot exist outside of a monitor screen, so composition is indicated.

 If you recall, composition models aggregation in which the life cycle of the objects being aggregated are under the control of the object performing the aggregation. If the object performing the aggregation goes out of scope, so should the objects it is composed of. The decision to use composition instead of aggregation comes down to a question of whether the composed class can exist on its own. If it can't, then composition is indicated; otherwise, aggregation is indicated.

Since inner classes are best used to model composition, I strongly suggest you stick to private and protected visibility for your inner classes.

Hierarchies of Inner Classes

Like normal classes, inner classes can exist in a hierarchy. In fact, inner classes can even carry the hierarchy restrictions of `abstract` and `final`. To understand these hierarchies, study the abstract inner class in Example 6-2.

Example 6-2. A basic monitor screen class

```
package oreilly.hcj.nested;
public abstract class BasicMonitorScreen {
  private Dimension resolution;

  public BasicMonitorScreen(final Dimension resolution) {
    this.resolution = resolution;
  }

  public Dimension getResolution() {
    return this.resolution;
  }

  protected abstract class PixelPoint {
    private int x;

    private int y;
```

Example 6-2. A basic monitor screen class (continued)

```
    public PixelPoint(final int x, final int y) {
      this.x = x;
      this.y = y;
    }

    public int getX( ) {
      return x;
    }

    public int getY( ) {
      return y;
    }
  }
}
```

The `BasicMonitorScreen` class provides the base class for all monitor screens in your overall class hierarchy. Since the screen is composed of pixels, which indicates composition, the `PixelPoint` class is declared as an inner class.

Note that both the enclosing class and the inner class are declared abstract. However, there is no connection at all between the two. The hierarchies for the enclosing class and inner class should be considered independently. In the example, the `BasicMonitorClass` is said to be abstract because it can't exist without more specificity. The `PixelPoint` class also has the same dynamics, but it could have been declared concrete and simply used by subclasses. In this case, however, the subclasses have to define a concrete subclass of `PixelPoint` to use it. Also, make sure that an abstract inner class *doesn't* make the enclosing class abstract, as with an abstract method.

Creating concrete classes within an abstract base class is a good way to model composition relationships in an inheritance hierarchy. You can declare the composed classes in the base class and let the subclasses use that composed class.

In this situation, you need to create a concrete type of `PixelPoint` to use it. The subclasses are shown in Example 6-3.

Example 6-3. A class for a color monitor

```
package oreilly.hcj.nested;
public class ColorMonitorScreen extends BasicMonitorScreen {
  public ColorMonitorScreen(final Dimension resolution) {
    super(resolution);
  }

  protected class ColorPixelPoint extends PixelPoint {
    private Color color;

    public ColorPixelPoint(final int x, final int y, final Color color) {
      super(x, y);
      this.color = color;
    }
```

Example 6-3. A class for a color monitor (continued)

```
    public Color getColor( ) {
      return this.color;
    }
  }
}
```

In this example, you create inheritance hierarchies for both the enclosing and inner classes. Now you have an inner class that can be instantiated in the virtual machine. However, watch out for one little gotcha with inherited inner classes:

```
    package oreilly.hcj.nested;
    public class ColorMonitorScreen extends BasicMonitorScreen {
      protected class ColorPixelPoint extends PixelPoint {
        public void someMethod( ) {
          System.out.println(resoultion); // <= compiler error
        }
      }
    }
```

Remembering that inner classes can access the members of their enclosing instance, try to access BasicMonitorScreen's resolution class variable in your ColorPixelPoint inner class. The compiler won't let you access resolution because the special privileged access to the enclosing class's members apply only to the inner classes declared in the enclosing class. This naturally follows since these inner classes are members of the enclosing class, but subclasses of them declared outside the enclosing class are not members. Since ColorPixelPoint is not a member of BasicMonitorScreen, access to BasicMonitorScreen's private and protected members is not allowed.

Finally, keep in mind that public inner classes can also be extended by classes that are *not* inner classes. However, since public inner classes are generally a bad idea, you shouldn't be doing this anyway. If you have an overwhelming compulsion to employ this technique, you should consider using static nested classes instead.

Limited-Scope Inner Classes

One of the strangest types of inner classes is the *limited-scoped inner class*. Limited-scoped classes are scoped to a particular block of code. Their declaration and usage all happen within that block. To get a better idea of how limited-scoped inner classes work, see Example 6-4.

Example 6-4. A limited-scope inner class scoped to a method

```
package oreilly.hcj.nested;
public class MethodInnerClassDemo extends JDialog {

  /** Holds the location of the logo image. */
  private static final String LOGO_LOCATION =
                  "oreilly/hcj/nested/oreilly_header3.gif";
```

Example 6-4. A limited-scope inner class scoped to a method (continued)

```
  static {
    LOGO = new ImageIcon(ClassLoader.getSystemClassLoader( )
                                    .getResource(LOGO_LOCATION));
  }

  /** Holds a reference to the content pane. */
  private final Container contentPane;

  /** holds a demo variable. */
  private String demo;

  public MethodInnerClassDemo(final int value) {
    super( );
    String title = "Inner Class Demo";
    setTitle(title);
    setModal(true);
    contentPane = getContentPane( );
    contentPane.setLayout(new BorderLayout( ));

    JLabel logoLabel = new JLabel(LOGO);
    contentPane.add(BorderLayout.NORTH, logoLabel);

    JButton btn = new JButton("Beep");

    class MyActionListener implements ActionListener {
      public void actionPerformed(final ActionEvent event) {
        Toolkit.getDefaultToolkit().beep( );
        System.out.println(value);
        System.out.println(LOGO_LOCATION);
        System.out.println(MethodInnerClassDemo.this.demo);
      }
    }
    btn.addActionListener(new MyActionListener( ));

    contentPane.add(BorderLayout.SOUTH, btn);
    pack( );
  }
}
```

Other than the fact that the declaration of the class occurs within the body of a method, this looks like any other class declaration. You can even use the keywords final and abstract on these declarations and develop class hierarchies all within one limited block. Once declared, you can use the class throughout the remainder of the method just like any other class. However, there are some important differences between limited-scope inner classes and normal classes.

First of all, limited-scope inner classes can access final variables of the declaring block. In Example 6-4, the actionPerformed( ) method of MyActionListener uses the variable value despite the fact that it hasn't declared this variable. In this case, value is a final parameter to the method; therefore, `MyActionListener` can access it. However, `MyActionListener` would not have access to the local variable `title`, as it is not `final`.

In addition to `final` variables of the enclosing block, a limited-scope inner class can access all members of the enclosing class, including the private variables. In Example 6-4, the `LOGO_LOCATION` and `demo` variables are class members; therefore, `MyActionListener` can use them within its methods despite the fact that both are private. Note especially the syntax used to access the demo variable in the outer declaring class:

```
System.out.println(MethodInnerClassDemo.this.demo);
```

This is the proper way to access an instance variable of an outer class from an inner class. The syntax specifies which `this` pointer to use, which is critical when your inner class has a variable with the same name as a variable in the outer class. If you use this syntax without the type specifier, you will get access only to the variable in the inner class.

Additionally, the limited-scope inner classes are subject to scoping rules that are unique to these classes. Example 6-5 shows a class that has several limited-scope inner classes.

Example 6-5. Various limited-scope inner classes

```
package oreilly.hcj.nested;
public class MethodInnerClassDemo extends JDialog {

  public MethodInnerClassDemo(final int value) {
    super();
    String title = "Inner Class Demo";
    setTitle(title);
    setModal(true);
    contentPane = getContentPane();
    contentPane.setLayout(new BorderLayout());

    JLabel logoLabel = new JLabel(LOGO);
    contentPane.add(BorderLayout.NORTH, logoLabel);

    JButton btn = new JButton("Beep");

    class MyActionListener implements ActionListener {
      public void actionPerformed(final ActionEvent event) {
        Toolkit.getDefaultToolkit().beep();
        System.out.println(value);
        System.out.println(LOGO_LOCATION);
        System.out.println(MethodInnerClassDemo.this.demo);
        // System.out.println(title); // <= compiler error
      }
    }
    btn.addActionListener(new MyActionListener());
```

Example 6-5. Various limited-scope inner classes (continued)

```
      contentPane.add(BorderLayout.SOUTH, btn);
      pack();
  }

  public MethodInnerClassDemo() {
    super();
    setTitle("Inner Class Demo");
    setModal(true);
    contentPane = getContentPane();
    contentPane.setLayout(new BorderLayout());

    JLabel logoLabel = new JLabel(LOGO);
    contentPane.add(BorderLayout.NORTH, logoLabel);

    JButton btn1 = new JButton("Beep");
    JButton btn2 = new JButton("Bell");

    class MyActionListener implements ActionListener {
      public void actionPerformed(final ActionEvent event) {
        Toolkit.getDefaultToolkit().beep();
      }
    }
    btn1.addActionListener(new MyActionListener());
    btn2.addActionListener(new MyActionListener());

    JPanel pnl = new JPanel(new GridLayout(1, 2));
    pnl.add(btn1);
    pnl.add(btn2);

    contentPane.add(BorderLayout.SOUTH, pnl);
    pack();
  }

  public void someMethod() {
    ActionListener listener =
        new MyActionListener(); // <= compiler error.
  }
}
```

In Example 6-5, you declare two different limited-scope inner classes in two differ-ent constructors. Each of these classes is in scope only within the method in which it is declared. Therefore, the MyActionListener class in the first constructor is a differ-ent class than the one in the second constructor despite the fact that they both have the same name. Furthermore, attempting to use one of the MyActionListener classes outside the method, which is done in someMethod(), will result in a compiler error—specifically, an undeclared type error.

These classes don't necessarily need to be scoped to a method. You could have sur-rounded them with curly braces, thereby scoping them to a particular block. In fact, many Java GUIs employ a specific type of limited-scope inner class, which is scoped only to a specific method call or assignment. These classes are called *anonymous classes*.

Anonymous Classes

The concept of anonymous classes often confuses Java developers. Essentially, anonymous classes are limited-scope classes that are declared but are not given a name by the programmer (hence the designation "anonymous") and have only a limited lifespan. Although they can be used for a wide variety of applications, they are most commonly used as event handlers in GUI programs. A common example of an anonymous class is shown in Example 6-6.

Example 6-6. An anonymous class

```
package oreilly.hcj.nested;
public class AnonymousDemo extends JDialog {

  public AnonymousDemo( ) {
    super( );
    setTitle("Anonymous Demo");
    setModal(true);
    contentPane = getContentPane( );
    contentPane.setLayout(new BorderLayout( ));

    JLabel logoLabel = new JLabel(LOGO);
    contentPane.add(BorderLayout.NORTH, logoLabel);

    JButton btn = new JButton("Beep");
    btn.addActionListener(new ActionListener( ) {
        public void actionPerformed(final ActionEvent event) {
          Toolkit.getDefaultToolkit().beep( );
        }
      });
    contentPane.add(BorderLayout.SOUTH, btn);
    pack( );
  }
}
```

This example declares an anonymous class that listens to and acts on the action events produced by a button. Because the syntax of the anonymous class is a little peculiar, it is worth studying in detail.

Anonymous class syntax

Anonymous classes can be used only once, so they must be used as a parameter to a method or assigned to a variable. Consequently, it is necessary to declare and institute the class in one move, which is why you start out using the keyword new to instantiate the class you are declaring. In this case, the anonymous class is declared, instantiated, and then passed to the addActionListener( ) method of the btn object:

```
btn.addActionListener(new ActionListener( ) {
  public void actionPerformed(final ActionEvent event) {
    Toolkit.getDefaultToolkit().beep( );
  }
});
```

The declaration of the anonymous class itself starts with the class name of the *super-type* of the anonymous class. In this case, you use the interface ActionListener as the supertype:

```
btn.addActionListener(new ActionListener( ) {
  public void actionPerformed(final ActionEvent event) {
    Toolkit.getDefaultToolkit().beep( );
  }
});
```

Anonymous classes can use any non-final interface or class as their supertype. If you use an interface, then the superclass of the anonymous class will automatically be java.lang.Object (see Chapter 1).

The parameters to the *superclass* constructor immediately follow the supertype. This allows you to pass arguments to the constructor of the superclass of your anonymous class. If there are multiple constructors to the superclass, you can pass parameters that are appropriate for any one of those constructors. In this case, the supertype of your anonymous class is an interface, and the superclass is java.lang.Object. Therefore, you don't need to pass any arguments to the superclass, and the parentheses are empty.

```
btn.addActionListener(new ActionListener( ) {
  public void actionPerformed(final ActionEvent event) {
    Toolkit.getDefaultToolkit().beep( );
  }
});
```

By contrast, here is an anonymous class declaration in which the programmer passed arguments to the constructor:

```
JButton btn = new JButton("Beep") {
  // ...contents omitted
};
```

In this case, the supertype of the anonymous class is javax.swing.JButton. The JButton class has several constructors; however, the programmer chose to pass arguments to the constructor that takes a single String parameter.

One difference between anonymous classes and limited-scope classes is that anonymous classes cannot use the keywords abstract or final. In fact, every anonymous class is considered to be final by default. When combined with the fact that these classes have no name, this means that it is impossible to declare hierarchies of anonymous classes.

The declaration of the contents of the class follows the parameters to the supertype constructor:

```
btn.addActionListener(new ActionListener() {
  public void actionPerformed(final ActionEvent event) {
    Toolkit.getDefaultToolkit().beep();
  }
});
```

In the example, you are declaring a class that implements `ActionListener`, so you have to override the `actionPerformed()` method in your anonymous class, just as if you had been writing a normal implementation class. If you want, you can also place other code within the body. The only thing that you can't place within an anonymous class is a constructor. In fact, it would be impossible to declare a constructor because constructors use the name of the class as the method name, and an anonymous class doesn't have a programmer-accessible type name.

The syntax for anonymous classes is a little weird and is not considered to be mainstream Java syntax. However, examining how the compiler deals with a declaration of your anonymous class will help you understand how it works. Here, the compiler views your anonymous class from Example 6-4:

```
public AnonymousDemo() {
  // ...snip

  class AnonymousDemo$1 implements ActionListener {
    public AnonymousDemo$1 () {
    }

    public void actionPerformed(final ActionEvent event) {
      Toolkit.getDefaultToolkit().beep();
    }
  }

  // ...snip
}
```

When the compiler sees an anonymous class declaration, the compiler creates a unique identifier for the anonymous class and then declares it as a normal method-scoped inner class.

The identifier that the compiler uses for your anonymous class is the position of the anonymous class in the order declared in the source file. In the case of the above example, you know that this anonymous class is the first one declared when reading from top to bottom in the source file. However, you can never depend on this name, so you can't reuse the class by instantiating it.

After the name declaration, the compiler adds the inheritance structure for the class. If `ActionListener` had been a class instead of an interface, the compiler would have used the keyword extends instead of `implements`. Finally, the compiler adds the body of the anonymous class to the newly declared class.

Once the class is declared, the virtual machine uses the new class in the method:

```
public AnonymousDemo(final in) {
    super();
    setTitle("Anonymous Demo");
    setModal(true);
    contentPane = getContentPane();
    contentPane.setLayout(new BorderLayout());

    JLabel logoLabel = new JLabel(LOGO);
    contentPane.add(BorderLayout.NORTH, logoLabel);

    JButton btn = new JButton("Beep");

    class AnonymousDemo$1 implements ActionListener {
        public AnonymousDemo$1 () {
        }

        public void actionPerformed(final ActionEvent event) {
            Toolkit.getDefaultToolkit().beep();
        }
    }

    btn.addActionListener(new AnonymousDemo$1());
    contentPane.add(BorderLayout.SOUTH, btn);
    pack();
}
```

In this example, the newly declared class is replaced in the source code with the expansion. Then the `addActionListener()` method line declares a new instance of this class to pass as a parameter. Although you don't have to know all of these details to use anonymous classes, it helps to track down bugs and understand the Java compiler—which are both important for hardcore Java programmers.

Problems with Limited-Scope Inner Classes

Since the syntax of anonymous classes is not considered to be mainstream Java syntax, anonymous classes are difficult to read and are often misunderstood. Furthermore, they tend to be overused, especially in GUI code. Example 6-7 shows a syntax that is similar to one I encountered in a GUI for a banking system.

Example 6-7. Anonymous classes galore

```
package oreilly.hcj.nested;
public class AnonymousDemo extends JDialog {
    public AnonymousDemo(final int exitDelay) {
```

Example 6-7. Anonymous classes galore (continued)

```
super();
setTitle("Anonymous Demo");
setModal(true);
contentPane = getContentPane();
contentPane.setLayout(new BorderLayout());

final String delayDisplay =
  new Object() {
      public String toString() {
        System.out.println(demo);
        if ((exitDelay) > 1000) {
          // Show in seconds.
          NumberFormat formatter = NumberFormat.getNumberInstance();
          formatter.setMinimumFractionDigits(2);
          double time = exitDelay / 1000.0;
          return (new String(formatter.format(time) + " seconds"));
        } else {
          // Show in Microseconds
          return new String(exitDelay + " microseconds");
        }
      }
    }.toString();

addWindowListener(new WindowAdapter() {
    public void windowClosing(final WindowEvent event) {
      try {
        System.out.println("Waiting for " + delayDisplay);
        Thread.sleep(exitDelay);
      } catch (final InterruptedException ex) {
        throw new RuntimeException(ex);
      }
    }
  });

JLabel logoLabel = new JLabel(LOGO);
contentPane.add(BorderLayout.NORTH, logoLabel);

JButton btn =
  new JButton("Beep") {
    public void fireActionPerformed(final ActionEvent event) {
      if (LOGGER.isDebugEnabled()) {
        LOGGER.debug(event);
        LOGGER.debug("This class is: " + this.getClass().getName());
      }
      super.fireActionPerformed(event);
    }
  };

btn.addActionListener(new ActionListener() {
    public void actionPerformed(final ActionEvent event) {
      doBeep();
```

Example 6-7. Anonymous classes galore (continued)

```
        }
    });
    contentPane.add(BorderLayout.SOUTH, btn);

    pack();
  }
}
```

In this single method, the programmer declared no less than four anonymous classes, all for different reasons. The code in Example 6-7 is a textbook demonstration of anonymous classes. However, anyone that writes code like this should probably be beaten to death with a code-readability guide. It's just far too difficult to comprehend at a glance.

The result achieved by the anonymous classes can be accomplished by implementing interfaces and proper method calls with much more clarity and maintainability. For example, the class itself could implement ActionListener and WindowListener to provide the event handling. Furthermore, the construction of the delayDisplay would have been easier to read if it had been in a method call instead. Even though the source code would have been longer, the maintenance situation would be far easier to understand.

Other limited-scope inner classes suffer from similar readability issues. When you embed a class declaration inside of a method block, you can easily confuse the reader and increase the time it takes to integrate new developers into a project.

Additionally, anonymous classes are not reusable at all. This goes against why you declare a class in the first place. The core of object-oriented programming is reusability; therefore, declaring a nonreusable class violates the principles of object-oriented engineering. In many GUIs, I've noticed instances in which programmers declare several anonymous classes that are nearly identical. Although this will work, it is not very object-oriented.

Finally, anonymous and other limited-scope inner classes make debugging code difficult and confusing. You could be stepping through code with a debugger and suddenly be transported to a piece of code in the middle of a method. It would require concentration and code awareness to realize that you are in a class declaration. Also, since anonymous classes don't have programmer-accessible names, errors that occur in that class are often difficult to locate.

All of these problems make limited-scope inner classes problematic. Therefore, I advise you to avoid them whenever possible. However, you should now be prepared when you encounter them in someone else's code. If you have a chance, I would recommend that you convert their code to use other techniques instead.

Static Nested Classes

A static nested class is, not surprisingly, a nested class that is declared with the keyword `static` on the declaration. Many developers call these classes "inner classes" as well. However, these developers are wrong. To be an inner class, a class has to have instance scope. To understand how static nested classes function, see Example 6-8.

Example 6-8. A static nested class

```
package oreilly.hcj.nested;
public class OuterClass {

  private static final String name = "Robert";
  private static String company = "O'Reilly";
  private int value = 5;

  public static class SomeClass {
    public void someMethod( ) {
      System.out.println(company);
      System.out.println(name);
      System.out.println(value); // <= Compiler error
    }
  }
}
```

This code declares a public static nested class. This nested class can access the various static members of the enclosing class. However, unlike inner classes, it cannot access any instance variables in the enclosing class. This is an important difference between static nested classes and inner classes. Formally, it can be said that an inner class is instance-scoped and a static nested class is class-scoped. The class scope of a static nested class makes it easier to use:

```
package oreilly.hcj.nested;
public class StaticNestedClassDemo {
  public static void main(final String[] args) {
    OuterClass.SomeClass obj = new OuterClass.SomeClass( );
    obj.someMethod( );
  }
}
```

To instantiate a public static nested class, you do not need an instance of the outer class. You can simply use the class as is to create new instances:

```
import oreilly.hcj.nested.OuterClass.SomeClass;
public class StaticNestedClassDemo {
  public static void main(final String[] args) {
    SomeClass obj = new SomeClass( );
    obj.someMethod( );
  }
}
```

With this import syntax, the class is quite easy to use. However, static nested classes can also use access specifiers. You can have public, private, protected, package, final, and even abstract static nested classes. If you try to access a static nested class outside of its visibility, your code won't compile, as the following snippet demonstrates:

```
package oreilly.hcj.nested;
public class OuterClass {
  private static class SomeOtherClass {
    // ...code
  }
}
```

```
package oreilly.hcj.nested;
public class StaticNestedClassDemo {
  public static void main(final String[] args) {
    OuterClass.SomeOtherClass prot =
        new OuterClass.SomeOtherClass(); // <= Compiler error
    OuterClass.doPrivate();
  }
}
```

Private and protected static nested classes have predictable visibility and specialized functions. Generally, they are used to implement internal features of a class or class hierarchy. For example, the Java collection classes use private static nested classes to implement the entries in their data structures. (For an example, see the source code to java.util.HashTable.) On the other hand, public static nested classes are often used to group classes together or give a group of classes access to private static resources.

When using static nested classes, your first concern should be whether package scope is sufficient for your class. If it isn't, then by all means use static nested classes. If package scope will suffice, then it is better, for the sake of readability, to declare the class normally.

Of all the nested classes, static nested classes are the easiest to use, read, and understand. Unless you positively need to access the instance variables of a class, I recommend you make your nested classes static whenever possible.

Double Nested Classes

One peculiar form of declaration that I came across while working for an aerospace company was a nested class within a nested class. The dynamics of this sort of declaration are similar to those of a normal nested class. The difference is that the dynamics extend to the subnested class as well as the nested class. See Example 6-9.

Example 6-9. A double nested class

```
package oreilly.hcj.nested;
public class DoubleNestedClass {
```

Example 6-9. A double nested class (continued)

```java
private static final String name = "Robert";
private static String company = "O'Reilly";

private int value = 5;

public static String getCompany() {
  return company;
}

public static String getName() {
  return name;
}

public int getValue() {
  return value;
}

public static class SomeClass {
  private final static String book = "Hardcore Java";

  public void someMethod() {
    System.out.println("In SomeClass.someMethod()");
    System.out.println(company);
    System.out.println(name);
    // System.out.println(value); // <= Compiler error
  }

  public static class SomeOtherClass {
    public void someMethod() {
      System.out.println("In SomeOtherClass.someMethod()");
      System.out.println(company);
      System.out.println(book);
    }
  }
}

}
```

In this example, the class SomeOtherClass is nested inside of the class SomeClass. Because of the double nesting, SomeOtherClass can access the private final static members of DoubleNestedClass as well as those of SomeClass. The dynamics extend down the nesting. Similar rules apply to method-scoped and instance-scoped double nested classes. For example, a method-scoped double nested class would have access to instance variables and final local variables of the declaring method. Regardless of how deep the nesting is, the rules propagate down.

However, just because you can use double nested classes doesn't necessarily mean you should. In fact, I can't think of a single legitimate reason for double nested classes. If you find yourself writing one of these, you should probably rethink your architecture. If you find yourself doing this routinely, you may want to consider taking a long vacation.

Nested Classes in Interfaces?

Java supports the concept of nested classes in interfaces. The syntax and dynamics work just like nested classes declared in a class. However, declaring a class nested inside an interface would be extremely bad programming. An interface is an abstraction of a concept, not an implementation of one. Therefore, implementation details should be left out of interfaces. Remember, just because you can cut off your hand with a saw doesn't mean that it's a particularly good idea.

Nested Interfaces

As with classes, you can nest interfaces inside an outer class or another interface. The dynamics are similar to nested classes. However, keep in mind that the classes that ultimately implement these nested interfaces don't have the special access to the class members that a nested class does; instead, they behave just like normally declared classes.

Nested Interfaces in Classes

The syntax for nested interfaces is the same as nested classes, but the results are quite different. Since you are defining only the interface and not the implementation, the user of the interface is free to implement the class any way he wants. A good example of a nested interface implementation is with a special collection. See Example 6-10.

Example 6-10. A nested interface

```
package oreilly.hcj.nested;
public class Inventory {
  public HashSet items;

  public Set getValues() {
    return Collections.unmodifiableSet(items);
  }

  public void addItem(final InventoryItem item) {
    items.add(item);
  }

  public Iterator iterator() {
    return items.iterator();
  }
```

Example 6-10. A nested interface (continued)

```
  public void removeElement(final InventoryItem item) {
    items.remove(item);
  }

  public static interface InventoryItem {
    public String getSKU();
  }
}
```

In this example, the special collection named `Inventory` will contain only objects that implement the `InventoryItem` interface (and therefore define the method `getSKU()`). Furthermore, since you don't want to tie down the inventory items to a particular superclass, you make an interface for the inventory items, which allows the user to implement that interface as he sees fit.

There are only a few good reasons why you should use inner interfaces. One is to model a composition relationship without restricting the implementation of the composed object. In this case, you would need an inner interface to model the compositional relationship and to let the user of the interface decide on the implementation.

Nested interfaces are useful on rare occasions, but most of the time you can achieve the same results simply by declaring the interface in its own file.

Nested Interfaces in Interfaces

It is also possible to nest interfaces within other interfaces, although this is rarely done. The syntax is the same as with nested classes. Although using interfaces nested in other interfaces is less crazy than nesting classes within an interface, it is still pretty weird.

Essentially, when you nest an interface inside another interface, you are describing a compositional relationship among interfaces. Conceptually, it is a rather strange thing to do. Therefore, I don't recommend nesting interfaces.

Ultimately, nesting classes or interfaces inside other interfaces should probably be blocked by the compiler because using them makes no sense in object-oriented programming. All you can hope to accomplish is to demonstrate some obscure aspects of Java for the admiration of your junior developers. Its practical usefulness is about zero.

Nested Class Rules

Nested classes have many confusing rules. Table 6-1 will help you keep them straight.

Table 6-1. *Nested class references*

Type	Scope			Access					Keywords		
	method	instance	class	method final	class final	class static	instance	abstract/final	private	protected	public
Anonymous	✓			✓	✓	✓	✓				
Limited-scope	✓			✓	✓	✓	✓	✓			
Inner		✓			✓	✓	✓	✓	✓	✓	✓
Static nested			✓		✓	✓		✓	✓	✓	✓

Although most of the nested classes in this chapter are not recommended for routine use, it is important that you understand their dynamics. You may come across these nested class types down the line, and knowing how they work could save you time and frustration.

Although many developers tend to overuse nested classes, they can be a valuable asset to your development process. When it comes to modeling composition relationships and implementing internals of a class that you want to hide, they can't be beat.

CHAPTER 7

All About Constants

The function of constants is a concept that is often taken for granted by most developers. On the surface, they seem simple and trivial. However, constants that are not used correctly can be a major source of development headaches.

Although most developers regard constants as a single concept, there are actually three categories of constants: substitution, bit field, and option. Each of these categories has different dynamics and different issues to deal with.

Substitution Constants

Substitution constants are the simplest type of constants. Basically, they are substituted for something else in code. See Example 7-1.

Example 7-1. Substitution constants

```
package oreilly.hcj.constants;
public class SubstitutionConstants {
  /** Holds the logging instance. */
  private static final Logger LOGGER =
                Logger.getLogger(SubstitutionConstants.class);

  /** A value for PI. */
  public static final double PI = 3.141;

  public double getCircleArea(final double radius) {
    double area = (Math.pow(radius, 2) * PI);
    LOGGER.debug("The calculated area is " + area);
    return area;
  }

  public float calculateInterest(final float rate,
                                 final float principal) {
    final String LOG_MSG1 =
                "Error: The interest rate cannot be less than ";
    final String LOG_MSG2 = ". The rate input = ";
    final double MIN_INTEREST = 0.0;
```

Example 7-1. Substitution constants (continued)

```
      // --
      if (rate < MIN_INTEREST) {
        LOGGER.error(LOG_MSG1 + MIN_INTEREST + LOG_MSG2 + rate);
        throw new IllegalArgumentException("rate");
      }
      return principal * rate;
  }
}
```

This code declares several substitution constants. The constant PI has class scope while the constants LOG_MSG1, LOG_MSG2, and MIN_INTEREST have method scope. All of these constants are declared and then later substituted in various parts of the application. In the case of the public final static primitives and String objects, the substitution occurs at compile time, according to the rules discussed in Chapter 2. In all other cases, it occurs at runtime.

The use of substitution constants is standard in most applications. However, there are a few things to note, even in this mundane bit of code. For instance, the only constant declared in the class scope is a public constant. If you remember the discussion of the final keyword, you will understand why. Since method-scoped constants are not accessible outside the method, it would be impossible to declare a public method-scoped constant. All of the other constants are used within only one method, so it would make no sense to declare them in class scope.

Also note that a 2 was placed in the line in which the area of the circle was calculated. Although a constant could be used for this number, it would be wasteful for two reasons. First, the number 2 is part of the formula for the area of a circle. Second, it is used only at one particular point in the method and has no effect on any other part of the method. You should avoid creating constants if they fall under such conditions.

However, MIN_INTEREST is a constant in the calculateInterest( ) method. This is because the minimum interest rate may change, and this interest rate is used twice in the code. If it ever does have to be changed, it's better to do so in one place instead of several.

While these rules are applicable to numerical values, String values are a little different. Whether to convert a String literal that is used only once to a constant generally depends on how the String is used. To illustrate, let's look at the following code fragment:

```
      package oreilly.hcj.constants;
      public class SubstitutionConstants {
        public float calculateInterest(final float rate,
                                       final float principal) {
          final String LOG_MSG1 =
                  "Error: The Interest rate cannot be less than ";
          final String LOG_MSG2 = ". The rate input = ";
          final double MIN_INTEREST = 0.0;
```

```
      // --
      if (rate < MIN_INTEREST) {
        LOGGER.error(LOG_MSG1 + MIN_INTEREST + LOG_MSG2 + rate);
        throw new IllegalArgumentException("rate");
      }
      return principal * rate;
    }

    protected String buildLogMessage(final Exception ex) {
      StringBuffer buf = new StringBuffer(200);
      StackTraceElement[] elements = ex.getStackTrace();
      buf.append("The exception ");
      buf.append(ex.getClass().getName());
      buf.append(" occurred at ");
      buf.append(Calendar.getInstance().getTime().toString());
      buf.append(" on line ");
      buf.append(elements[0].getLineNumber());
      return buf.toString();
    }
  }
```

In this code, constants are used in the first method but not in the second. Since the strings in question are used only once in both methods, the question of whether to use constants may seem arbitrary. However, there is a good reason why they are used in the first method: they improve readability. In the first method, the String objects used in the log message are long. If you tried to put them together within the structure of the log message, the result would be a long, multiline concatenation of strings. This would clearly be less readable. However, in the second method, the String objects are short, so it wouldn't make much sense to turn them into constants. On the other hand, if the String object is being used more than once, it should be a constant.

Although they appear to be trivial, you need to consider substitution constants when designing your code. They can turn messy, unreadable code into code that is easy to understand.

Internationalizing with Substitution Constants

Internationalizing an application's strings gives you the perfect opportunity to show off the power of substitution constants. Although most programs are internationalized in other ways, using substitution constants can eliminate a great deal of overhead from the process. To understand how this is done, you must first learn how to internationalize strings in an application. You can then use this technique to improve the performance and maintainability of your applications.

Common internationalization techniques

To internationalize a program, a class called ResourceBundle is used. A resource bundle allows you to access strings within a properties file. To use this bundle, build a

---

small class called I18N to load the bundle and access it. Consequently, you will not have to initialize the bundle for every class that wants to use the strings. Example 7-2 shows the code for I18N.

Example 7-2. A resource bundle accessor

```
package oreilly.hcj.constants;

import java.util.MissingResourceException;
import java.util.ResourceBundle;

public final class I18N {
  private final static String BUNDLE_NAME = "oreilly/hcj/constants/I18N";

  private final static ResourceBundle BUNDLE=
    ResourceBundle.getBundle(BUNDLE_NAME);

  private I18N( ) {
  }

  public static String getString(final String key) {
    try {
      return BUNDLE.getString(key);
    } catch (final MissingResourceException ex) {
      return '!' + key + '!';
    }
  }
}
```

When the class is statically initialized, the resource bundle is initialized. To initialize the bundle, the ResourceBundle class looks for a file with the same name as BUNDLE_NAME in the classpath. In this case, it finds the *I18N.properties* file, which stores a list of key/value pairs that looks like the following:

```
# I18N.properties
OK=OK
CANCEL=Cancel
REFRESH=Refresh
```

Once the resource bundle is initialized, you can use getString( ) to fetch a string value for any key. If the value isn't found, simply return the key enclosed in exclamation points.

Using the resource bundle allows you to store the actual value of your strings in a file that doesn't need to be recompiled if you want to change the strings. This is beneficial to the program's translators, who are often not programmers themselves. They simply need to find all of the *I18N.properties* files in a project and change them with a text editor.

To use the new I18N class, call getString( ):

```
package oreilly.hcj.constants;

public class SomeApp {
  public final static void main(final String[] args) {
    System.out.println(I18N.getString("OK"));
    System.out.println(I18N.getString("CANCEL"));
    System.out.println(I18N.getString("REFRESH"));
    System.out.println(I18N.getString("SOME_STRING"));
  }
}
```

If you run this class, it will produce the following output:

```
C:\...\hcj>java -cp build/ oreilly.hcj.constants.SomeApp
OK
Cancel
Refresh
!SOME_STRING!
```

This class is run differently than the other examples because the locale will be altered in a later run.

The class found all of the strings except SOME_STRING. Although this code is useful, what makes resource bundles magical is that they automatically find the resources for the locale that is set in the virtual machine. You can write another file for German versions of your strings and it will select the correct file at runtime. The German version looks like the following:

```
# I18N_de.properties
OK=OK
CANCEL=Abbrechen
REFRESH=Aktualisieren
```

You now have one file named *I18N.properties* and one named *I18N_de.properties*. The first file contains the English strings; the second contains the German strings. Now the ResourceBundle class will find the correct file based on the locale of the virtual machine.

To change the locale, pass the user.language property to the virtual machine. Rerun the example using the German locale:

```
C:\...\hcj>java -Duser.language=de -cp build/ oreilly.hcj.constants.SomeApp
OK
Abbrechen
Aktualisieren
!SOME_STRING!
```

The ResourceBundle class magically found the other strings and printed out the German versions to the console. Since SOME_STRING also isn't defined in the German file, it was returned in the same way as in the previous run. If the ResourceBundle class can't find a version of the bundle for your particular locale, it will default to the version with no extension:

```
C:\dev\hcj>java -Duser.language=fr -cp build/ oreilly.hcj.constants.SomeApp
OK
Cancel
Refresh
!SOME_STRING!
```

Since you don't have an *I18N_fr.properties* file, the ResourceBundle class used the *I18N.properties* file instead.

Improving internationalization performance

Although the internationalization technique shown in the last section is useful, it has a few problems. When the resource bundle is initialized, it is loaded with the key/value pairs. Whenever you access it using getString( ), the bundle looks up the key in the hash map. While the program is executing, these keys don't change at all. Therefore, it would be wasteful to use a large data structure that takes up memory to accommodate them.

The second problem with the previous internationalization technique is that the keys are given to the resource bundle as quoted strings. This is annoying for two reasons. First, it introduces the possibility of a typo in a key. In your application, finding a typo would be easy. In an application with hundreds of classes accessing these strings, it wouldn't be so much fun; you would have to search for every class that used the string and fix it. The second annoyance is that whenever you look up a resource, you have to type several lines of code, which increases the size of your application and makes it look ugly.

You can make internationalization fast, clean, and neat by using substitution constants. All you have to do is rewrite the I18N class:

```
package oreilly.hcj.constants;

import java.util.MissingResourceException;
import java.util.ResourceBundle;

public final class I18N2 {
  public static final String OK;
  public static final String CANCEL;
  public static final String REFRESH;

  static {
    final String BUNDLE_NAME = "oreilly/hcj/constants/I18N";
    final ResourceBundle BUNDLE = ResourceBundle.getBundle(BUNDLE_NAME);

    // --
    OK = getString(BUNDLE, "OK");
```

```
      CANCEL = getString(BUNDLE, "CANCEL");
      REFRESH = getString(BUNDLE, "REFRESH");
   }

   private I18N2() {
   }

   private static String getString(final ResourceBundle bundle,
                                   final String key) {
      try {
         return bundle.getString(key);
      } catch (final MissingResourceException ex) {
         assert (false) : ex.getMessage();
         return '!' + key + '!';
      }
   }
}
```

This version of the I18N class takes advantage of deferred final static initialization. In the static initializer, you look up the resource bundle by name and initialize it. You then use the bundle to get the values for the strings and initialize them to the proper values. When getting the string values, you add an assert to the getString( ) method, which helps you catch missing strings. Since assertions don't have to be caught—and indeed shouldn't be caught—this won't require you to use a try-catch block in the initializer.

Now that the strings are initialized, the user can use them, as shown in this new version of SomeApp:

```
package oreilly.hcj.constants;

public class SomeApp2 {
   public final static void main(final String[] args) {
      System.out.println(I18N2.OK);
      System.out.println(I18N2.CANCEL);
      System.out.println(I18N2.REFRESH);
      // System.out.println(I18N2.SOME_STRING); // <== compiler error
   }
}
```

The new version is much cleaner and easier to use than the old version. Since the only quoted strings are in the actual initializer for the I18N2 class, any typos will be located there as well as fixed there. Also, you gain two performance benefits. First, since the resource bundle is scoped to the static initializer, it will be garbage-collected and not take up the extra memory after the initializer exits. Second, accessing a substitution constant is significantly faster than calling a method to perform a lookup in a map. You don't have to create a new variable for the quoted string, call a method, set up a try-catch block, or perform any of the other myriad operations needed to look up constants the old way.

One final thing to consider when using substitution constants is that it is safe to change a constant in the I18N2 file without recompiling all of the classes that use the constants. Although the constants are final static strings, they are not replaced at compile time by optimizers because they are initialized using method calls. Therefore, instead of optimizing them out, the compiler will put them in the variable space for the application and use them just like references to any other variable.

Bit Fields

A *bit field* is a memory-saving tool that was developed early in the history of computer science. It saves memory by combining several true-false options into one byte. For example, a car may have several options that are either present or not present. These true or false options can be grouped into a bit field rather than using an entire byte for each of the options, which would be the case if you used booleans. The options in the bit field are represented as set or unset according to the status of a specific bit in the byte. These options can then be checked and compared using logical operators. One implementation of the hypothetical Car class is shown in Example 7-3.

Example 7-3. A car class that uses bit field constants

```
package oreilly.hcj.constants;
public class Car {
  public final static int POWER_WINDOWS = 1;
  public final static int POWER_LOCKS = 2;
  public final static int SNOW_TIRES = 4;
  public final static int STANDARD_TIRES = 8;
  public final static int CRUISE_CONTROL = 16;
  public final static int CD_PLAYER = 32;
  public final static int AIR_CONDITIONING = 64;

  private int options;

  public Car( ) {
  }

  public void setOptions(final int options) {
    this.options = options;
  }

  public int getOptions( ) {
    return this.options;
  }
}
```

In this example, a car can have several options, such as power windows and air conditioning. Each of the options are combined into a bit field and stored in the integer variable options. The bit field constants, such as POWER_WINDOWS, define which bit, within the `options` variable, represents that particular option. Since bits in a byte ascend in powers of two, these bit field constants will always be in powers of two as well. This is one easy way to distinguish bit fields from other types of constants.

If you want to determine whether the car has power windows, all that matters is the zero bit in the `options` integer variable. In Figure 7-1, a bit field is mapped out in memory.

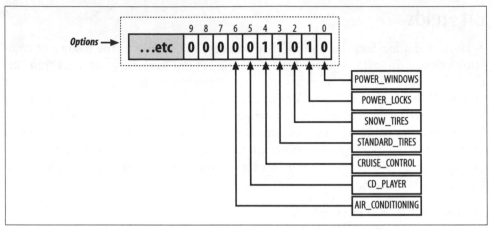

Figure 7-1. A memory map of a bit field

The zero bit in the field corresponds to the option `POWER_WINDOWS`. When that bit is set, the car has power windows. On the other hand, when the zero bit isn't set, the car does not have power windows. The situation is similar for each of the successive bits in the bit field. The car shown in Figure 7-1 has cruise control, standard tires, and power door locks.

Altering Bit Fields

To change the options on your car, use logical operators:

```
package oreilly.hcj.constants;
public class BitFieldDemo {
  public void setBitFields() {
    this.myCar = new Car();
    myCar.setOptions(Car.CRUISE_CONTROL |
                     Car.STANDARD_TIRES |
                     Car.POWER_LOCKS);
    System.out.println(myCar.getOptions());
  }
}
```

The result of the combination of options shown here will produce the bit field mapped in Figure 7-1. To create the bit field, use a logical OR (the | operator) operator to combine the various bits into a single number and then set this number in the options variable. The options variable will then contain the number 26, (CRUISE_CONTROL + STANDARD_TIRES + POWER_LOCKS, or 16 + 8 + 2). This encoding is the primary reason why bit field constants can't be sequential—since bit fields are binary, a value of 3 would mean that the zero and one bits are both set. This would lead to ambiguous results.

If you want to remove standard tires from your hypothetical car, you can use an exclusive OR (XOR—the ^ operator) operator:

```
package oreilly.hcj.constants;
public class BitFieldDemo {
  public void clearStandardTires( ) {
    myCar.setOptions(myCar.getOptions( ) ^ Car.STANDARD_TIRES);
    System.out.println(myCar.getOptions( ));
  }
}
```

This piece of code removes the standard tires from the bit field. By applying an XOR against the field, you clear the set bit. However, realize that if the bit hadn't been set, you would have just set it. The only way to clear an entire bit, whether the bit is set or not, is to create a bit field mask of all bits *except* for the one you want to clear. After you create the mask, you must use a logical AND operator to combine the mask and the target bit field:

```
myCar.setOptions(myCar.getOptions( ) & (Car.POWER_WINDOWS |
                                        Car.POWER_LOCKS |
                                        Car.SNOW_TIRES |
                                        Car.CRUISE_CONTROL |
                                        Car.CD_PLAYER |
                                        Car.AIR_CONDITIONING));
```

Since the only bit left unset in the call was STANDARD_TIRES, that bit was zero. When you use a logical AND against the current setting of the bit fields, you can be sure that the bit was removed. Setting a bit is simply a matter of using the OR operator again, as when the bit field was created (see Figure 7-1).

Comparing Bit Fields

Comparing bit fields can also be done with logical operators. For example, if you want to know whether a car has power windows and power locks, you can use the code in Example 7-4.

Example 7-4. Examining bit fields

```
package oreilly.hcj.constants;
public class BitFieldDemo {
public void printCarOptions( ) {
    System.out.println("-- Options --");
    if ((myCar.getOptions( ) & Car.POWER_WINDOWS) > 0) {
      System.out.println("Power Windows");
    }
```

Example 7-4. Examining bit fields (continued)

```
    if ((myCar.getOptions() & Car.POWER_LOCKS) > 0) {
      System.out.println("Power Locks");
    }
  }
}
```

This code uses logical AND operators to compare the bit field against the bit field constants. Since the bit field constant contains 0 for all bits except its target bit, the AND operation will result in a 1 or a 0. In this case, the car has power locks only, so the method would output the following:

```
-- Options --
Power Locks
```

Problems with Bit Fields

Although bit fields are an interesting concept, you may wonder what relevance they have to Java. The fact is, bit fields perform several different functions inside the JDK. One of their most prominent functions occurs in the various reflection methods, in which they are used to store the modifiers for a field, class, constructor, or method. There is a bit for abstract, a bit for final, and so on. However, the modifiers bit field reveals a glaring problem with the bit field concept itself.

Mutual exclusivity

In the Car class, there is a bit for standard tires and another for snow tires. However, a car can have only one or the other. If someone set the bits for both types of tires, the data would be corrupted.

In fact, this is a common misuse of the bit field concept. If you think the previous example is contrived, consider the modifiers with regards to reflection. Example 7-5[*] is a snippet from the JDK that shows the definitions of these modifiers.

Example 7-5. Modifier snippet from the JDK

```
package java.lang;
public class Modifier {
  public static final int PUBLIC       = 0x00000001;
  public static final int PRIVATE      = 0x00000002;
  public static final int PROTECTED    = 0x00000004;
}
```

In this case, the JDK assigns different bits for each of the visibility specifiers. The problem with this is that the options represented by these bits are mutually exclusive. A method, class, constructor, or attribute cannot be both private and protected

---

[*] From the JDK source, © 2002 by Sun Microsystems.

at the same time. Fortunately, in the case of the JDK, it's impossible to set the modifiers programmatically on a method, class, constructor, or attribute because the virtual machine creates these bit fields and doesn't let you change them. However, the Car class is not so fortunate.

In fact, determining the type of tires on the car would have been easier if it was done with constants and properties. You could use various tire constants to name the possible tire configurations, and then use a property, tireType, to hold one of these constants. Although this would fix the mutual exclusivity problem, there would still be a bigger problem that you haven't fixed yet.

Limited expandability

The bit field may work for now, but what if the car company comes along and tells you that it has added a tape player to the list of options for the car. In this case, you can use bit seven for a TAPE_PLAYER constant. However, if all of the department heads call a meeting the next day in which they decide to add 75 more options to the car, you *will* have a problem. Since an int doesn't have 82 bits, there is no more space left in the bit field. Suddenly, you have a large refactoring job on your hands. Not only may you have to change hundreds of lines of code, you may also have to tell the very unhappy departments that they need to wait six months for their new options.

The problem with bit fields is that they have limited space, while companies have no limit on the number of things they can change in your program. Since you must expect companies to change your requirements, using bit fields is not an optimal solution. Even if there were no problems in changing code, bit fields would still not be a good idea because they violate the basic object-oriented concept of encapsulation.

Improper encapsulation

Object-oriented engineering is based on the concept of encapsulation—that is, whatever is in an object should be hidden from the class's user. Bit fields are an example of poor encapsulation because they expose the internal implementation of the storage of options to the user. They also combine multiple attributes into one, which muddles the interface. When a user wants to know whether a class has power door locks, he shouldn't have to decode the information from several other options.

A class has a certain set of attributes and behaviors. Combining multiple attributes into one is just bad design. If, instead, you modeled your car options differently, you would be able to preserve the concepts of object-oriented engineering and have an unlimited amount of options. You could, for example, make a set in the car class and use that set to store non–mutually exclusive options for your car.

Bit fields are just far too cryptic and constraining to be of much use in Java applications. The only time you should use them is when you truly have no other choice. However, they are something that you will have to deal with frequently in legacy code. Whenever you get the chance to convert them to option constants, I highly advise you do so.

Option Constants

Option constants often bear a striking resemblance to bit field constants. However, the main difference between them is that a bit field uses powers of two for successive constants, while option constants are often numbered sequentially and use combinations that wouldn't make sense for a bit field. For example, consider this constant:

```
public final static int CONSTANT = 3;
```

If you see a constant such as this, the value of 3 is a dead giveaway that it isn't a bit field constant.

Option constants also differ from substitution constants in that they represent a concept and are not merely there for efficiency or readability. If you consider a constant other than an option constant, the situation becomes a bit easier to understand:

```
public final static int MAX_COKES_PER_DAY = 200;
```

Clearly, this constant is there to hold a significant value. However, the constant itself doesn't signify anything in particular. Compare that with the following examples of option constants:

```
public final static String LOCALE_US = 0;
public final static String LOCALE_UK = 1;
public final static String LOCALE_DE = 2;
```

Here, the constant represents various available options. Your code may use constants such as these to represent the three locales used in your GUI.

The most common kind of option constant is the integral option constant, which uses integral numbers to distinguish between option values, such as in the previous code snippet. However, you can use anything as the value of the option constant as long as there are no other constants for the same option that use the same value. The following code is valid even though integers are not used to distinguish option constants (although it is probably a little silly):

```
public final static int LOCALE_US = "fred";
public final static int LOCALE_UK = "joe";
public final static int LOCALE_DE = "john";
```

Option constants are concerned only with differentiation between the various constants, not with how this differentiation is accomplished. However, most option constants use integral values because these don't take as long to compare as string values.

Option constants are used rather heavily in the JDK, as well as in other code. They are used for everything from text alignment in a GUI to exception error codes. However, option constants suffer from several design flaws.

Defects of Option Constants

Option constants suffer from a few critical problems that make using them a danger-ous task. To illustrate, consider some constants used to represent countries, as shown in Example 7-6.

Example 7-6. Option constants for countries

```
package oreilly.hcj.constants;
public class Country {
  public static final int CANADA = 0;
  public static final int CROATIA = 1;
  public static final int GERMANY = 2;
  public static final int ITALY = 3;
  public static final int MEXICO = 4;
  public static final int UK = 5;
  public static final int USA = 6;
}
```

This approach should be familiar. The problems with the approach result from the constants. Here is what happens if they are used:

```
package oreilly.hcj.constants;
public class Address {
  private int country;

  public void setCountry(final int country) {
    this.country = country;
  }

  public int getCountry() {
    return this.country;
  }
}
```

Although this code looks normal, it suffers from a gaping hole. The user can pass the setCountry( ) method any integer she wants, whether it represents a valid country or not. To block this attempt, you need to alter your original Country class and add a couple more static members:

```
package oreilly.hcj.constants;
public class Country {
  public static final int CANADA = 0;
  public static final int CROATIA = 1;
  public static final int GERMANY = 2;
  public static final int ITALY = 3;
  public static final int MEXICO = 4;
  public static final int UK = 5;
  public static final int USA = 6;
  public static final int MIN_VALUE = 0;
  public static final int MAX_VALUE = 6;
}
```

Now that you have the MIN_VALUE and MAX_VALUE constants and can change the setter to implement range checking, as shown here:

```
package oreilly.hcj.constants;
public class Address {
  public void setCountry2(final int country) {
    if ((country < Country.MIN_VALUE) || (country > Country.MAX_VALUE)) {
      throw new IllegalArgumentException( );
    }
    this.country = country;
  }
}
```

simply check the incoming integer to make sure it is within the range of the bounded constants. If it isn't, then throw an IllegalArgumentException. Now the user has to give the setter a valid country. Unfortunately, throughout the program, you will have to provide the same validation. This checking code will be all over your server-side code, client-side code, and so on. It will be the responsibility of the *user* of the Country class to determine whether a value of this class is valid. This violates the principles of object-oriented engineering.

If that doesn't bother you, it gets worse. If you want to add a new country to your list, you could make the following change:

```
package oreilly.hcj.constants;
public class Country {
  public static final int CANADA = 0;
  public static final int CROATIA = 1;
  public static final int GERMANY = 2;
  public static final int ITALY = 3;
  public static final int MEXICO = 4;
  public static final int UK = 5;
  public static final int USA = 6;
  public static final int VENEZUELA = 7;
  public static final int MIN_VALUE = 0;
  public static final int MAX_VALUE = 6;
}
```

The code looks okay, but it has a nasty, lurking bug. In the example, the MAX_VALUE constant was not incremented to preserve your checking code. It's a good thing you saw this error now or you may have been in big trouble when the system deployed. The only time you would have encountered this bug would have been when a user tried to set a country value as VENEZUELA and was rejected by the checking code. Since a live system would be far more complex than this example, locating this tiny bug could take hours.

There are a number of other ways to complicate things. If two countries had the same value, this would be a huge problem. Suppose you introduce the country of Uruguay and give it the value 1 by accident. Then if a user tries to set an address as being in the U.S.A., the system may interpret the value as Uruguay.

The situation with integral option constants gets even worse when you consider the code in Example 7-7.

Example 7-7. Exception type constants

```
package oreilly.hcj.constants;
public class NetAppException extends Exception {
  /** An undefined network exception. */
  public static final int NETWORK_UNDEFINED = 100;

  /** A network exception caused by the server dropping you. */
  public static final int NETWORK_SEVER_RESET = 101;

  /** A network exception caused by undefined hostname. */
  public static final int NETWORK_INVALID_HOST_NAME = 102;

  /** A bad parameter exception. */
  public static final int LOGIC_BAD_PARAMETER = 200;

  /** An exception caused by failed authorization. */
  public static final int LOGIC_AUTHORIZATION_FAILED = 201;
}
```

In this code, you declare a number of exception type codes to be used in generated exceptions. The exception type codes in Example 7-6 are grouped by type. All of the type codes for network errors are in the 100 to 199 range, and all of the ones for logic errors are in the 200 to 299 range. The organization of your constants in this manner helps you when you want to add new exception types to your system. Since you have room in between the values, you can easily insert them.

A Private Constructor?

In Chapter 1, I warned you about using private constructors. However, the situation in Example 7-7 is one time when using them is acceptable.

In this case, the class declares only static members. Inheriting this class into another would be pointless because the user of the subclass would still have to refer to the static members by the name of the base class. For example, if your subclass was SomeExceptionType, referencing SomeExceptionType.LOGIC_BAD_PARAMETER would cause a compiler error.

However, note that in addition to the private constructor being created, the class was declared as final. Always be explicit. If there is a reason to make a class final, come right out and say it.

But now your entire MIN_VALUE and MAX_VALUE validation solution is trash. To fix this, you could build an array for validation or a set of valid constants. To implement this, you will have to change all of the locations in the program where these constants are used—a very unpleasant and boring job.

Even after doing all of that work, the object-oriented problem remains unsolved: the *users* of this class are still responsible for validation. If the junior programmer working on your GUI is sleepy one day and forgets these rules, you could have a horrible hidden bug in your system. Clearly, you need an alternative to this archaic type of constant declaration. That is where constant objects come into the picture.

Constant Objects

Earlier, I said that you can use anything to differentiate option constants. Constant objects use `final` instances of `final` classes to declare constants and differentiate them. Each constant is an object that is an instance of the constant class. The constant object class groups options together by theme. To understand how constant objects work, look at the constant object class in Example 7-8.

Example 7-8. Exception types as constant objects

```
package oreilly.hcj.constants;
public final class NetAppException2 extends Exception {
  /** An undefined network exception. */
  public static final NetAppException2 NETWORK_UNDEFINED =
    new NetAppException2("NETWORK_UNDEFINED");

  /** A network exception caused by the server dropping you. */
  public static final NetAppException2 NETWORK_SEVER_RESET =
    new NetAppException2("NETWORK_SEVER_RESET");

  /** A network exception caused by undefined hostname. */
  public static final NetAppException2 NETWORK_INVALID_HOST_NAME =
    new NetAppException2("NETWORK_INVALID_HOST_NAME");

  /** A bad parameter exception. */
  public static final NetAppException2 LOGIC_BAD_PARAMETER =
    new NetAppException2("LOGIC_BAD_PARAMETER");

  /** An exception caused by failed authorization. */
  public static final NetAppException2 LOGIC_AUTHORIZATION_FAILED =
    new NetAppException2("LOGIC_AUTHORIZATION_FAILED");

  /** Holds the name of this constant. */
  private final String name;

  /**
   * Creates a new NetAppException2 object.
   *
   * @param name The name for the exception type.
   */
```

Example 7-8. Exception types as constant objects (continued)

```
private NetAppException2(final String name) {
  this.name = name;
}

/**
 * Get the name of this NetAppException2.
 *
 * @return The name of the NetAppException2.
 */
public String getName( ) {
  return this.name;
}
```

In this code, constants are defined not by integers but by objects. Each constant is initialized during static initialization with a call to the private constructor and passes its name to the constructor for storage in a read-only variable.

This technique saves you hundreds of lines of code. To demonstrate, let's revisit the Country and Address classes. First, convert the Country class into the constant objects paradigm. The results of the conversion are shown in Example 7-9.

Example 7-9. Country as a constant object

```
package oreilly.hcj.constants;
public class Country2 {
  public static final Country2 CANADA = new Country2("CANADA");
  public static final Country2 CROATIA = new Country2("CROATIA");
  public static final Country2 GERMANY = new Country2("GERMANY");
  public static final Country2 ITALY  = new Country2("ITALY");
  public static final Country2 MEXICO  = new Country2("MEXICO");
  public static final Country2 UK  = new Country2("UK ");
  public static final Country2 USA  = new Country2("USA");
  public static final Country2 VENEZUELA  = new Country2("VENEZUELA");

  /** Holds the name of this country.*/
  private final String name;

  /**
   * Creates a new Country2.
   *
   * @param name The name for the exception type.
   */
  private Country2(final String name) {
    this.name = name;
  }

  /**
   * Get the name of this country.
   *
   * @return The name of the exception.
   */
```

Example 7-9. Country as a constant object (continued)

```
  public String getName( ) {
    return this.name;
  }
}
```

Now that you have a revised Country class, it's time to revisit the problems discussed earlier. Let's start with the unchecked setter:

```
  package oreilly.hcj.constants;
  public class Address2 {
    private Country2 country;

    public void setCountry(final Country2 country) {
      this.country = country;
    }
  }
```

Since the new setter takes an object of type Country2, the user can't pass you anything except a Country2 object. Furthermore, since the constructor to Country2 is private, a user cannot create a new Country2 object. There is absolutely no need to validate the country here or anywhere else in the code! The users of the class no longer have to do any validation; the object-oriented engineering principle remains intact. If that isn't enough to sell you on the concept of constant objects, there are still more benefits.

Since your countries are declared as objects and don't need to be ordered sequentially, you can declare them in any order you want. You can alphabetize them, sort them by continent, or even organize them by preferred travel destination. Also, since order doesn't matter, you can introduce new constants without doing lots of extra work. There is no need to renumber old constants to restore numbering sequencing, nor do you need to change logic throughout the code base. Simply drop in the new constant and go.

Finally, as a bonus, you also get a convenient name to associate with the constant. Since you differentiate your option constants by object instance and not by integer, you never have to look up a constant based on an integer value; instead, you merely call getName( ) whenever you want to know which constant is set in the variable.

 This can come in handy during debugging. If you've ever had to figure out what exception type number 2034 is from a stack trace, you can appreciate the benefit of seeing LOGIC_CREDIT_REFUSED instead of having to look it up.

Constant objects provide you with all of these benefits simply by the nature of their declaration. Clearly, they are superior to integral option constants.

Performance of Constant Objects

If you decide to use constant objects, it's good to know that the performance hit is near zero. In fact, constant objects consistently outperform integral option constants.

When the constant objects are constructed, you incur a slight performance overhead. However, since this is done at static initialization time, the cost to you is minimal. A delay of 50 milliseconds in the setup of your program will not be noticeable.

Integral constants, which are public final static constants and primitives, are substituted at compile time with their values. This may sound great, but making sure that all the classes that use the constant were recompiled is often more trouble than it's worth. Also, the checking code that constantly has to validate integral constants will not be optimized out of the code at compile time. Therefore, by using integral option constants, you save perhaps 50 milliseconds in program setup, but end up spending several minutes of CPU time executing checking code that you don't need for constant objects.

However, when you compare their execution, there is virtually no difference between integral option constants and constant objects. Consider the following:

```
if (address.getCountry( ) == Country.US)
```

If Country.US is an integral option constant, the code becomes a comparison of two integers. If Country.US is a constant object, the code becomes a comparison of two memory locations. There is virtually no difference between the two.

Given the benefits of constant objects, they are far better than traditional integral option constants. Constant objects can be considered to be *cheap insurance*, which is a term for a small task that prevents a large number of things from going wrong. Savvy project managers go for whatever cheap insurance they can find.

Indexing Constant Objects

Constant objects give you another advantage. Consider the two XML snippets in Example 7-10.

Example 7-10. An XML-encoded address

```
<!-- With Integral constants -->
<address >
  <street value="21 Main Street"/>
  <postal_code value="56756"/>
  <city value="Gainsville, FL"/>
  <country id="1"/>
</address>

<!-- With named constants -->
<address >
  <street value="21 Main Street"/>
```

Example 7-10. An XML-encoded address (continued)

```
  <postal_code value="56756"/>
  <city value="Gainsville, FL"/>
  <country id="USA"/>
</address>
```

Obviously, the second version of the XML file is much easier to read and understand than the first. With the named constant, you know the meaning of the country field of the address. When you consider the first example, it's easy to be confused about what country 1 represents. To find out, you would have to look it up in the code, most likely with integral constants. This would be clumsy and ineffective, especially if there were several of these constants. In an XML file, the named constant objects win again.

The XML file in Example 7-10 also introduces a desired feature in your application. With the constant objects in the example, it would be easy to write out the constant as shown in the XML file, but what about reading the constant? It would be nice if there was a method that could return the constant object if you give it a name. Fortunately, you already have most of the tools you need to accomplish this.

Since all of the constant objects are created by the same constructor, you can simply use the constructor as an indexing mechanism. This mechanism can then store all of the constants in a lookup table. Example 7-11 shows how the indexing mechanism works.

Example 7-11. An indexed constant object

```
package oreilly.hcj.constants;
public class Country3 {
  /** Holds the Index of the country objects. */
  private static final Map INDEX = new HashMap( );

  public static final Country3 CANADA = new Country3("CANADA");
  public static final Country3 CROATIA = new Country3("CROATIA");
  public static final Country3 GERMANY = new Country3("GERMANY");
  public static final Country3 ITALY = new Country3("ITALY");
  public static final Country3 MEXICO = new Country3("MEXICO");
  public static final Country3 UK = new Country3("UK");
  public static final Country3 USA = new Country3("USA");
  public static final Country3 VENEZUELA = new Country3("VENEZUELA");

  /** Holds the name of this country. */
  private final String name;

  private Country3(final String name) {
    this.name = name;
    INDEX.put(name, this);
  }

  public String getName( ) {
    return this.name;
  }
```

Example 7-11. An indexed constant object (continued)

```
/**
 * Looks up a String to find the associated Country3 object.
 *
 * @param name The name to look up.
 *
 * @return The object or null if it does not exist.
 */
public static Country3 lookup(final String name) {
    return (Country3)INDEX.get(name);
}
}
```

When the user calls lookup( ) with a valid country name, the actual constant object used to represent the country is returned. This will allow you to use the constant class with a SAX content handler, a DOM parser, or any other mechanism for reading XML or plain text. Once you have a string, you simply input it into the lookup( ) method to get back the correct object.

> Remember that since static initializers work in order of declaration, you will have to declare the INDEX *before* declaring the constant objects. If you change the order, you will get a NullPointerException when the first constant is constructed. Refer to Chapter 1 for more information on static initializers.

Also, since the constant objects are created at static initialization, you can be sure that they are all created and loaded into the virtual machine whenever one of them is used. It is a chain reaction. The first time the program uses the constant object, the virtual machine looks for that class. If it hasn't been loaded, then the virtual machine loads the class and runs the static initialization. This causes all of the constants to be created and indexed.

Serialized Constant Objects

Your country objects wouldn't be very useful if they couldn't be written or read on different virtual machines or in different sessions. The natural solution to this problem is to change the constant object to be serializable, as shown here:

```
package oreilly.hcj.constants;
public class Country4 implements Serializable {
    // ...same as Country3
}
```

> Serialization is a large and involved topic, which is thoroughly explained in *Java I/O* by Elliotte Rusty Harold (O'Reilly). I encourage you to check out this book if you are unfamiliar with the mechanisms behind serialization.

Now that your constant object is serializable, you can write it to disk and read it back. Furthermore, you can use it in an EJB or RMI application, which require passed data to be Serializable. Everything seems to be perfect, but there is one problem: simply marking the object as Serializable is not enough.

The Serializable constant object can result in *two* instances of Country4.GERMANY in memory. You may think that since the constant object is final and static, this will guarantee that only one instance of each constant object will be in memory. I used to think the same thing until I was blindsided by a vicious bug in a genetic research system.

I was debugging a particular piece of code that was failing a rule check, even though the data input should have passed the rule check. The particular data I was working with came from an EJB over serialization. It never occurred to me that there could be *two* instances of the same constant object in memory at the same time. I will show you how I solved the problem with something as mundane as file I/O:

```
// From oreilly.hcj.constants.SerialTest
public class SerialTest {
  public static void writeCountry4() throws IOException {
    FileOutputStream fos = new FileOutputStream(getFilename());
    ObjectOutputStream oos = new ObjectOutputStream(fos);
    oos.writeObject(Country4.GERMANY);
  }
}
```

This snippet is the write portion of the test. It is fairly mundane serialization to a file. The target country of GERMANY is simply stored to a file. After you store the country, you immediately read it back from the file:

```
// From oreilly.hcj.constants.SerialTest
public class SerialTest {
  public static void readCountry4()
      throws FileNotFoundException, IOException, ClassNotFoundException {
    // --
    System.out.println("Country4 in VM");
    System.out.println("Type = " + Country4.GERMANY.getClass());
    System.out.println("Name = " + Country4.GERMANY.getName());
    System.out.println("Hashcode = " + Country4.GERMANY.hashCode());
    // --
    FileInputStream fis = new FileInputStream(getFilename());
    ObjectInputStream ois = new ObjectInputStream(fis);
    Country4 inCountry = (Country4)ois.readObject();
    // --
    System.out.println("----------------");
    System.out.println("Country4 read in");
    System.out.println("Type = " + inCountry.getClass());
    System.out.println("Name = " + inCountry.getName());
    System.out.println("Hashcode = " + inCountry.hashCode());
    // --
    System.out.println("----------------");
    System.out.println("Identical = " + (inCountry == Country4.GERMANY));
  }
}
```

The first thing this method does is write out the details of the `Country4.GERMANY` object to the console. It then opens the file you created in the write portion of the program, reads the `Country4` object, and writes out its details. Finally, it compares the two objects. The output is shown here:

```
>ant -Dexample=oreilly.hcj.constants.SerialTest run_example
run_example:
     [java] Country4 in VM
     [java] Type = class oreilly.hcj.constants.Country4
     [java] Name = GERMANY
     [java] Hashcode = 17870931
     [java] ----------------
     [java] Country4 read in
     [java] Type = class oreilly.hcj.constants.Country4
     [java] Name = GERMANY
     [java] Hashcode = 4660784
     [java] ----------------
     [java] Identical = false
```

After the read phase is run, there are *two* `Country4.GERMANY` objects in the virtual machine. The same results would be obtained regardless of which constant object you used. Both versions of the object are the same. The problem is that the hash code, which is based on their memory location (unless you override that method), is different. In the sample run, the virtual machine first ran the static initializer for `Country4` and then initialized the version for itself. However, when the object was read in from the file, the virtual machine placed this object in its own memory location. There are two instances in memory; since your rule checked for equals based on identity, your rule check failed.

The correct resolution to the problem is to fix the serialization mechanism used in the `Country4` object.

To fix the serialization, you have to override a "magic" method that will return a different object if the user reads a `Country4` object. The new variation, called `Country5`, shows how this works:

```
package oreilly.hcj.constants;
public class Country5 implements Serializable {

  // ...same as Country3 and Country4

  protected Object readResolve() throws ObjectStreamException {
    Object result = Country5.lookup(this.getName());
    if (result == null) {
      throw new RuntimeException(
          "Constant not found for name: " + this.getName());
    }
    return result;
  }
}
```

The readResolve( ) method is a "magic" method because it is not required by any interface or superclass; however, it is found by the serialization mechanism if it is declared. The serialization reads in the Country5 object and then looks to see whether a readResolve( ) method was defined for this class. Since it was, this method is called by the serialization mechanism. Inside your method, use the handy index to find the correct object already in the virtual machine (if it exists) and return it rather than returning a new object instance. The original object that was read in goes out of scope and is dumped on the next garbage-collection pass—problem solved.

Also note that there is a writeResolve( ) method as well. This method performs the inverse of the readResolve( ) method. That is, before the object is written, this method is called, and the object you return is used in the write operation. In this case, you don't need to use this method because you need only to write out the string value of the constant, so the default serialization mechanism is sufficient. On the other hand, if you had to write out the object in a format other than the natural serialization format, you would have had to override writeResolve( ).

Now that your object is resolved, you can try your test again, this time with the repaired Country5 object. The result is shown here:

```
>ant -Dexample=oreilly.hcj.constants.SerialTest run_example
run_example:

    ... old output snipped ...

    [java] Country5 in VM
    [java] Type = class oreilly.hcj.constants.Country5
    [java] Name = GERMANY
    [java] Hashcode = 16399041
    [java] ----------------
    [java] Country5 read in
    [java] Type = class oreilly.hcj.constants.Country5
    [java] Name = GERMANY
    [java] Hashcode = 16399041
    [java] ----------------
    [java] Identical = true
```

This is perfect. The objects read in and write out exactly as they should.

 This serialization fix will work for any kind of constant object or other static object.

Accounting for Multiple Constant Object Types

Since creating constant objects is such a common task, it would be beneficial if you could abstract out some of the common details into a base class that can be used by developers who need this functionality. To accomplish this, you need to create a class named ConstantObject in your oreilly.hcj.constants package.

The ConstantObject class is a general-purpose class that would normally reside in a utility library separate from application-specific code. However, for the sake of this book, I don't want to complicate things, so I keep it in the same package. Upon publication of this book, many of its general-purpose tools will be submitted to the Jakarta commons libraries, available at *http://jakarta.apache.org/*.

The ConstantObject class has some interesting aspects of its own. Since the class will provide a lookup mechanism for members of all descendants, you need to slightly alter your storage mechanism. Consequently, the constructor gets a little more complicated, as shown in Example 7-12.

Example 7-12. A constructor for a constant object utility

```
package oreilly.hcj.constants;
public abstract class ConstantObject implements Serializable {
  private static final Map CONSTANTS_MASTER_INDEX = new HashMap();

  /** Holds value of property name. */
  private final String name;

  protected ConstantObject(final String name) {
    if (name == null) {
      throw new NullPointerException("The name may not be null.");
    }
    Map constMap = (Map)CONSTANTS_MASTER_INDEX.get(this.getClass());
    if (constMap == null) {
      constMap = new HashMap();
      CONSTANTS_MASTER_INDEX.put(this.getClass(), constMap);
    }
    if (constMap.containsKey(name)) {
      throw new IllegalArgumentException(ERR_DUP_NAME);
    }
    this.name = name;
    constMap.put(name, this);
  }

  public final String getName() {
    return this.name;
  }
}
```

To make things easier on the derived classes, the read-only name property and the indexing are in the base class. However, unlike the constructor in the Country5 class, this constructor must index multiple classes worth of constant objects. To accomplish this, create a map of maps, the outer map keyed by class and the inner map keyed by constant name. Then simply store the constant in the correct map for its class. Since the class is indexed when it is initialized (which happens only once per run in your program) the overhead in indexing the constants is minimal.

Your `ConstantObject` constructor is protected to prevent the user from instantiating the objects. It also has a bonus cheap insurance feature. It checks the name of the object you are creating and makes sure that the name isn't already being used. So, if you are in a rush and forget to change the name, this code will catch the problem.

 While writing this book, the cheap insurance that blocks duplicate names actually caught a mistake I made while working on the sample code.

Now all you have to do is provide a way to look up the objects. The method that does the lookup is shown here:

```
package .utilities;
public abstract class ConstantObject {
  public static final ConstantObject lookup(final Class dataType,
                                            final String name) {
    return (ConstantObject)
        ((Map)CONSTANTS_MASTER_INDEX.get(dataType)).get(name);
  }

  public static final Map lookup(final Class dataType) {
    return Collections.unmodifiableMap(
            (Map)CONSTANTS_MASTER_INDEX.get(dataType));
  }
}
```

Looking up the constant is merely a matter of finding the correct class map for the given data type and then the correct key. Also, a utility was added that allows you to get a map of all of the constants for a particular constant class. This map is returned as an unmodifiable map to prevent any accidental changes.

Finally, you need to alter your serialization to account for the problem shown in the last section. The following code shows the changed method:

```
package oreilly.hcj.constants;
public abstract class ConstantObject {
  protected Object readResolve() throws ObjectStreamException {
    Object result = lookup(getClass(),getName());
    if (result == null) {
      throw new RuntimeException(
        "Constant not found for name: " + getName());
    }
    return result;
  }
}
```

Once you have the correct data type, obtained with `getClass()`, simply employ the lookup mechanism to get the correct constant and then return that constant. This will work flawlessly for any class that the virtual machine can access.

Using the ConstantObject class is extremely easy. To illustrate, let's convert the old country class to use the ConstantObject class. Example 7-13 shows the result of this conversion.

Example 7-13. Using the constant object utility

```
package oreilly.hcj.constants;
public final class Country6 extends ConstantObject {
  public static final Country6 CANADA = new Country4("CANADA");
  public static final Country6 CROATIA = new Country4("CROATIA");
  public static final Country6 GERMANY = new Country4("GERMANY");
  public static final Country6 ITALY = new Country4("ITALY");
  public static final Country6 MEXICO = new Country4("MEXICO");
  public static final Country6 UK = new Country4("UK");
  public static final Country6 USA = new Country4("USA");
  public static final Country6 VENEZUELA = new Country4("VENEZUELA");

  private Country6(final String name) {
    super(name);
  }
}
```

It's that easy! The revised Country6 class simply calls its superclass constructor, which does all of the difficult work. You can use this mechanism to create any kind of constant object you want.

Constant Encapsulation

One final thing to note about constant objects is that they allow you a great deal of flexibility. You can put any kind of data in a derived constant object. For example, you may want abbreviations of commonly referenced country names. Example 7-14 shows an expanded constant object class with country abbreviations.

Example 7-14. Countries with abbreviations

```
package oreilly.hcj.constants;
public final class Country7 extends ConstantObject {
  public static final Country7 CANADA = new Country7("CANADA", "CA");
  public static final Country7 CROATIA = new Country7("CROATIA", "HR");
  public static final Country7 GERMANY = new Country7("GERMANY", "DE");
  public static final Country7 ITALY = new Country7("ITALY", "IT");
  public static final Country7 MEXICO = new Country7("MEXICO", "MX");
  public static final Country7 UK = new Country7("UK", "UK");
  public static final Country7 USA = new Country7("USA", "US");
  public static final Country7 VENEZUELA =
                          new Country7("VENEZUELA", "VZ");

  /** Holds the abbreviation for the Country. */
  private final String abbreviation;
```

Example 7-14. Countries with abbreviations (continued)

```
  private Country7(final String name, final String abbreviation) {
    super(name);
    this.abbreviation = abbreviation;
  }

  public final String getAbbreviation() {
    return this.abbreviation;
  }
}
```

Adding the abbreviation information is easy. You retain all the benefits of constant objects and can define more information than a simple cryptic number. There is practically no limit to the information you can add to constant objects.

However, like any power tool, constant objects can hurt you if you're not careful. Example 7-15 shows a trap you need to watch out for.

Example 7-15. A country object with a read/write property

```
package oreilly.hcj.constants;
public final class Country8 extends ConstantObject {
  public static final Country8 CANADA = new Country8("CANADA", 31.90f);
  public static final Country8 CROATIA = new Country8("CROATIA", 4.39f);
  public static final Country8 GERMANY = new Country8("GERMANY", 83.25f);
  public static final Country8 ITALY = new Country8("ITALY", 57.71f);
  public static final Country8 MEXICO = new Country8("MEXICO", 103.40f);
  public static final Country8 UK = new Country8("UK", 59.77f);
  public static final Country8 USA = new Country8("USA", 280.56f);
  public static final Country8 VENEZUELA =
                              new Country8("VENEZUELA", 24.28f);

  /** Holds the abbreviation for the Country in millions. */
  private float population;

  private Country8(final String name, final float population) {
    super(name);
    this.population = population;
  }

  public final void setPopulation(final float population) {
    this.population = population;
  }

  public final float getPopulation() {
    return this.population;
  }
}
```

In this code, the programmer added the population of the country to the constant object subclass Country8. Since he was aware that populations change, he made population a read/write property so he can update the populations as necessary.

However, having read/write properties in constant objects is a bad thing to do for a number of reasons, the most important being that it violates the object-oriented paradigm that constant objects represent. A constant object should be *entirely* constant. Objects that are partially constant and partially nonconstant complicate the situation because the user of a constant object expects things to stay the way they are and not change from day to day.

Additionally, the read of these constant objects via serialization is now ambiguous. Which population is the correct one? Is it the one in the file being read or the one already in the virtual machine? Does it depend on when the constant was written to the disk? These are just a couple of the questions that the confused programmer would have to deal with when using mixed-mode objects.

It is best to avoid these objects completely in your code. Instead of adding variable information to constant objects, create a new class called CountryInformation with a member that is a constant object and other members that contain the variable information. This provides a cleaner separation and less confusion.

Speaking of separation, you should also consider one other common mistake shown in Example 7-16.

Example 7-16. Mixed constants

```
package oreilly.hcj.constants;
public class OptionConstant extends ConstantObject {
  /** An error message type. */
  public static final OptionConstant ERROR_MESSAGE =
    new OptionConstant("ERROR_MESSAGE");

  /** An information message type. */
  public static final OptionConstant INFORMATION_MESSAGE =
    new OptionConstant("INFORMATION_MESSAGE");

  /** An warining message type. */
  public static final OptionConstant WARNING_MESSAGE =
    new OptionConstant("WARNING_MESSAGE");

  /** An question message type. */
  public static final OptionConstant QUESTION_MESSAGE =
    new OptionConstant("QUESTION_MESSAGE");

  /** An plain message type. */
  public static final OptionConstant PLAIN_MESSAGE =
    new OptionConstant("PLAIN_MESSAGE");

  /** Use default buttons. */
  public static final OptionConstant DEFAULT_OPTION =
    new OptionConstant("DEFAULT_OPTION");

  /** Use yes/no buttons. */
  public static final OptionConstant YES_NO_OPTION =
    new OptionConstant("YES_NO_OPTION");
```

Example 7-16. Mixed constants (continued)

```
/** Use yes/no/cancel buttons. */
public static final OptionConstant YES_NO_CANCEL_OPTION =
  new OptionConstant("YES_NO_CANCEL_OPTION");

/** Use ok/cancel buttons. */
public static final OptionConstant OK_CANCEL_OPTION =
  new OptionConstant("OK_CANCEL_OPTION");

public OptionConstant(String name) {
  super(name);
}
}
```

In this class, several constant objects are declared. There are five constants for the type of message that is displayed and four constants for the type of buttons to use.

The problem with this class is that the constants are mixed together. Imagine what could happen if a user gave OK_CANCEL_OPTION as a message type. The programmer of this constant object class should have separated the constants into distinct classes, each with its own purpose, instead of mixing them.

Those of you who do a lot of Swing coding may recognize this as the ConstantObject rendering of the constants in the JOptionPane class. However, the real JOptionPane uses integral constants for each of the options, making the situation worse. For example, a user of the JOptionPane class may want to make a JOptionPane of the yes/no warning variety. So he writes the following code:

```
JOptionPane.showOptionDialog(null, "Save before Exiting?",
                  "Warning", JOptionPane.WARNING_MESSAGE,
                  JOptionPane.YES_NO_CANCEL_OPTION,
                  myIcon, null, null);
```

However, since the programmer accidentally put the message type in the button options parameter and the button options in the message type parameter, he is presented with a information message with OK and Cancel buttons. The compiler doesn't catch the error, and something trivial ends up being an annoying bug. If the options to JOptionPane were constant objects separated by type, this wouldn't happen.

As long as you remember not to mix various types of constant objects together or to make mixed-mode constant/nonconstant objects, the ConstantObject paradigm will be an enormous asset to the development of your programs. Constant objects provide much more functionality, security, and safety than integral option constants.

CHAPTER 8

Data Modeling

A *data model* is a set of objects designed to hold data concerning a particular business concept or application. A *data model object* is a component of a data model. A data model object differs from a regular object that holds data in that it must represent a particular business concept.

For example, the class `Point` from the `java.awt` package is an object that contains data but is not a data model object. Although it has a role in the system, it doesn't represent any particular business concept. On the other hand, a class such as `Customer` is a data model object.

This distinction is important because business data is sacred. Regardless of what you do in a software system, you should avoid corrupting a data model at all costs. It is the life blood of a business. Since data model objects are so important to the survivability of a business, you have to spend more time on them than you would on other objects. Your data model objects need to be more solid and bug-free than every other part of the code. This necessarily means that you will have to employ checking and error-detection procedures that you would normally not concern yourself with.

For example, consider the difference between an object that holds the items of a list box and a data model object. If the GUI object is corrupted with false data, the worst that could happen is that the GUI crashes or displays an address where it should display customer names. However, if a data model object is corrupted, your company could accidentally order 50,000 of the wrong type of part and consequently loose millions. Therefore, you can't afford to make mistakes; data should be modeled and checked 50 times by both you and your company before anyone touches a piece of business logic code.

Modeling data is the first step in the implementation of a software system. In fact, the data model forms the core of any software project. Without the data model, there is little point to the software application. Therefore, it is important to examine how data models are created by professional programmers. To explore this concept, let's take a quick break from our pure Java work to discuss some key concepts.

The Requirements Document

Ideally, a data model begins with a requirements document, in which the customer specifies all aspects of the system. Once this document is delivered, the architects analyze it and extract the data model. Unfortunately, real life is usually not so simple.

An Iterative Process

Customers rarely know enough about what they want in the software to write a full requirements document. While the people you work with may be quite intelligent, it's likely that their minds aren't attuned to organizing information for use in a piece of software. The solution to this problem is that you must write the requirements document for them. By talking to the customer's employees, you can learn a great deal about the company and its operations. This should enable you to write a first draft of the requirements document.

> A good example of a company not being able to provide a requirements document is a genetics research company I worked for in Munich. Although the biologists and chemists I worked with were nothing less than brilliant, their minds were oriented toward biology and chemistry and not toward the organization of information within software. Recognizing that each person should stick to their gifts, I knew that I would never get an appropriate requirements document out of this group any more than they would get me to understand the finer points of genetics.
>
> I set about preparing the requirements document by learning all I could about the business. Through long meetings, I discovered the core needs of the business. Since the job was rather large, I broke it up among the various developers working for me. One was responsible for working out the process flow while another was responsible for gathering GUI requirements. I arranged the information and coordinated the effort. Through various presentations and discussions, the information was altered and corrected by the biologists and chemists in an iterative manner until we had a document that was scientifically accurate.

Once you have the first draft of the requirements document, it is much easier for the customer to understand how their software will be built. The next step is to present the document to the customer and ask whether the document explains *exactly* what he wants. Invariably, he will say that it is close but needs some modifications. This is the start of an iterative process in which the customer proposes changes to the requirements document, and these changes are incorporated into the document. The process continues until you and the customer agree on what is feasible yet still satisfies the needs of the business. Although this may seem easy, it is actually the most difficult part of a new project.

Getting Approval of Requirements

Whatever you do, *don't proceed without a requirements document*. The problems of having to improvise are too costly. One of the biggest problems with a fast-and-loose approach is that you have no measure by which to judge the project as complete. Also, without a requirements document specifying the business processes, a concept or critical piece of information could be completely wrong. Such a mistake could cost you weeks, even months, of work and blow your deadlines to pieces.

If the customer seems reluctant, or "too busy," to read a requirements document, there are a couple of tricks you can use to motivate him. The first is simply to say, "This is what I am going to build for you if you make no changes." This usually galvanizes the customer to study the document. The second trick is to ask the customer to sign off on the document. Since people are reluctant to sign their name to something that they haven't read, it is likely the customer will carefully review the document and suggest changes; of course, this is exactly what you want to happen.

Closing the Gap

You should make the customer explain *everything* about his business. Although you may know quite a bit about the field for which you are writing the software, it is often important that the customer explain everything to you; just as he is no expert in computers, you are most likely not an expert in his field. When a customer talks about his business, it often makes him think about his problems in ways he has never considered before. Your goal should be to act as the bridge between the business and the computing world.

Before you present the first draft of the requirements document, you should brush up on your communication skills. Just as you may not know what RNA transcription is, the customer is not likely to know what a decorator pattern is, or the difference between inheritance and aggregation. Dispense with the jargon and use plenty of metaphors during the requirements meeting. Compare such terms as inheritance to concepts with which the customer is familiar. It doesn't matter if he doesn't understand the finer points of the concept. He just needs to know enough to understand you. For example, when talking to a business development manager, you can use the concept of one business owning another to represent the idea of aggregation or composition. By speaking in metaphors, you will be able to communicate productively with the customer.

 Many senior developers find it difficult to communicate with management because they cannot dispense with jargon. Such communication gaps are extremely destructive to productive software engineering. If the customer cannot understand you, or you cannot understand him, it will be impossible for you to deliver what he wants. Focus your efforts on removing these communication gaps.

Using these techniques will help you extract a requirements document out of even the most recalcitrant customer. Once the requirements document is completed, use it extensively and update it religiously. If your developers routinely have the requirements document open on their machines or on their desk in hardcopy, then you did a good job in preparing it.

Natural Language Modeling

The next step is to turn the requirements document into a data model. For a simple system, it is not really difficult to figure out where to start. However, in a real-world setting, converting a requirements document to a data model can be an extremely daunting task. The *natural language modeling* approach makes this conversion much easier.

Natural language modeling looks at the requirements document as a discourse on the final state of the application. From this discourse, you can filter various elements, much like straining spaghetti. To do this, you need to be able to recognize which parts of the document to filter and which to leave intact.

 I vividly recall a time when I was developing a huge application used in a genetic research company. One morning, I was sitting in my office staring at the 300-page requirements document. Using natural language modeling, I was able to extract a first draft of the more than 100-class data model.

Noun Sets

Your data model is the *noun set* of your application. If you pour the requirements document through the "major noun strainer," you will find the data model of the application. The major nouns are simply the words that define business concepts, such as *account* or *customer*. Once you have identified these nouns, start organizing them into hierarchies of objects. Meanwhile, toss out the nonessential items that will inevitably seep in, and you're off to a flying start. By filtering parts of the requirement document, you begin to develop large chunks of your program. The initial picture will not be complete, but it will get you started. In fact, you should actually draw a picture at this point. Grab your modeling tool and start structuring classes and associations.

 In the later stages of your development, you can pour the requirements document through a *verb filter* to organize all of the actions being done to the nouns. These verbs will help you create use cases to figure out which actions need to be supported in the system. For example, the requirement "A user can change her password" suggests that you need a use case to change passwords.

An Application of Natural Language Modeling

Let's explore an actual application of how to build a data model. For the purposes of this example, you will create a data model to encapsulate a small subset of functionality used in the banking industry. Here is a small requirements document for your data model:

Online Only Bank, Inc. System Specification

The goal of this document is to describe the system that will control the financial aspects of Online Only Bank, Inc. The software to be built from this document will be the interface for internal and online customer banking.

1. The system will support the online checking, savings, loan, and credit card account types.

2. Online checking accounts will not pay interest to account holders.

3. Online checking accounts will allow account holders to execute a transfer of funds from their accounts to any other account within the system electronically.

4. Payment of bank fees or automatic payments will be processed in the following order. First, an attempt will be made to obtain the payment from the account holder's online checking account. Upon failure, the payment will be applied versus the account holder's savings account. Upon failure of this payment, a notice will be emailed to the customer requesting funds to be deposited to account for the payment.

5. Online checking accounts will allow the account holder to execute an external transfer of funds to an external entity, given a bank routing number and account number.

6. Online checking accounts will have a variable credit limit that will allow the account holder to temporarily hold the account under zero. A bank officer will be needed to set this limit.

7. Savings accounts will allow only transactions conducted by bank employees. These employees can transfer money only from the savings account to other accounts held by the savings account holder. No transactions from a savings account may go directly to a third party.

8. The bank will offer phone support for personal interaction with customers.

9. Savings account holders will be paid interest for the amounts in their account.

10. Loan accounts are special accounts for repayment of credit extending to the customer. These accounts have a duration of payments and an interest rate charged by the bank for the loan. Loan payment will be collected in accordance with requirement 4 of this specification.

11. Credit card accounts will have a credit limit set by a banking official.

12. Normal banking tellers will not be able to set credit card limits.

13. Credit card accounts will automatically pay the minimum payment, calculated as a percent of balance, according to requirement 4 of this specification.

14. Account holders will be issued monthly statements detailing the status of their accounts and the transactions of the preceding month. Due to ecological concerns, these transactions will be delivered by email only.

15. Customers will be able to apply for a loan online.

16. An online loan application will require the account holder's ID and information relevant to processing the loan. The required information will include the purpose for the loan, a description of any collateral offered, the required amount of the loan, and the duration of the loan in months.

17. Only a bank officer can approve an online loan application. This bank officer will assign either a fixed or variable interest rate to the loan depending on his sole judgment.

18. Customers will be informed by email as to their approval or rejection status for loans.

19. Customers will be informed yearly of the amount of interest paid on a loan.

20. Online access to the banking system will be protected by appropriate security measures to prevent unauthorized access.

21. On the phone, all customers will be required to have a pass phrase in addition to their online password to identify themselves to bank personnel.

22. Customers will be able to change their password online.

23. Bank fees will be administered via transfer to the bank's own internal accounts.

24. Each officer will have an administrative code for payroll issues not related to this product. This code will be a positive 8-digit number.

If you are a professional programmer, this requirements document probably looks familiar. For some of you, these requirements may look a bit overwhelming, but they aren't too bad when you apply your natural language modeling approach.

Creating the noun set

Whenever you find a *major noun*—which is a noun that stands alone without help and represents a business concept—write it down in your list of candidate objects. After working through the requirements, the resulting list would look something like the following:

- Online Checking Account
- Savings Account
- Credit Card Account
- Loan Account
- Transfer of Funds
- External Transfer of Funds
- Automatic Payment
- Transaction
- Employee
- Bank Officer
- Account Holder
- Customer
- Loan Application

You should know that if the requirements document is changed, you will have to update the list of nouns. This is why it is so important to complete the document as much as possible before starting on the noun set!

Although most of the elements in this noun list are fairly clear, the "Transfer of Funds" and "External Transfer of Funds" elements require additional explanation. For every transfer of funds that takes place, you need to record data that specifies the transfer information, such as source and destination. Therefore, you need an object to hold this information. By inheritance, External Transfer of Funds is a noun because it is a special type of Transfer of Funds.

On the other hand, the action in requirement 22 does not require any extra support. Since the password is stored in the user's account, and changing it is simply a matter of providing an interface to accomplish the task, you do not need to create a helper object to store data. However, if the document required that you store the date that the user changed the password, then you would need to implement some support. While working through the document, make sure you keep an eye out for verb helper objects and handle them appropriately.

Moving to a data model

Once the requirements document is signed, you may want to start planning the database tables and entity-relationship diagram. However, at this stage, the *data model* should be the prime focus, not the *database*. The database should be viewed as just another storage mechanism, which is irrelevant at this stage of planning. Therefore, you should define the data model using object-oriented principles and then figure out a way to actually store the data.

With the list of major nouns, the proposed system doesn't look so complex anymore. Now that you have a list, you can start creating some classes in your unified modeling language (UML) modeling tool.

 UML is the best language in which to model data or other programming concepts, not because it is superior to other alternatives but because it is almost universally understood by all senior programmers. Also, many executives understand or can easily learn the basics of UML. This helps close communication gaps. A good UML tool is critical to the success of large projects.

Start planning the data model by creating empty classes, one for each major noun, and have your modeling tool leave content for later. Once you have your empty classes, try to organize the objects into hierarchies and groups. While organizing the objects, make sure you remove any conceptual duplicates. For example, you can eliminate AccountHolder because it is the same as Customer. Continue to refine the structure and look for commonalties among the objects until a cohesive model emerges. While refining, remember not to worry about the details of the model. At this point, you should just try to get the skeleton of your data model in place; once this is done, the skeleton will give you a much better platform for incorporating the details of the model.

Relationships and attributes

Now that the skeleton is complete, you can fill in your data model with relationships and attributes. Again, consult the requirements document and note each occurrence of the core objects in the document. For example, consider requirement #5:

> 5. *Online checking accounts* will allow the account holder to execute an *external transfer of funds* to an external entity, given a *bank routing number* and *account number*.

From this requirement, you know that there should be a relationship between the `OnlineCheckingAccount` and `ExternalTransaction` classes. Furthermore, the `ExternalTransaction` class requires that the bank routing number and account number be added as attributes. As you work through the document, fill in the data model of the application with details such as these.

Once you are done analyzing the requirements document, begin the second pass, in which you examine each of your objects and consider them separately. For example, you never mention in the requirements document that a `Person` needs to have a first and last name. However, this data is implied, so you should add it. Continue this type of analysis until you feel that you have a fairly complete data model. In this case, a sample data model is shown in Figure 8-1.

The first draft

Now that you have a draft of the model, take the model back to the customer and let him pick it to pieces. At this point, it is absolutely critical that you don't forget that your customers are not programmers. If you email this diagram to the customer and ask for his input, I guarantee you will be greeted with silence. All of the symbols used in UML are second nature to you, but often look like Greek to a customer.

Instead, present the data model to the customer in small pieces that focus on individual concepts. The best way to do this is to meet face-to-face with the customers at a location where he can focus on the data model and not be distracted by other concerns. The meeting will also give him a chance to ask questions. You will also be able to ask any questions *you* have, and ensure that the customer sticks to concepts that are realistically achievable.

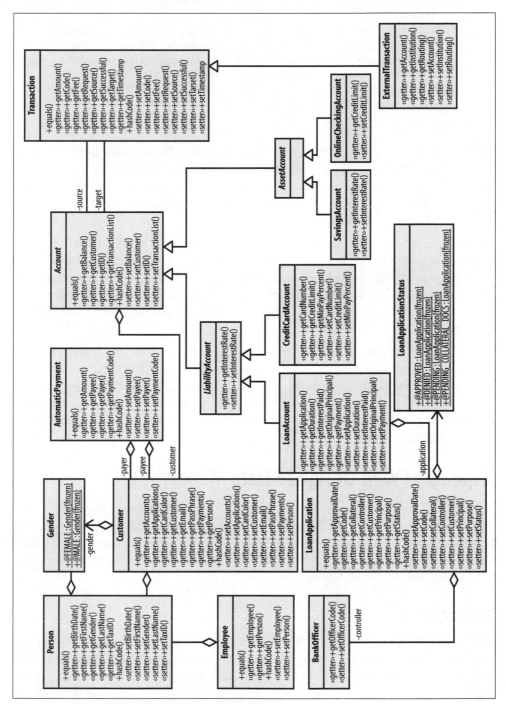

Figure 8-1. Online bank data model

During the data model meetings with the genetics research company, employees often requested that an object "know" that an animal was "ready" for the next step in their process. Of course, computers don't "know" anything. Therefore, I had to extract several additional details from them. This example demonstrates that meeting with a customer can turn generic concepts in their minds into specific concepts in an application.

During the data model presentation, be sure to explain the symbols and notation in the simplest terms possible. It isn't important that the difference between aggregation and composition is clear; what is important is that your customers understand why there is a line connecting two objects. As I said, your goal should be to get verbal or, preferably, written approval.

Once the customer signs off on the requirements and data model, the story is not over. In fact, the analysis and modification of the requirements and data model will be a recurring theme throughout the development as the requirements change, new concepts are discovered, and old questions are answered. It is a simple reality of business that your model and requirements will be altered while you complete the project.

Even after the software is released, there will be more requirements and data model changes. New requirements should go in their own section of the requirements document to separate them from the original requirements. You will have to integrate data model changes constantly, but try not to do so without a requirements specification. It is much easier to change a sentence in a document or a line in a drawing than to change code.

Aspects of Well-Designed Data Models

For an application in a book, the data model is fairy substantive. However, it still doesn't encapsulate all of the functionality needed in a real banking application. You have necessarily limited its scope so that you can focus on concepts and not the intricacies of designing banking applications. This section will cover some of the more interesting aspects of data models.

Ghost Classes

One thing that you should notice about the Online Only Bank data model is that the AssetAccount class has no attributes or relationships (see Figure 8-1). The AssetAccount class is a special type of class called a *ghost class*. A ghost class marks a conceptual shift.

In your data model, the OnlineCheckingAccount and SavingsAccount classes are both assets to your customers. On the other hand, the CreditCardAccount and LoanAccount classes are liabilities to your customer. Without a marker class separating assets from liabilities, all four of these classes would inherit from `Account`, removing the important distinction between assets and liabilities.

By creating the ghost class `AssetAccount`, you gain much more flexibility, power, and long-term survivability in your data model. Since the `OnlineCheckingAccount` and `SavingsAccount` classes represent a conceptual difference between the other two accounts, you could conceive of a piece of logic that would have to make decisions based on this conceptual difference. For example, the officers of your bank may want to write a report of all the assets recorded for a particular customer. To complete this report, he would want to examine only the asset account objects.

Of course, you may consider using a flag in each class, and letting the flag differentiate between assets and liabilities. However, placing a flag in the class signaling whether the class is an asset or a liability is the wrong approach because if you think of another category of accounts and want to implement it in later revisions, a simple flag will not work. To fix this, you would have to go through all of the business logic and change the logic to account for the new account type. However, if your classes are conceptually divided with a ghost class, this work would be unnecessary. You would simply create a new ghost class for each new type of account, and the structure would be preserved. With this technique, the structure of the model itself is used to encapsulate information.

Also, because `AssetAccount` represents a conceptual shift, it isn't difficult to imagine a subsequent requirement that would require a data member in the `Asset` class. Suppose six months down the line, your boss comes in and tells you to add a new attribute to the system. If you had used a flag instead of a ghost class, you now have a choice. Either you make some kind of sloppy kludge, or you refactor the data model to include an `AssetAccount` class. Either choice is not appealing. It's better simply to use a ghost class at the beginning and save yourself the trouble.

Proper Relationships

You may have noticed that inheritance was not used in the `Customer` and `Employee` classes to extend the `Person` class. This is because it is not warranted at this point. Many developers tend to use inheritance when aggregation would be more appropriate. In this case, a `Person` can assume the role of a `Customer`, an `Employee`, or both.

In object-oriented engineering, there are three traditional questions that determine relationships between objects. The "is a," "has a," and "uses a" questions each define different relationships with different semantics. Using each kind of relationship properly is critical in creating a cohesive and stable data model.

Is a

The "is a" question determines inheritance. If you say that one object *is* another object, then you use inheritance. In the case of a `SavingsAccount`, you can say that a `SavingsAccount` is a type of `AssetAccount`. This relationship is shown in Figure 8-2.

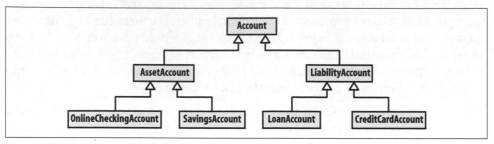

Figure 8-2. Accounts in the Online Only Bank

However, with the `Customer` class, the question gets tricky. You may say that a `Customer` is a `Person`; however, a `Customer` is *not* a type of `Person`. Instead, the `Customer` is one of many roles played by a `Person`; the `Person` is a part of the customer concept, so aggregation (see the next section) is required. If you change the traditional "is a" question to "is a type of," then the results become much clearer: a `BankOfficer` is a type of `Employee` but a `Customer` is not a type of `Person`.

Using inheritance improperly is a common data-modeling mistake, one that can cause a number of undesirable side effects. For example, if you modeled `Customer` and `Employee` as inheriting from `Person`, then the same person could be in your system twice: for the employee of the company and when that person opens a new account. When you change the person's address, remember to change both instances of the person. This type of data duplication is just asking for bugs to be introduced into the system.

 I have read some books that advise "avoid inheritance." I feel that these books are overly concerned with this issue. Inheritance has a pivotal role in object-oriented engineering. You shouldn't avoid it, but make sure you employ it only when the situation calls for it.

Has a

The "has a" question determines aggregation. If you say that one object *has* another object, then the object that has the other object aggregates it. For example, a customer *has* a person associated with it.

Aggregation is really a special kind of association that models a relationship in which the object performing the aggregation is the whole, and the object that is aggregated is a part. This type of aggregation is often called *shared aggregation* because several classes can aggregate the aggregated class. For example, `Person` and `Customer` share an aggregation relationship because the person forms a part of the customer; furthermore, the person can also be an employee, which means the aggregation is shared. See Figure 8-3.

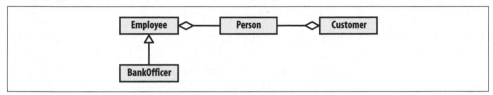

Figure 8-3. People in the Online Only Bank

There is also a special type of aggregation called *composition*, which occurs when an object aggregates another object and has life-cycle control over that object. For example, the HashMap class from Chapter 4 uses an inner class called Entry to implement its storage buckets. These Entry objects can exist only within the context of a HashMap; they cannot exist on their own. See Figure 8-4.

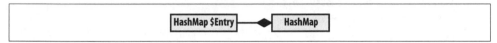

Figure 8-4. A composition relationship

Composition also implies that only one class can compose an object; other classes can use it, but just one class can be its owner. In practice, composed objects are rarely shared but are isolated in private access. An Entry to a HashMap can be created only by the HashMap itself.

Uses a

The "uses a" question indicates plain association, in which a class can navigate to another class and use the services of that class. In association, the classes are conceptually on the same level. For example, a transaction *uses* an account and is therefore associated with it. However, Account and Transaction are on the same conceptual level, and neither is a part of the other, but you need to navigate between the two, so you use a plain association. See Figure 8-5.

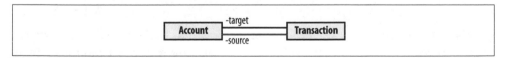

Figure 8-5. A plain association

If you want more information on the concepts behind UML modeling, pick up a copy *of The Unified Modeling Language User Guide* by Booch, Rumbaugh, and Jacobson (Addison-Wesley).

A Primitive Question

Throughout the Online Only Bank data model, wrapper types are used for all primitives. No primitive objects are used in the model. This decision is rooted in a simple question, "How do you deal with null on a primitive field?"

There are times when a value may be null in your data model without being an error. Consider the Transaction class. In this class, there is a Boolean indicating the success or failure of the transaction. However, if the transaction has not been submitted, this attribute could legally be null. If you wrote the class with primitives, the property methods would look like this:

```
public class Transaction {
  public boolean successful;

  public void setSuccessful(final boolean successful) {
    this.successful = successful;
  }

  public boolean getSuccessful() {
    return this.successful;
  }
}
```

Since the success attribute in this example is a primitive, you cannot set its value to null. To compensate, you could state that transactions are failed until they succeed. However, this would give misleading information to your customers. They would log in to check their transaction list, find several failed transactions, and start to wonder why. On the other hand, if you use a wrapper type instead of a primitive, you would have the following code for your property:

```
public class Transaction {
  public Boolean successful;

  public void setSuccessful(final Boolean successful) {
    this.successful = successful;
  }

  public Boolean getSuccessful() {
    return this.successful;
  }
}
```

In this case, you can legally set the value of successful as null. Since the property is a Boolean object, it can contain the value null. In this case, you can avoid the ambiguity of transactions that have not been submitted by setting their success to null.

Throughout your data model, you need to decide whether to use primitives. One option is to use only wrapper types for the properties that can be null. A second option is to convert every primitive in the data model to their related wrapper classes.

Partial use of primitives

Using wrappers for only the attributes that can legally be `null` can save a small amount of memory per object. However, this extra memory is almost negligible unless you are storing thousands of numbers, in which case you would most likely use a complex data structure such as an array anyway. The array attribute can already contain `null` as a value.

Also, using primitives for part of the data model cleans up the mathematics with the primitive variables:

```
public void calcMonthlyInterest(final LoanAccount loan) {
  // -- Using Primitives
  float interest = loan.getBalance() * loan.getInterestRate();

  // -- Using Wrappers
  float interest = loan.getBalance().floatValue() *
                   loan.getInterestRate().floatValue();
}
```

Primitive attributes also eliminate the need to create objects when calling a setter:

```
public void adjustLoan(final LoanAccount loan) {
   // -- Using Primitives
   loan.setInterestRate(0.0565);

   // -- Using Wrappers
   loan.setInterestRate(new Float(0.0565));
}
```

Using only wrapper types

Using wrapper types for all primitives can clear up the semantics when dealing with the model. If you use only primitive wrappers, everything is an object. All getters return objects, and all setters take objects as arguments. This is convenient when dealing with reflection, as you will see in Chapter 9.

Also, using primitive wrappers exclusively eliminates the need for many temporary objects, which would be required if the attribute was a primitive. For example, consider your basic bound property setter:

```
// -- Using Primitives
public void setInterestRate(final float interestRate) {
  float oldInterestRate = this.interestRate;
  this. interestRate = interestRate;
  propertyChangeSupport.firePropertyChange("interestRate ",
      new Float(interestRate), new Float(interestRate));
}

// -- Using Wrappers.
public void setInterestRate (final Float interestRate) {
  Float oldInterestRate = this. interestRate;
  this. interestRate = interestRate;
```

```
    propertyChangeSupport.firePropertyChange("interestRate ",
        interestRate, interestRate);
}
```

You save two object instantiations per call by using a wrapped type; the instantiations are traded for one instantiation in the call to the setter. Since creating new objects on the heap is a relatively time-consuming task, avoiding it saves some CPU time.

Even if there is a lot of math, the wrappers shouldn't affect performance. If you follow the principles of code efficiency, the difference between wrappers and primitives ceases to be an issue. Consider the following problematic example:

```
// -- Using Primitives
public void doMath (final MyFactorObject obj) {
  float result;
  while(someCondition) {
    result = result * obj.getFactor();
  }
}

// -- Using Wrappers.
public void doMath(final MyFactorObject obj) {
  float result;
  while(someCondition) {
    result = result * obj.getFactor().floatValue();
  }
}
```

This common type of code shows the difference between using a wrapper and a primitive type. Whenever you iterate through the loop, you have to make an extra method call. However, this code is poorly designed. Calling a method that always returns the same result many times in the same method is bad practice. Calling a method that always returns the same result in a loop is even worse. With every iteration of the loop, you lose several clock cycles. To solve this problem, you can refactor the method:

```
// -- Using Primitives
public void doMath (final MyFactorObject obj) {
  float result;
  float factor = obj.getFactor();
  while(someCondition) {
    result = result * factor;
  }
}

// -- Using Wrappers.
public void doMath(final MyFactorObject obj) {
  float result;
  float factor = obj.getFactor().floatValue();
  while(someCondition) {
    result = result * factor; // <-- Speedy!!!
  }
}
```

The difference between the two optimized methods is now only one call to floatValue( )—a fairly minor bit of overhead. You could eliminate this extra call by using primitives, but then you would lose all the advantages of these values being actual objects. When performing most math operations, there will be similar minor differences between using primitives and wrappers. Although you can save these minor amounts of overhead using primitives, you sacrifice consistency and flexibility in your data model.

In the end, going with pure wrapper types has more advantages than disadvantages. The speed increase that primitives give you does not outweigh the clarity and flexibility of using wrappers. I suggest you use wrappers instead of primitives in data model objects.

Mutable Objects

In the data model, all of the objects fall under two categories. They are either constant objects, as in the case of Gender and LoanApplicationStatus, or they are mutable data model objects, as in the case of Person and Account.

The mutable objects in the model have much in common. Since they are all Java beans, and all of their properties are bound, they all need property change support for their events. Since they all need it, simply push this support into a base class called MutableObject, which is shown in Example 8-1.

Example 8-1. MutableObject

```
package oreilly.hcj.datamodeling;
public abstract class MutableObject implements Serializable {
  private static final transient Logger LOGGER =
                      Logger.getLogger(MutableObject.class);

  private static final long serialVersionUID = 7902971632143872731L;

  protected final transient PropertyChangeSupport propertyChangeSupport =
    new PropertyChangeSupport(this);

  protected MutableObject( ) {
  }

  public void addPropertyChangeListener(
                              final PropertyChangeListener listener) {
    propertyChangeSupport.addPropertyChangeListener(listener);
  }

  public void addPropertyChangeListener(final String property,
                              final PropertyChangeListener listener) {
    propertyChangeSupport.addPropertyChangeListener(property, listener);
  }
```

Example 8-1. MutableObject (continued)

```
  public void removePropertyChangeListener(
                          final PropertyChangeListener listener) {
    propertyChangeSupport.removePropertyChangeListener(listener);
  }

  public void removePropertyChangeListener(final String property,
                          final PropertyChangeListener listener) {
    propertyChangeSupport.removePropertyChangeListener(property,
                                              listener);
  }

}
```

If you were developing software for a company, you would put MutableObject in a software common package so that other applications can use its services. The MutableObject class would form the base class for all of the data model objects. Throughout this book, we will place more functionality into the MutableObject class to give your data models even more power.

Identity and equality for all objects

There is one other small problem in your data model. Recall from Chapter 4 that the default implementation of the equals() method in java.lang.Object compares objects by identity rather than equality. Since you have not overridden the default method, you can't tell when one object is equivalent to another.

This problem is easily solved by remembering to declare both an equals() and hashCode() method on all of the data objects or their superclasses, where appropriate. For example, you can declare that Account objects and all of their descendants use the ID property to compare for equivalence. Therefore, you can declare equals() and hashCode() methods in Account, which will apply to all descendants:

```
    package oreilly.hcj.bankdata;
    public abstract class Account extends MutableObject {
      /**
       * @see java.lang.Object#equals(java.lang.Object)
       */
      public boolean equals(final Object obj) {
        if (!(obj instanceof Account)) {
          return false;
        } else {
          return (((Account)obj).getID().equals(this.ID));
        }
      }

      /**
       * @see java.lang.Object#hashCode()
       */
```

```
public int hashCode( ) {
  return this.ID.hashCode( );
}
}
```

 Since the ID property is of type Integer, using the == operator wouldn't work. It would only check to see whether the two instances are the same object in memory. You must use the equals( ) method to compare the values of the two integers. Be careful when using the == operator, especially when comparing primitives or constants objects.

This will work for all of the account subtypes. Now you simply need to go through all the other data objects and repeat the process.

However, if you forget to implement methods for one of your data objects, you would have a serious problem. Since the equals( ) and hashCode( ) methods are declared in Object, there would be no compiler error or warning. You may notice the problem only after you pull an all-night debugging session trying to figure out why your manager's reports don't include the loan accounts. Fortunately, there is a way to avoid this before it happens.

One of the interesting and little known aspects of Java is that you can reabstract a method from a base class. As long as a method is not declared as final when you inherit the method in your class, you can add the keyword abstract to its declaration; this will force the users of your class to implement the method. You can alter MutableObject to reabstract equals( ) and hashCode( ):

```
package oreilly.hcj.datamodeling;
public abstract class MutableObject implements Serializable {
  public abstract boolean equals(Object obj);

  public abstract int hashCode( );
}
```

Now that hashCode( ) and equals( ) are abstract, any class descending from MutableObject will have to implement these two methods somewhere along its class hierarchy. If the methods aren't declared, the compiler will object that the class needs to be declared as abstract. This trick is an invaluable tool in forcing descendants of a class to implement certain features.

Reusable Data Constraints

When placing data into the data model, you allow users to place practically anything into the various fields as long as they use the correct data type. For example, the user could input null for the interest rate and crash the system when it tries to calculate the interest. Even worse, a user could easily input -5.45 for the interest rate on her credit card. The bank may find it to be a little expensive to pay the customer

545% interest for running up her credit card! Obviously, you need to put some constraints on the data members throughout the model.

For the problematic interest rate, the natural thing to do would be to add checking code to the setter of the interest rate in the `LiabilityAccount` class. This code would prevent any negative values and constrain the rate to 1.0 or less. Your modified property setter would look like the following:

```
public void setInterestRate(final Float interestRate) {
    if ((interestRate.floatValue( ) > 1.0f) ||
        (interestRate.floatValue( ) < 0.0f)) {
      throw new IllegalArgumentException( );
    }
    final Float oldInterestRate = this.interestRate;
    this.interestRate = interestRate;
    propertyChangeSupport.firePropertyChange("interestRate",
        oldInterestRate, this.interestRate);
}
```

Although this checking code will work, it isn't very elegant or reusable. For example, if the GUI for your bank wants to display an entry field for the interest rate, it would have no idea what the legal values are. Also, if you hardcode the legal values into the GUI, you would have two sets of validation code to maintain. Instead, you should write a validator that can validate the interest rate whenever it is needed. Even better, the validator could tell you which rules it is applying so you could display them in a tool tip or in a text field in a web form.

You can do this by designing special-purpose validator objects that can be interrogated by other pieces of code to find out their rules. To start with, you will need a way to indicate that a validation failed.

The ConstraintException

To facilitate the validation, you need to create a runtime exception that you can throw if validation fails. You can make `ConstraintException` a `RuntimeException` subclass because the concept of `ConstraintException` is similar to `IllegalArgumentException`.

The Constraint Hierarchy

Now that you can indicate if a validation failed, you need to be able to perform the data validation. Your validator should implement essentially the same code used in the embedded validation code. It should also provide information on the rules it enforces. To do this, introduce a hierarchy of classes known as constraints, which are reusable and immutable objects that validate pieces of data. The `Constraint` class shown in Example 8-2 forms the base of your new hierarchy.

Example 8-2. The base of all constraints

```
package oreilly.hcj.datamodel.constraints;
public abstract class Constraint {
  private String name;

  protected Constraint(final String name) {
    this.name = name;
  }

  public String getName() {
    return this.name;
  }
}
```

This is a basic abstract constraint class. Since all constraints in the architecture should name the property they are constraining, it is useful to have this in the base class. It isn't until you get to the derived classes that the code actually starts to get interesting.

Primitive constraints

After the base class, you have to split the hierarchy into two directions: one that is suitable for validating primitives, and one that is suitable for validating objects. The code for the primitives is rather mundane and repetitive. Since primitives are not objects, you need one validator for each type of primitive; they all follow the same pattern as IntValidator, shown in Example 8-3.

Example 8-3. The int type constraint

```
package  mirror.datamodel.constraints;
public class IntConstraint extends Constraint {
  private int maxValue;
  private int minValue;

  public IntConstraint(final String name, final int minValue,
                       final int maxValue) {
    super(name);
    this.minValue = minValue;
    this.maxValue = maxValue;
  }

  public int getMaxValue() {
    return this.maxValue;
  }

  public int getMinValue() {
    return this.minValue;
  }

  public void validate(final int value) {
    if (minValue > value) {
```

Example 8-3. The int type constraint (continued)

```
      throw new ConstraintException(
            ConstraintExceptionType.VALUE_BELOW_MINIMUM);
    }
    if (maxValue < value) {
      throw new ConstraintException(
            ConstraintExceptionType.VALUE_ABOVE_MAXIMUM);
    }
  }
}
```

Most of this code is mundane, but it demonstrates the basic plan for all constraints. Ideally, the user would build an immutable validator with the legal values of the property. Whenever the user tries to set that property, the setter would call validate( ) with the integer to be validated as a parameter. If the rules are broken, you would get an exception.

Also, another piece of code can ask this validator what its minimum and maximum values are through its getMinValue( ) and getMaxValue( ) methods. For example, a GUI could use these methods to configure a spinner control with minimal effort and coding.

You will need one of these primitive validators for float, one for long, and so on. Unfortunately, other than the change in the data types, the validators for primitives are all identical. However, they have all been prepared for you. You can find them in the mirror.datamodel.constraints package.

Object constraints

Constraints get more interesting when you consider how they apply to objects. Objects themselves can be null-valued, which is one of the core reasons why wrapper types are used throughout the model. Example 8-4 illustrates the basic object constraint.

Example 8-4. The object constraint

```
package mirror.datamodel.constraints;
public class ObjectConstraint extends Constraint {
  private static final String ERR_PRIMITIVE =
          "The dataType cannot be a primitive";

  /** Holds value of property dataType. */
  private Class dataType;

  /** Holds value of property optional. */
  private boolean optional;

  public ObjectConstraint(final String name, final boolean optional,
                          final Class dataType) {
    super(name);
```

Example 8-4. The object constraint (continued)

```
  if (dataType.isPrimitive()) {
    throw new IllegalArgumentException(ERR_PRIMITIVE);
  }
  this.optional = optional;
  this.dataType = dataType;
}

public Class getDataType() {
  return this.dataType;
}

public boolean isOptional() {
  return this.optional;
}

public void validate(final Object obj) {
  if (obj == null) {
    if (!optional) {
      throw new ConstraintException(
             ConstraintExceptionType.NULL_NOT_ALLOWED);
    }
  } else if (!dataType.isAssignableFrom(obj.getClass())) {
      throw new ConstraintException(
             ConstraintExceptionType.INVALID_DATA_TYPE);
  }
 }
}
```

This class allows you to validate any kind of object to determine whether it should allow the value to be null. Since primitives cannot be null, this class does not allow you to create a constraint with int.class or with any other primitive class. To accomplish this, it simply asks the class that you pass in whether it is a primitive class.

> Using isPrimitive() in the validator is a basic component of reflection. We will cover this and the other reflection methods in Chapter 9.

In the ObjectConstraint validate() method, the data type is validated and it is determined whether a null value is allowed. In this manner, you can easily use the method to verify simple properties. A snippet of the Account class from your data model shows how it is used:

```
package oreilly.hcj.bankdata;
public abstract class Account extends MutableObject {

  /** Constraint for the customer property. */
  public static final ObjectConstraint CUSTOMER_CONSTRAINT =
    new ObjectConstraint("customer", false, Customer.class);
```

```
/**
 * Setter for property customer.
 *
 * @param customer New value of property customer.
 */
public void setCustomer(final Customer customer) {
  CUSTOMER_CONSTRAINT.validate(customer);
  final Customer oldCustomer = this.customer;
  this.customer = customer;
  propertyChangeSupport.firePropertyChange("customer",
                      oldCustomer, this.customer);
  }
}
```

Once the user creates the constraint, it can be easily used in the setter. The proposed change to the setter is passed to the validator, and the data is validated according to optional requirements and data type. As a bonus, a dynamic web engine can interrogate CUSTOMER_CONSTRAINT to determine whether it should place a red star next to the field in the form to indicate that the field is required.

A numerical object constraint

One of the benefits of object validators is that they allow you to validate all numerical primitive wrappers in one validator. See Example 8-5.

Example 8-5. A numerical validator

```
package mirror.datamodel.constraints;
public class NumericConstraint extends ObjectConstraint {
  private static final String ERR_NOT_NUMBER =
    "The dataType must be a Number";
  private static final String ERR_MISMATCH =
    "The min and max value type must match the data type.";

  private Number maxValue;
  private Number minValue;

  public NumericConstraint(final String name, final boolean optional,
                           final Class dataType, final Number minValue,
                           final Number maxValue) {
    super(name, optional, dataType);
    if (!Number.class.isAssignableFrom(dataType)) {
      throw new IllegalArgumentException(ERR_NOT_NUMBER);
    }
    if (!(minValue.getClass().equals(dataType))) {
      throw new IllegalArgumentException(ERR_MISMATCH);
    }
    if (!(maxValue.getClass().equals(dataType))) {
      throw new IllegalArgumentException(ERR_MISMATCH);
    }

    // ** validation done
    this.minValue = minValue;
```

Example 8-5. A numerical validator (continued)

```
    this.maxValue = maxValue;
  }

  public Number getMaxValue( ) {
    return this.maxValue;
  }

  public Number getMinValue( ) {
    return this.minValue;
  }

  public void validate(final Object obj) {
    super.validate(obj);
    if (obj != null) {
      if (((Comparable)obj).compareTo(minValue) < 0) {
        throw new ConstraintException(
                  ConstraintExceptionType.VALUE_BELOW_MINIMUM);
      }
      if (((Comparable)obj).compareTo(maxValue) > 0) {
        throw new ConstraintException(
                  ConstraintExceptionType.VALUE_ABOVE_MAXIMUM);
      }
    }
  }
}
```

NumericConstraint takes advantage of the fact that all of the wrapper types extend the Number class and implement Comparable. Instead of defining one constraint for each type of number, you can do them all in one swipe. This numerical validator will work for every numerical wrapper type. It first invokes the superclass ObjectConstraint to validate data type and optionality and then proceeds to validate the range.

Setting up the NumericConstraint is similar to using the object validator; the validator simply requires a few more arguments:

```
    package oreilly.hcj.bankdata;
    public abstract class Account extends MutableObject {
      /** Constraint for the ID property. */
      public static final NumericConstraint ID_CONSTRAINT =
        new NumericConstraint("ID", false, Integer.class,
                    new Integer(1000000),
                    new Integer(Integer.MAX_VALUE));
    }
```

Once the constraint is set up, use it as you would an ObjectConstraint.

Constraints for collections

Validating collections is a bit more complicated than validating primitives or numerical types because of the lack of parameterized types in the JDK. Parameterized types should be familiar to those of you who have experience in C++—they allow you to make type-safe collections and maps. Since no bad data can get into a type-safe set, this makes the validation much simpler. Unfortunately, since a user can place any kind of object in your set, which is supposed to contain only Account objects, you will have to check not only the type of the set but the entire contents of the set as well.

Many programmers have tried to compensate for the lack of type safety in Java collections, but all of their solutions have serious drawbacks. For example, source code generation can significantly increase the size of the source code base, which is a distinct project risk; simply put, the more code you have, the higher the potential for bugs. Unfortunately, there isn't a quick solution, so you have to do your validation the hard way.

To illustrate how to validate a collection, here's the validate() method of the CollectionConstraint class:

```
package mirror.datamodel.constraints;
public class CollectionConstraint extends ObjectConstraint {

  public void validate(final Object obj) {
    if (obj == null) {
      throw new ConstraintException(
              ConstraintExceptionType.NULL_NOT_ALLOWED);
    }
    if (!getDataType().isAssignableFrom(obj.getClass())) {
      throw new ConstraintException(
              ConstraintExceptionType.INVALID_DATA_TYPE);
    }
    Collection coll = (Collection)obj;
    if (coll.isEmpty() && (!isOptional())) {
        throw new ConstraintException(
                ConstraintExceptionType.COLLECTION_CANNOT_BE_EMPTY);
    }
    if (containedType != null) {
      Iterator iter = coll.iterator();
      while (iter.hasNext()) {
        if (!(iter.next().getClass().equals(containedType))) {
          throw new ConstraintException(
                  ConstraintExceptionType.INVALID_SET_MEMBER);
        }
      }
    }
  }

}
```

If the emphasized code seems to be a bit bulky and a performance hog, you are correct. However, you have little choice—if you don't validate the collection data type itself, along with every object inside the collection, a user could place an invalid object in the collection. But the setters won't be called that often. In the interest of a solid data model, you will have to deal with the performance overhead of calling set-ters on collection methods.

By contrast, the same validation with parameterized types would look like the following:

```
public void validate(final Object obj) {
    if (obj == null) {
        throw new ConstraintException(ConstraintExceptionType.
                                      NULL_NOT_ALLOWED);
    }
    if (!getDataType().isAssignableFrom(obj.getClass())) {
        throw new ConstraintException(ConstraintExceptionType.
                                      INVALID_DATA_TYPE);
    }
    Collection coll = (Collection)obj;
    if (coll.isEmpty() && (!isOptional())) {
        throw new ConstraintException(
                ConstraintExceptionType.COLLECTION_CANNOT_BE_EMPTY);
    }
}
```

In this version, you don't have to validate the objects in the collection because the user would describe his collections, as in the following code:

```
/** The list of transactions executed on thsi account. */
private Set transactionList = new HashSet<Transaction>();
```

This example declares a HashSet that can have members of type Transaction only. Since the set declared in this example is type-safe, you can be certain there are no illegal values inside it. However, until parameterized types are available, you will need to make a series of validators the hard way.

Note that you will need only a Collection validator and a Map validator. All of the collection and map classes implement these two interfaces, and you do not need any special features of their implementation classes for the validator. Therefore, you can get away with two validators only.

Using Constraints

Throughout the data model, you use constraints to bind data only within accepted ranges. This allows you to build interfaces that do not depend on hardcoded values. Interactive constraints will open up your data model so it can provide much more information than if you had coded each property individually. Also, since the con-straints are reusable, you can easily constrain data in other applications.

The Account class in the oreilly.hcj.bankdata package shows how several types of constraints are used. First, the class sets up its constraints as final objects:

```
package  oreilly.hcj.bankdata;
public abstract class Account extends MutableObject {
    /** Constraint for the ID property. */
    public static final NumericConstraint ID_CONSTRAINT =
```

```
        new NumericConstraint("ID", false, Integer.class,
                              new Integer(1000000),
                              new Integer(Integer.MAX_VALUE));

  /** Constraint for the customer property. */
  public static final ObjectConstraint CUSTOMER_CONSTRAINT =
    new ObjectConstraint("customer", false, Customer.class);

  /** Constraint for the balance property. */
  public static final NumericConstraint BALANCE_CONSTRAINT =
    new NumericConstraint("balance", false, Float.class,
                          new Float(Float.MIN_VALUE),
                          new Float(Float.MAX_VALUE));

  /** Constraint for the transactionList property. */
  public static final CollectionConstraint TRANSACTION_LIST_CONSTRAINT =
    new CollectionConstraint("transactionList", false, Set.class,
                             Transaction.class);
  }
```

Here, several constraints are defined for the various properties of Account. Note that a common naming standard was used to define these constraints; each constraint is in uppercase with the words separated by underscores, followed by the _CONSTRAINT suffix. (This will be useful later when you try to look up constraints dynamically.) Also, defining the constraints as final objects in the class means that if you ever have to change a range for a particular property, you can do it in one place, and all of the users of the constraint will be updated automatically. This will save you enormous amounts of time when your requirements change. Once the constraints are set up, each individual setter uses them:

```
package oreilly.hcj.bankdata;
public abstract class Account extends MutableObject {

  public void setBalance(final Float balance) {
    BALANCE_CONSTRAINT.validate(balance);
    final Float oldBalance = this.balance;
    this.balance = balance;
    propertyChangeSupport.firePropertyChange("balance",
        oldBalance, this.balance);
  }
}
```

Since the ConstraintException is a RuntimeException subtype, you don't need to declare it in the throws clause of the method. If the validate( ) method fails, the appropriate ConstraintException will be thrown, which will cause the method to exit without changing any members of the class.

Using the constraints in a GUI is also a simple matter. For example, you can use INTEREST_RATE_CONSTRAINT from LiabilityAccount to validate data in a GUI. Example 8-6 shows a dialog box for entering interest rates for liability accounts.

Example 8-6. An interest rate dialog

```java
package oreilly.hcj.datamodeling;
public class InterestRateDialog extends JDialog implements ActionListener {

  private JButton okBtn;
  private JTextField interestRateField;

  private InterestRateDialog() {
    setModal(true);

    final Container contentPane = getContentPane();
    contentPane.setLayout(new GridLayout(3,1));

    JLabel interestRateLabel =
      new JLabel("Enter an Interest Rate (Between " +
                   LiabilityAccount.INTEREST_RATE_CONSTRAINT
                              .getMinValue() + " and " +
                   LiabilityAccount.INTEREST_RATE_CONSTRAINT
                              .getMaxValue() + ")");
    contentPane.add(interestRateLabel);

    interestRateField = new JTextField(15);
    contentPane.add(interestRateField);

    okBtn = new JButton("OK");
    okBtn.addActionListener(this);
    contentPane.add(okBtn);

    pack();
  }

  /**
   * Run the demo.
   *
   * @param args Command line arguments.
   */
  public static final void main(final String[] args) {
    InterestRateDialog demo = new InterestRateDialog();
    demo.show();
    System.exit(0);
  }

  public void actionPerformed(final ActionEvent event) {
    Object src = event.getSource();
    if (src == okBtn) {
      float value = Float.parseFloat(interestRateField.getText());
      try {
        LiabilityAccount.INTEREST_RATE_CONSTRAINT
                          .validate(new Float(value));
        // do something with the value.
        dispose();
      } catch (final ConstraintException ex) {
        Toolkit.getDefaultToolkit().beep();
```

Example 8-6. An interest rate dialog (continued)

```
        interestRateField.requestFocus();
        interestRateField.selectAll();
      }
    }
  }
}
```

The dialog in the constructor interrogates the INTEREST_RATE_CONSTRAINT to find out what the minimum and maximum values are. It then concatenates these values to the label. In the actionPerformed() method, the constraint is used to check the input value to see whether it is a legal value for interest rates. If it isn't, the user is prompted to enter a valid interest rate.

The reusable nature of constraints makes it easy to build GUIs that check values. Also, you can use a constraint in a JSP page to annotate a form. There are many possible uses of constraints. Once you learn about reflection in Chapter 9, you will be able to discover these constraints dynamically, which will make them even more useful.

Creating New Constraint Types

In the package mirror.datamodel.constraints, there are a wide variety of constraints that can be used with any data model you care to write. Each is constructed in a similar manner as the NumericConstraint class. You should need to create a new constraint type only when the code for validation is significantly different than the constraints that come with Mirror.

Do not use constraints as a substitute for proper checking on construction. For example, you could create a constraint for the java.awt.Color class to validate that the red, green, and blue values are between 0 and 256. However, this is misplaced logic; it is the Color class itself that should do validation upon construction, not an outside constraint. Furthermore, if only a set of distinct colors is allowed, the best bet would be to create a constant object class instead of a custom constraint.

Generally, you should have to create new constraint types only if you want to use new data types in your model that have a range of possibilities, but only a few of them are legal in the context of your class. Essentially, constraints check legality based on context and not on type, and should be created only when unique types of contexts present themselves.

Persistence

Now that you have a data model that is nearly complete, you can start to consider where to store it. Although many developers automatically think of JDBC when someone says "persistence," that isn't the only way you can store your data. In fact, storing data in a relational database management system (RDBMS) may be the *wrong* choice.

RDBMS Versus OODBMS

Although RDBMSs are the most common data storage solution used in Java programming, they are often the wrong choice. Many systems would benefit far more from an object-oriented database management system (OODBMS). To understand why, it's important that you know the differences between relational and object databases.

Relational databases organize information into tables. These tables have columns for each piece of data and rows that organize the data into records. Each row is one record, and each column is a piece of that record. Connections between records of different types are made with relations. These databases can be easily expressed with an entity-relationship diagram such as the one in Figure 8-6.

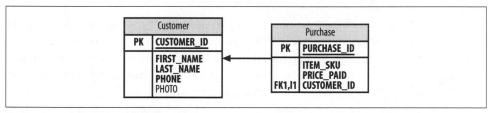

Figure 8-6. An entity-relationship diagram

In this case, there are two tables, one with five columns and one with four. Each customer's purchases are stored in the Purchase table and are linked to the Customer table via a foreign key. To find a customer's purchases, execute a SQL statement such as the following:

```
select PURCHASE_ID from Purchase
    where Purchase.CUSTOMER_ID = 80543
```

Those of you who have worked with relational databases are already familiar with this concept. However, the above statement has a deeper meaning that many developers fail to consider.

In the example, the select statement prompts the database to look through the Purchase table, checking each record for the proper CUSTOMER_ID. The more purchases there are, the longer this process will take.

Object databases work differently. Consider the UML diagram in Figure 8-6 rendered in an object-oriented manner, as shown in Figure 8-7.

The purchase is an object that is aggregated into the customer object. If you render this code into Java, you will use a list to contain each customer's purchases. Once you have a customer object, you simply navigate to the desired purchases.

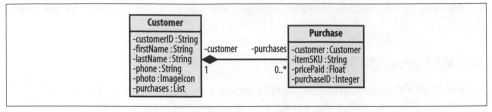

Figure 8-7. UML diagram of a customer schema

This is exactly how object databases work. They store the entire objects in their systems and navigate from one object to another using a device called a *smart pointer*, which replaces the standard reference with a reference that has more functionality. With the object database, the individual purchase objects are stored on the disk. In the list that contains the purchases, the database mechanism stores these locations using various proprietary methods, such as an object ID (OID). When you navigate to the object, the persistence mechanism finds the OID and goes directly to the object.

This mechanism is much faster. Since the database doesn't have to search the list of records for a particular OID, but instead goes directly to the record on the disk, a costly step is removed. Also, when navigating deeply, the situation improves because you simply jump from place to place on the disk instead of searching through thousands of records. Finally, since the object database stores the objects as objects, there is no need to flatten map objects that may be multidimensional. Instead of flattening hierarchies, you simply tell the engine to "store this," and it does.

Object databases provide superior performance in object navigation; however, an object database is not necessarily superior in all instances. Since the objects are stored in an object database as objects and not in a single table, parametric searches with object databases are much slower than those with relational databases.

For example, suppose you try to write a report on the purchases in your store. If you want to record every customer that purchased barbecue equipment (SKU starts with BBQ) that cost over $40, you would need a parametric search. In this case, the parameters are "SKU begins with BBQ and price > 40 dollars." With a relational database, the results are found by using a SQL statement. Object databases have something similar; however, the relational database will always perform faster because its records are already optimized to perform parametric searches. The object database, on the other hand, has to locate each customer and then navigate each to their purchases, checking each against the search criteria.

So the question of whether to use an object database or a relational database depends on your application. If you are writing an application in which the vast majority of work will be parametric searches, then your best bet is to use a relational database. On the other hand, if the vast majority of work will be navigation, then your best bet is to use an object database.

But there is another problem with object databases: there is no free (or even inexpensive) object database—they are not cheap. Some of the best, such as Versant and ObjectStore, can cost as much as Oracle. If you can afford Oracle, you can probably afford an object database, and I strongly encourage you to check one out. If you are building a small web application for your company, and you can't afford an object database, you may be stuck with the relational database.

Java Data Objects to the Rescue

Although it is a relatively new technology, Java data objects (JDO) are based on some fairly old ideas, such as providing a single solution to make object persistence transparent. The Object Data Management Group (ODMG) tried to standardize this, but it never really caught on for one reason or another. However, with the failure of CMP, the transparent-persistence problem was once again brought to the forefront. A team of experts from the Java Community Process (JCP) took on the issue, and the result was JDO.

JDO is designed to persist any object. Whether you want to persist an object you built or one that you bought from another company, JDO allows you to do so. Also, JDO doesn't reengineer the object, as other techniques, such as CMP, require. JDO simply looks at the object, determines its fields, and stores them. See the book *Java Data Objects* by David Jordan and Craig Russel (O'Reilly) for more information on JDO.

For my JDO work, I use a product called Kodo JDO from SolarMetric (*http://www.solarmetric.com/*). There are many products out there, but, unfortunately, none are both fully JDO-compliant and free. However, SolarMetric provides a community edition and evaluation copies so that you can experiment with the relevant code in this book.

Essentially, using JDO is a three-step process. First, you write, or otherwise acquire, the objects you want to store. Then you run them through a process called enhancement. Finally, you use them.

The first step is relatively simple because you can use JDO with virtually any Java object. The second step to JDO persistence is a process called enhancement, in which methods are added to a compiled class file to enhance the object. This is done with a JDO enhancer, which looks at the class file, analyzes it, and then adds various methods that the PersistenceManager, the boss of JDO, needs to manage the object. The resulting object is then ready to be persisted. Normally, enhancement is done with an IDE such as Eclipse or with Ant. Kodo JDO, for example, provides a number of plug-ins for various IDEs.

After the objects are enhanced, you can proceed with an optional step: object identification. There are two ways to identify objects in JDO. You can either let the JDO engine define its own IDs, called *data store identity*, or you can define your own ID classes, called *application identity*. Whichever approach you use depends on your application and the data you are trying to persist. If you are trying to persist classes that weren't originally designed to be persisted, you will probably have to use data store identity. If you have designed data model classes yourself, then you will probably have to use application identity. Either way, the JDO vendor usually has tools to help you. With Kodo, for example, there is a tool that will generate application identity classes.

Finally, the objects are ready to be used in the application. The beauty of JDO is that the objects are used as objects, stored as objects, and read as objects. Even the query language for JDO, JDOQL, is object-oriented. All of the details of writing to the database, caching, and reading are managed by the `PersistenceManager`. Furthermore, the user can use a relational or object database for the persistence, and the interface will stay the same. If you decide to switch to an object database, you don't need to rewrite the code.

Also, JDO vendors usually offer tools to assist in enterprise development. For example, Kodo has an enterprise cache that will allow several Enterprise JavaBeans (EJBs) to share the same cache. JDO can handle the transactional issues and the overhead of using the data objects. Using JDO will make your life much easier. I use JDO as my persistence mechanism in all my projects.

CHAPTER 9

Practical Reflection

Reflection is one of the least understood aspects of Java, but also one of the most powerful. Reflection is used in almost every major production product on the market, yet it often has to be learned from developers who are already experts, and these developers are often few and far between.

The reason for using reflection is because of the difficulties in building complex projects in a short time. As your projects become more advanced, you may find that you have less time to finish them.

For example, consider the Online Only Bank data model from Chapter 8. It was relatively small and simple to understand. When designing a GUI to manipulate this data model, you may be tempted to fire up a GUI builder tool and start making forms for each of the objects. In the end, you would have as many forms as there are data model objects. In fact, this is how most GUIs are built today.

However, consider if you used the same technique on a data model with over 200 data model objects and thousands of relationships among the items. In this situation, the idea of using the GUI builder tool is much less appealing—you would need to budget months of man-hours to complete the project. Furthermore, whenever any of these objects changes, even slightly, you would need to go back and fix all of the panels of the affected object. The icing on this particularly bitter cake is that you would have to create new panels each time a new object is introduced into the system. Clearly, this is not an effective method of delivering software in a timely manner.

 GUI builders certainly have their uses, such as to prototype applications. However, you should be reluctant to rely on them in production products. Since they must be very general to be useful, the code that drives them is often bulky and inefficient. This is a major reason why Java GUIs are considered slow.

Because of this complexity, the current rage in the Java programming industry is to turn everything into a web application. In fact, many applications that should be GUI-based have been turned into web applications for this very reason. However, even if you decide to go the web application route, the problem of building efficient GUIs remains. Now, instead of having to build GUI panels, you have to build JSP pages for each of your data model objects. Again, the 200 data model objects require much more time to develop than you can spare. Clearly, you need a solution to this problem, and reflection may provide that solution.

Reflection allows you to build tools rather than panels. In fact, you can use reflection to build panels that construct themselves on the fly according to the structure of the object they are displaying. Instead of designing 200 panels, you can design a tool that builds panels and works for any object. Despite the added complexity of the code introduced by using reflection, creating systems with reflection-based tools is significantly faster and much cheaper to maintain.

The Basics

Suppose you are walking down the street and a stranger approaches and hands you an object. What would you do? Naturally, you would look at whatever was handed to you. You inspect the item, and in an instant determine that the object is a piece of paper. Instantly, you know many things about this object: one can write on it; it can have messages such as advertisements, warnings, news, and other useful information printed on it; and you can even crush it into a ball and play basketball when your boss isn't looking.

Though this is a silly example, it does illustrate the basic idea of reflection, which allows you to conduct a similar inspection of Java objects and classes. Using a combination of reflection and introspection, you can determine the nature and possible function of an object that you didn't know about at compile time. Furthermore, you can use this information to execute methods or set field values on the object.

To see how reflection works, let's start with a class from your Online Only Bank data model. In Example 9-1, the Person class from the data model is displayed without any comments or content from its methods.

Example 9-1. A Person in a bank data model

```
package oreilly.hcj.bankdata;

public class Person extends MutableObject {
  public static final ObjectConstraint GENDER_CONSTRAINT =
    new ObjectConstraint("gender", false, Gender.class);

  public static final StringConstraint FIRST_NAME_CONSTRAINT =
    new StringConstraint("firstName", false, 20);
```

Example 9-1. A Person in a bank data model (continued)

```java
public static final StringConstraint LAST_NAME_CONSTRAINT =
    new StringConstraint("lastName", false, 40);

public static final DateConstraint BIRTH_DATE_CONSTRAINT =
    new DateConstraint("birthDate", false, "01/01/1900",
                       "12/31/3000", Locale.US);

public static final StringConstraint TAX_ID_CONSTRAINT =
    new StringConstraint("taxID", false, 40);

private Date birthDate = Calendar.getInstance()
                                 .getTime();

private Gender gender = Gender.MALE;

/** The first name of the person. */
private String firstName = "<<NEW PERSON>>";

private String lastName = "<<NEW PERSON>>";

private String taxID = new String();

public void setBirthDate(final Date birthDate) {  }

public Date getBirthDate() {  }

public void setFirstName(final String firstName) {  }

public String getFirstName() {  }

public void setGender(final Gender gender) {  }

public Gender getGender() {  }

public void setLastName(final String lastName) {  }

public String getLastName() {  }

public void setTaxID(final String taxID) {  }

public String getTaxID() {  }

public boolean equals(final Object obj) {  }

public int hashCode() {  }
}
```

All of your Online Only Bank data model classes roughly look like this. They are all JavaBeans—that is, they conform to the naming standard that is set for JavaBeans. Since all constructed classes in Java ultimately inherit from java.lang.Object (see

Chapter 1), you can pass an instance of this class as an object to a method and then figure out which properties, methods, inner interfaces, etc., the class contains, as Example 9-2 demonstrates.

Example 9-2. Getting method information on an object

```java
package oreilly.hcj.reflection;
import java.lang.reflect.Method;
import oreilly.hcj.bankdata.Person;
import oreilly.hcj.bankdata.Gender;

public class MethodInfoDemo {

  public static void printMethodInfo(final Object obj) {
    Class type = obj.getClass();
    final Method[] methods = type.getMethods();
    for (int idx = 0; idx < methods.length; idx++) {
      System.out.println(methods[idx]);
    }
  }

  /**
   * Demo method.
   *
   * @param args Command line arguments.
   */
  public static void main(final String[] args) {
    Person p = new Person();
    p.setFirstName("Robert");
    p.setLastName("Simmons");
    p.setGender(Gender.MALE);
    p.setTaxID("123abc456");

    printMethodInfo(p);
  }
}
```

Inside `printMethodInfo( )`, inspect the object passed to you. After you determine the class of the object, examine contents of the class and print the string version of the methods:

```
>ant -Dexample=oreilly.hcj.reflection.MethodInfoDemo run_example
run_example:
    [java] public int oreilly.hcj.bankdata.Person.hashCode( )
    [java] public boolean oreilly.hcj.bankdata.Person.equals(java.lang.Object)
    [java] public void oreilly.hcj.bankdata.Person.setFirstName(java.lang.String)
    [java] public void oreilly.hcj.bankdata.Person.setLastName(java.lang.String)
    [java] public void oreilly.hcj.bankdata.Person.setGender
           (oreilly.hcj.bankdata.Gender)
    [java] public void oreilly.hcj.bankdata.Person.setTaxID(java.lang.String)
    [java] public void oreilly.hcj.bankdata.Person.setBirthDate(java.util.Date)
```

```
[java] public java.util.Date oreilly.hcj.bankdata.Person.getBirthDate( )
[java] public java.lang.String oreilly.hcj.bankdata.Person.getFirstName( )
[java] public oreilly.hcj.bankdata.Gender
       oreilly.hcj.bankdata.Person.getGender( )
[java] public java.lang.String oreilly.hcj.bankdata.Person.getLastName( )
[java] public java.lang.String oreilly.hcj.bankdata.Person.getTaxID( )
[java] public java.lang.String oreilly.hcj.datamodeling.MutableObject.toString( )
[java] public void oreilly.hcj.datamodeling.MutableObject.
       addPropertyChangeListener
       (java.lang.String,java.beans.PropertyChangeListener)
[java] public void oreilly.hcj.datamodeling.MutableObject.
       addPropertyChangeListener(java.beans.PropertyChangeListener)
[java] public void oreilly.hcj.datamodeling.MutableObject.
       removePropertyChangeListener
       (java.lang.String,java.beans.PropertyChangeListener)
[java] public void oreilly.hcj.datamodeling.MutableObject.
       removePropertyChangeListener(java.beans.PropertyChangeListener)
[java] public final native java.lang.Class java.lang.Object.getClass( )
[java] public final void java.lang.Object.wait(long,int) throws
       java.lang.InterruptedException
[java] public final void java.lang.Object.wait( ) throws
       java.lang.InterruptedException
[java] public final native void java.lang.Object.wait(long) throws
       java.lang.InterruptedException
[java] public final native void java.lang.Object.notify( )
[java] public final native void java.lang.Object.notifyAll( )
```

The getMethods( ) call in printMethodInfo( ) returned an array of Method objects from the java.lang.reflect package; the string version of these Method objects was then written to the console. The getMethods( ) call extracted each of the public members of the Person class, including the members it inherited from other classes such as MutableObject. The emphasized lines contain the setters and getters for the Person class. The nice thing about printMethodInfo( ) is that it will work for any object you pass to it.

> If you want to get only the methods of the class without the inherited methods, you can use the getDeclaredMethods( ) method defined on Class. However, getDeclaredMethods( ) will also return private and protected members of the class.

In addition to printing out the Method objects, you can use them to execute the methods. This is demonstrated in Example 9-3 with a method that will set all string properties in a class as empty strings.

Example 9-3. Dynamically invoking methods

```
package oreilly.hcj.reflection;
public class MethodInfoDemo {
  public static void emptyStrings(final Object obj)
      throws IllegalAccessException, InvocationTargetException {
    final String PREFIX = "set";
```

Example 9-3. Dynamically invoking methods (continued)

```
        Method[] methods = obj.getClass()
                            .getMethods();
        for (int idx = 0; idx < methods.length; idx++) {
          if (methods[idx].getName()
                      .startsWith(PREFIX)) {
            if (methods[idx].getParameterTypes()[0] == String.class) {
              methods[idx].invoke(obj, new Object[] { new String() });
            }
          }
        }
      }
    }
}
```

This method looks for all of the methods in a class that start with the word "set" and take a single `String` as a parameter. It then invokes these methods by passing an array of objects filled with only a single empty string to the method.

The nice thing about the last two methods in the example is that they will work for any object passed to them, not just the `Person` object. If you have complex code in this demonstration class, you could apply it to a wide variety of objects, just like a carpenter applies a saw to many kinds of wood.

> Many pieces of professional software expand on this ability to implement exceedingly complex functionality. For example, the Eclipse IDE is based on a plug-in architecture and uses reflection to invoke plug-ins that the programmers of Eclipse have never seen.

Reflection and Greater Reflection

The tools available to a reflection programmer are not limited to the `java.lang.reflect` package, as you may expect. In fact, they are spread all over the core of the JDK. All the tools used in reflection are often referred to as *greater reflection*. In this section, you will address each of the relevant packages and the tools within those packages and assemble an arsenal of reflection tools that will improve your programming.

> Although this book isn't intended as a reference manual explaining how to use the individual methods on the reflection tools, there are several examples in the `oreilly.hcj.reflection` package. These examples demonstrate many of the methods and basic techniques of reflection.

Package java.lang

This package contains the core functionality of reflection as well as the JDK itself. Since all classes ultimately inherit from `java.lang.Object`, the `java.lang` package plays a pivotal role in obtaining information about classes and objects.

Class java.lang.Class

This class contains information about the object's class, such as which fields and methods it contains, and which package it is in. You used it before to obtain information about the methods in a class. See Example 9-2.

Class java.lang.Object

From this class, you can get the Class instance for any object. Also, since the Object class is the basis for all constructed types in Java, it is used to pass parameters or get results from reflexively invoked methods and fields.

Class java.lang.Package

This class encapsulates the runtime manifestation of a package. However, Package is not a particularly useful class because you can't ask it for all of the classes in a package. I rarely use this class in my reflection programming.

Package java.lang.reflect

This package contains utilities for dynamic invocation of methods and for dynamic assignment and retrieval of fields. When you get catalogs of fields and methods from Class, they will be returned to you as instances of classes within java.lang.reflect. This package is one of the critical tools in building dynamic code, and it is used often in reflection code.

Class java.lang.reflect.Field

This class contains a description of a field and the means to access the field. With this class, you can dynamically set or retrieve field values.

Class java.lang.reflect.Method

This class contains a description of a method and the means to dynamically invoke it. You can use instances of this class to dynamically invoke methods. See Example 9-3.

Class java.lang.reflect.Modifier

This class is used to decode the bit field modifiers of a class, field, or method. Using Modifier, you can determine whether a field is public, private, static, transient, and so on. The modifiers are set by the native reflection code in the virtual machine that examines the actual Java byte code. These modifiers are read-only.

Class java.lang.reflect.Proxy

This class is used to create dynamic proxy classes, which are then used to create objects that implement specific interfaces. Usually, these classes are used to hide pieces of the implementation of a class from a user. For example, you could create a Proxy to the data object that presents an immutable interface to the object.

Class java.lang.reflect.AccessibleObject

This is the base class from which Method, Field, and the other descriptors inherit. It allows you to bypass class access constraints such as "private," which allows you to execute methods and set fields that would normally be blocked by visibility specifiers. Serialization often uses this class because it must have access to private fields to serialize an object. In EJB, this class is off-limits.

Although this class can be useful, I caution against using it unless you have no other choice. Forcibly breaking the encapsulation on an object can lead to enormously confusing code that is difficult to debug.

Package java.beans

The java.beans package was designed to allow developers to build GUIs using visual tools. However, there are many classes within this package that can be used with reflection. This package has classes that provide convenient access to various parts of reflection that you would otherwise have to search for in several places.

Although this package contains some powerful tools, it is quite old. Most of the classes in this package were introduced long before the collections framework of Java Foundation Classes (JFC) were finalized. Therefore, this package deals with arrays and not with the superior collection classes in the java.util package.

 This package has much more functionality than is covered in this chapter. Most of the JavaBeans programming paradigm is outside the scope of this book, so I don't delve into the world of customizers and other JavaBeans-specific concepts. Instead, I focus on the aspects of the java.beans package that are applicable to reflection as a whole and not just JavaBeans, which is one application of reflection.

Class java.beans.Introspector

This is a singleton class that can be used to obtain property information about a class declared with the JavaBeans naming specification. One important benefit of this class is that it caches the lookup of class information, which significantly speeds up the reflection process.

Although `Introspector` is useful, it does have some significant drawbacks. First, it does not detect polymorphic properties. Consider the following property:

```
public void setValue(final int value);
public int getValue();
```

This property is declared using the JavaBeans naming specification. However, it can also be expressed using polymorphic notation:

```
public void value(final int value);
public int value();
```

This notation uses the context of the method to determine whether the method is a getter or setter. The syntax is much cleaner since a field does not need to be capitalized. These properties are often used in products such as the Simple Widget Toolkit (SWT), which is used to build the Eclipse GUI.

To detect polymorphic properties, you can try to extend `Introspector`. However, if you do this, you encounter the second major disadvantage of this class. The `Introspector` class is implicitly private (see Chapter 2), which means that you cannot extend its functionality. Although it isn't declared as a `final` class, all of its constructors are private instead of protected, which means you can't extend it.

 `Introspector` is a good example of why you should use protected methods instead of secured methods, and use private attributes instead of secured attributes. You never know when someone will want to extend your class, so you should give them as many options as possible. Therefore, make a method private only if there is an important reason why it shouldn't be available to subclasses.

Class java.beans.PropertyDescriptor

This class encapsulates the field, setter, and getter of a property all in one location. Essentially, it is a package where you get all of the information about a property in one place instead of having to look it up using `Class`.

Unfortunately, neither this class nor any of its subclasses support collection properties with `add` and `remove` methods. The `PropertyDescriptor` class is used to provide a convenient interface to properties of a class. Most reflection tools use this class often.

One problem with `PropertyDescriptor` is that it allows the user to set the read and write methods for a property manually. Although this appears to be a good idea, it can lead to some confusing results if multiple methods and classes are using the same property descriptor. For example, consider a GUI that views an object that is also being viewed in another panel showing a tree view of the object's structure. If one panel changes the accessor methods, the other panel would access the old method and could be corrupted. This is a good example of an object that should be immutable.

Class java.beans.IndexedPropertyDescriptor

This class is similar to `PropertyDescriptor` but has extra functionality to handle properties that are arrays (also referred to as indexed properties). Here is a simple example of an indexed property:

```
package oreilly.hcj.reflection;
public class SomeClass {
  private String[] values = new String[0];

  public void setValues(String[] values) {
    this.values = values;
  }

  public void setValues(final String value, final int index) {
    this.values[index] = value;
  }

  public String[] getValues() {
    return values;
  }

  public String getValues(final int index) {
    return values[index];
  }
}
```

In this case, the `values` property is an indexed property because it is an array and has methods to set or get individual values in the array.

The `IndexedPropertyDescriptor` class will allow you to access the get and set methods of the property and the indexed get and set methods of the property.

Classes MethodDescriptor and ParameterDescriptor

These classes encapsulate information on methods and their parameters. The `MethodDescriptor` class allows you to retrieve the information about a method in a class, and `ParameterDescriptor` allows you to get information about the method's parameters. These classes are useful for beans programming because they contain display information about the method and its parameters. However, for reflection, they don't provide any significant functionality above `java.lang.reflect.Method`. Therefore, these classes are rarely used in mainstream reflection programming.

Interface java.beans.BeanInfo

This class holds all of the information about a particular JavaBean. It provides a convenient place from which you can look up various descriptors and other information about the class. The `Introspector` is used to look up and cache `BeanInfo` instances.

However, the one major problem with the BeanInfo class is that it doesn't provide access to the property descriptors by name. Unfortunately, extending this class isn't possible because the Introspector is implicitly private. To get an Introspector to find your extended BeanInfo class, you would either have to define the objects manually on every class (which would defeat the point of reflection) or reimplement the Introspector from the ground up (which is not a small task).

Applying Reflection to MutableObject

Now that you have a thorough understanding of the tools used in reflection, it's time to put them to work to solve a practical problem.

In Chapter 8, we discussed how to implement a data model to encapsulate the data in a hypothetical bank. Most of the data model objects in this model are structurally the same. They differ only in the number, name, and types of properties they contain. Reflection can be used on this data model to implement several key features.

Reflecting on toString( )

In your Online Only Bank data model, there are many classes that encapsulate data, and each has several properties. Although you can compare them and obtain their hashCode( ), you cannot print them to the console. This is the job of the toString( ) method. However, the default toString( ) method defined on class Object will print only the hash code and type of object. This is not enough information to do any serious debugging with these classes. What you really need is for the toString( ) method to print the values of the properties in the mutable object.

One tactic you could implement is to reabstract the toString( ) method and make each class declare its own toString( ) method. This would force developers to implement the method on each class, which would solve the problem. However, the implementations of the toString( ) method on each class would be the same, except for the names of the properties and classes; also, the method would have to be modified manually if new properties are added or removed. It would be better if you could save the users of MutableObject all of this work by implementing a toString( ) method in the MutableObject class that would print the properties of the derived classes. You can do this with reflection (see Example 9-4).

Example 9-4. The toString() method of MutableObject

```
package oreilly.hcj.datamodeling;
public abstract class MutableObject implements Serializable {

public String toString( ) {
    try {
```

Example 9-4. The toString() method of MutableObject (continued)

```
final BeanInfo info = Introspector.getBeanInfo(this.getClass(),
                                               Object.class);
final PropertyDescriptor[] props = info.getPropertyDescriptors();
final StringBuffer buf = new StringBuffer(500);
Object value = null;
buf.append(getClass().getName());
buf.append("@");
buf.append(hashCode());
buf.append("={");
for (int idx = 0; idx < props.length; idx++) {
  if (idx != 0) {
    buf.append(", ");
  }
  buf.append(props[idx].getName());
  buf.append("=");
  if (props[idx].getReadMethod() != null) {
    value = props[idx].getReadMethod()
                      .invoke(this, null);
    if (value instanceof MutableObject) {
      buf.append("@");
      buf.append(value.hashCode());
    } else if (value instanceof Collection) {
      buf.append("{");
      for (Iterator iter = ((Collection)value).iterator();
           iter.hasNext();) {
        Object element = iter.next();
        if (element instanceof MutableObject) {
          buf.append("@");
          buf.append(element.hashCode());
        } else {
          buf.append(element.toString());
        }
      }
      buf.append("}");
    } else if (value instanceof Map) {
      buf.append("{");
      Map map = (Map)value;
      for (Iterator iter = map.keySet()
                             .iterator(); iter.hasNext();) {
        Object key = iter.next();
        Object element = map.get(key);
        buf.append(key.toString());
        buf.append("=");
        if (element instanceof MutableObject) {
          buf.append("@");
          buf.append(element.hashCode());
        } else {
          buf.append(element.toString());
        }
      }
```

Example 9-4. The toString() method of MutableObject (continued)

```
          buf.append("}");
        } else {
          buf.append(value);
        }
      }
    }
    buf.append("}");
    return buf.toString();
  } catch (Exception ex) {
    throw new RuntimeException(ex);
  }
} }
```

Although this method may seem long for such a simple task, it is a fraction of the cut-and-paste code that would be required to implement toString( ) methods on all of the individual MutableObject types in a large data model. Furthermore, the reflexive toString( ) method doesn't require maintenance if you decide to add a new property to your data model object. It automatically updates itself.

Most of the code in Example 9-4 is fairly mundane string construction. However, the emphasized portions show various uses of the reflection toolkit. First, ask the Introspector for the BeanInfo on the object and its superclasses up to, but not including, Object. Then get the PropertyDescriptor objects for that class, which will give you access to the properties. At this point, you can loop through the properties, but make sure you check for a null read method, which could happen if the property is write-only.

While looping through the properties, you also have to watch out for recursive reflection. If you used the toString( ) method to print MutableObjects that are members of a MutableObject, then you could get caught in an endless loop. For example, if you used toString( ) on Account, the toString( ) method would be accessed on the Customer class; however, since Customer has a member holding its Accounts, you would recurse back into the Account object and end up in a loop. For this reason, you print only the hashCode( ) of members that are MutableObjects. Additionally, since the collection and map properties may also contain MutableObject descendants, you have to iterate through them to make sure you don't get caught in a loop.

Once the toString( ) method is compiled, it will work for any MutableObject descendant that you can dream up. Whether you have 4 data model objects or 40,000, you won't have to lift another finger to give your objects the ability to print their contents. Let's try it on some of your objects:

```
package oreilly.hcj.reflection;
public class DemoToStringUsage {

  public static void main(String[] args) {
    // Create some objects.
    Person p = new Person();
```

```
    p.setFirstName("Robert");
    p.setLastName("Simmons");
    p.setGender(Gender.MALE);
    p.setTaxID("123abc456");

    Customer c = new Customer( );
    c.setPerson(p);
    c.setCustomerID(new Integer(414122));
    c.setEmail("foo@bar.com");

    SavingsAccount a = new SavingsAccount( );
    a.setCustomer(c);
    a.setBalance(new Float(2212.5f));
    a.setID(new Integer(412413789));
    a.setInterestRate(new Float(0.062f));

    Set accounts = new HashSet( );
    accounts.add(a);
    c.setAccounts(accounts);

    // Now print them.
    System.out.println(p);
    System.out.println(c);
    System.out.println(a);
  }
}
```

Using this code, let's examine the new toString( ) method. The resulting output of
this code is shown here:

```
>ant -Dexample=oreilly.hcj.reflection.DemoToStringUsage run_example
run_example:
    [java] oreilly.hcj.bankdata.Person@-1989116069={birthDate=Sun Dec 07 18:04:11
CET 2003, firstName=Robert, gender=oreilly.hcj.bankdata.Gender.MALE,
lastName=Simmons, taxID=123abc456}
    [java] oreilly.hcj.bankdata.Customer@414122={accounts={@412413789},
applications={}, cardColor=java.awt.Color[r=0,g=0,b=255], customerID=414122,
email=foo@bar.com, passPhrase=null, payments={}, person=@-1989116069}
    [java] oreilly.hcj.bankdata.SavingsAccount@412413789={ID=412413789,
balance=2212.5, customer=@414122, interestRate=0.062, transactionList={}}
```

Each of the objects is printed correctly with each of their properties without any
additional input from the developer of the data model.

Although this is a good demonstration of how reflection is used, it just scratches the
surface of its capabilities.

Fetching Constraints

Since the constraints that you put on your data model objects are designed to be
accessible to panels, JSP pages, and other classes using these objects, it would be
convenient if there was a way to fetch the constraints from the model. Rather than

having the developer specify the constraints at compile time in a data structure, you can use reflection to fetch the constraints. Example 9-5 shows how you can build a map of the constraints on a MutableObject descendant. The emphasized lines use reflection.

Example 9-5. Fetching constraints on a MutableObject descendant

```
package oreilly.hcj.datamodeling;
public abstract class MutableObject implements Serializable {
  public static final Map buildConstraintMap(final Class dataType)
    throws IllegalAccessException {
    final int modifiers = Modifier.PUBLIC | Modifier.FINAL |
                          Modifier.STATIC;

    // --
    Map constraintMap = new HashMap();
    final Field[] fields = dataType.getFields();
    Object value = null;
    for (int idx = 0; idx < fields.length; idx++) {
      if ((fields[idx].getModifiers() & modifiers) == modifiers) {
        value = fields[idx].get(null);
        if (value instanceof ObjectConstraint) {
          constraintMap.put(((ObjectConstraint)value).getName(), value);
        }
      }
    }
    return Collections.unmodifiableMap(constraintMap);
  }
}
```

Get the fields in the target class and then check each of the public static final fields to see whether they contain instances of the class ObjectConstraint. If they do, put the constraint in the map and key it with the name of the property it constrains (which you can get from the ObjectConstraint class). The buildConstraintMap() method will give you references to the constraints on your objects, which you can use in your GUI or web page form validation.

However, there is one problem with the constraint mechanism. Although reflection is a powerful tool, the process of introspection (analyzing a class to determine its contents) takes up a lot of CPU time. If the users of MutableObject have to fetch the constraints in this manner every time they need them, your programs would run slowly. You need to cache your constraints in MutableObject. You can create a simple catalog to do this:

```
package oreilly.hcj.datamodeling;
public abstract class MutableObject implements Serializable {
  private static final Map CONSTRAINT_CACHE = new HashMap();

  public static ObjectConstraint getConstraint(final Class dataType,
                                               final String name) {
```

```
    Map constraintMap = getConstraintMap(dataType);
    return (ObjectConstraint)constraintMap.get(name);
  }

  public static final Map getConstraintMap(final Class dataType)
    throws RuntimeException {
    try {
      Map constraintMap = (Map)CONSTRAINT_CACHE.get(dataType);
      if (constraintMap == null) {
        constraintMap = buildConstraintMap(dataType);
        CONSTRAINT_CACHE.put(dataType, constraintMap);
        return constraintMap;
      }
      Collections.unmodifiableMap(constraintMap)
    } catch (final IllegalAccessException ex) {
      throw new RuntimeException(ex);
    }
  }
}
```

This code will cache each of the constraint maps the first time they are fetched. Now
all you have to do is change the visibility of buildConstraintMap( ) to protected to
force the users to call the caching methods:

```
package oreilly.hcj.reflection;
public class ConstraintMapDemo {
  public static final void main(final String[] args) {
    Map constraints = MutableObject.getConstraintMap(Customer.class);
    Iterator iter = constraints.values( )
                              .iterator( );
    ObjectConstraint constraint = null;
    while (iter.hasNext( )) {
      constraint = (ObjectConstraint)iter.next( );
      System.out.println("Property=" + constraint.getName( ) + " Type="
                        + constraint.getClass( ).getName( ));
    }

    constraint = MutableObject.getConstraint(SavingsAccount.class,
                                             "interestRate");
    System.out.println("\nSavingsAccount interestRate property");
    System.out.println("dataType = "
                      + ((NumericConstraint)constraint).getDataType( )
                                                      .getName( ));
    System.out.println("minValue = " +
                      ((NumericConstraint)constraint).getMinValue( ));
    System.out.println("maxValue = " +
                      ((NumericConstraint)constraint).getMaxValue( ));
  }
}
```

This results in the following output:

```
>ant -Dexample=oreilly.hcj.reflection.ConstraintMapDemo run_example
run_example:
```

```
[java] Property=accounts
       Type=oreilly.hcj.datamodeling.constraints.CollectionConstraint
[java] Property=cardColor
       Type=oreilly.hcj.datamodeling.constraints.ObjectConstraint
[java] Property=person
       Type=oreilly.hcj.datamodeling.constraints.ObjectConstraint
[java] Property=passPhrase
       Type=oreilly.hcj.datamodeling.constraints.StringConstraint
[java] Property=email Type=oreilly.hcj.datamodeling.constraints.StringConstraint
[java] Property=applications
       Type=oreilly.hcj.datamodeling.constraints.CollectionConstraint
[java] Property=payments
       Type=oreilly.hcj.datamodeling.constraints.CollectionConstraint
[java] Property=customerID
       Type=oreilly.hcj.datamodeling.constraints.NumericConstraint

[java] SavingsAccount interestRate property
[java] dataType = java.lang.Float
[java] minValue = 0.0
[java] maxValue = 1.0
```

As with toString( ), adding more data objects, properties, and constraints to your model will not require any more work. The MutableObject class adapts to your code.

Performance of Reflection

Our discussion of caching constraint maps leads to the question of reflection's performance. I am frequently asked how expensive reflection is in terms of CPU and memory.

The answer is that reflection can be cheap or expensive depending on how you use it. No tool in any programming language has zero cost. Example 9-6 shows how reflection performs.

Example 9-6. Measuring reflection's performance

```
package oreilly.hcj.reflection;
public class ReflexiveInvocation {
  /** Holds value of property value. */
  private String value = "some value";

  public ReflexiveInvocation( ) {
  }

  public static void main(final String[] args) {
    try {
      final int CALL_AMOUNT = 1000000;
      final ReflexiveInvocation ri = new ReflexiveInvocation( );
      int idx = 0;
```

Example 9-6. Measuring reflection's performance (continued)

```
    // Call the method without using reflection.
    long millis = System.currentTimeMillis();

    for (idx = 0; idx < CALL_AMOUNT; idx++) {
      ri.getValue();
    }

    System.out.println("Calling method " + CALL_AMOUNT
                    + " times programatically took "
                    + (System.currentTimeMillis() - millis)
                    + " millis");

    // Call while looking up the method at each iteration.
    Method md = null;
    millis = System.currentTimeMillis();

    for (idx = 0; idx < CALL_AMOUNT; idx++) {
      md = ri.getClass()
          .getMethod("getValue", null);
      md.invoke(ri, null);
    }

    System.out.println("Calling method " + CALL_AMOUNT
                    + " times reflexively with lookup took "
                    + (System.currentTimeMillis() - millis)
                    + " millis");

    // Call using a cache of the method.
    md = ri.getClass()
        .getMethod("getValue", null);
    millis = System.currentTimeMillis();

    for (idx = 0; idx < CALL_AMOUNT; idx++) {
      md.invoke(ri, null);
    }

    System.out.println("Calling method " + CALL_AMOUNT
                    + " times reflexively with cache took "
                    + (System.currentTimeMillis() - millis)
                    + " millis");
  } catch (final NoSuchMethodException ex) {
    throw new RuntimeException(ex);
  } catch (final InvocationTargetException ex) {
    throw new RuntimeException(ex);
  } catch (final IllegalAccessException ex) {
    throw new RuntimeException(ex);
  }
}
```

Example 9-6. Measuring reflection's performance (continued)

```
  public String getValue( ) {
    return this.value;
  }
}
```

In the first part of this test, you measure the time it takes to call the getter of the class normally 1 million times. In the second phase, you measure the time it takes to call the getter 1 million times using a reflection-based invocation, in which the getter method is looked up each time the loop is iterated. Finally, you cache the lookup of the getter and invoke the getter method 1 million times using the cached Method object. The results of running this class are shown here:

```
>ant -Dexample=oreilly.hcj.reflection.ReflexiveInvocation run_example
run_example:
    [java] Calling method 1000000 times normally took 20 millis
    [java] Calling method 1000000 times reflexively with lookup took 5618 millis
    [java] Calling method 1000000 times reflexively with cache took 270 millis
```

 Your times may vary depending on the capabilities of your computer, but generally, the ratios will be the same.

The phase during which the Method object was cached was significantly faster than the phase during which the Method object was looked up at each iteration. Naturally, both phases were slower than invoking the method normally.

This test teaches a couple of lessons. First, looking up the Method object is the most expensive part of reflection. If you cache the method, you can dramatically improve performance. Second, reflection is slower than invoking methods normally. However, this performance loss is compensated with the benefit of producing your products significantly faster and with fewer bugs. In most cases, the benefits of reflection are well worth the cost of 0.25 seconds over 1 million calls.

Reflection + JUnit = Stable Code

When designing architecture code, unit testing can be an important process. With unit testing, units of the code are tested in a controlled environment before they are incorporated into the entire system. Unit testing allows developers to catch bugs before the code is integrated with several other classes. Also, creating reusable unit tests with frameworks such as JUnit allows the programmer to perform a regression test when other features are implemented; they simply need to run the test to verify that nothing was broken. The most important and common question surrounding unit testing is how much of the code should be tested.

Ideally, you should test everything in the product. Unfortunately, this is often not possible because of deadlines and other pressures. You could easily spend more time writing tests than code. However, all architecture code should be tested because of the weight of the system that will be resting on that code.

You may believe that testing is not worth the effort; after all, these objects are only beans that hold data and not business processes. However, reflection allows you to have your cake and eat it too.

With reflection, you can test a data model object regardless of which properties it declares:

```java
package oreilly.hcj.reflection;
public class TestMutableObject extends TestCase {
  private Class type = null;

  protected TestMutableObject(final Class type, final String testName) {
    super(testName);
    assert (type != null);
    assert (MutableObject.class.isAssignableFrom(type));
    this.type = type;
  }

  public static Test suite(final Class type) {
    if (type == null) {
      throw new NullPointerException("type");
    }
    if (!MutableObject.class.isAssignableFrom(type)) {
      throw new IllegalArgumentException("type");
    }

    TestSuite suite = new TestSuite(type.getName());
    suite.addTest(new TestMutableObject(type, "testConstraintsExist"));
    return suite;
  }

  public void testConstraintsExist() {
    try {
      final PropertyDescriptor[] props =
        Introspector.getBeanInfo(type, Object.class)
                    .getPropertyDescriptors();

      for (int idx = 0; idx < props.length; idx++) {
        ObjectConstraint constraint =
          MutableObject.getConstraint(type, props[idx].getName());
        assertNotNull("Property " + props[idx].getName()
                      + " does not have a constraint.", constraint);
      }
    } catch (final IntrospectionException ex) {
      throw new RuntimeException();
    }
  }
}
```

This class is a standard JUnit test case with a twist. It does not know what kind of class it will be testing until the suite of test cases is created with the suite( ) method. The user of the test case passes the class that he wants to test into the suite( ) method, and the test is built for that particular class:

```
package oreilly.hcj.reflection;
public class BankDataTests {
  public static Test suite( ) {
    TestSuite suite = new TestSuite("Online-Only Bank Datamodel Tests");
    suite.addTest(TestMutableObject.suite(Account.class));
    suite.addTest(TestMutableObject.suite(AssetAccount.class));
    suite.addTest(TestMutableObject.suite(AutomaticPayment.class));
    suite.addTest(TestMutableObject.suite(BankOfficer.class));
    suite.addTest(TestMutableObject.suite(CreditCardAccount.class));
    suite.addTest(TestMutableObject.suite(Customer.class));
    suite.addTest(TestMutableObject.suite(Employee.class));
    suite.addTest(TestMutableObject.suite(ExternalTransaction.class));
    suite.addTest(TestMutableObject.suite(LiabilityAccount.class));
    suite.addTest(TestMutableObject.suite(LoanAccount.class));
    suite.addTest(TestMutableObject.suite(LoanApplication.class));
    suite.addTest(TestMutableObject.suite(OnlineCheckingAccount.class));
    suite.addTest(TestMutableObject.suite(Person.class));
    suite.addTest(TestMutableObject.suite(SavingsAccount.class));
    suite.addTest(TestMutableObject.suite(Transaction.class));
    return suite;
  }

  public static void main(final String[] args) {
    TestRunner.run(BankDataTests.class);
  }
}
```

You can run this test using the ant script:

```
>ant -Dexample=oreilly.hcj.reflection.BankDataTests run_example
```

This will bring up the JUnit test window and run each of the tests. On your healthy data model, the results will look like Figure 9-1.

However, if you comment out the constraint on the balance property of Account, your test case will acquire the defect in every class that inherits from Account (see Figure 9-2).

The Account class, as well as classes that inherit from Account, shows an error indicating that there isn't a constraint on the balance property.

Unit testing can be expanded to test almost all facets of your data model to make sure it conforms to the rules of your design specification. Also, you can use unit testing to write tests for other objects. With this technique, you can implement tests in one location and apply them to many classes.

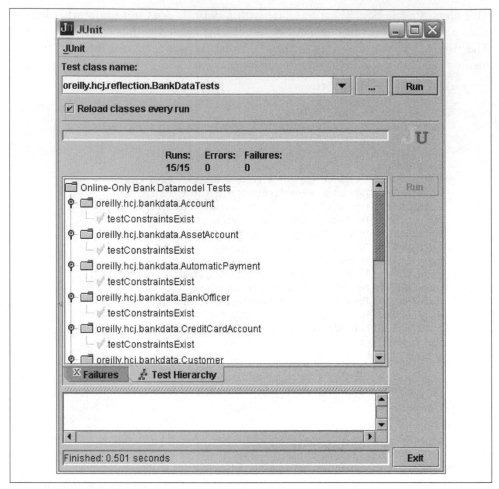

Figure 9-1. Testing the constraints in a healthy data model

Reflection can be used for a wide variety of other problems as well. This chapter has touched on only a fraction of the large number of things you can do with reflection. As you expand your reflection skills, you will find that you are designing more and more tools and copying less and less code. In the end, your code will be more solid and easier to maintain.

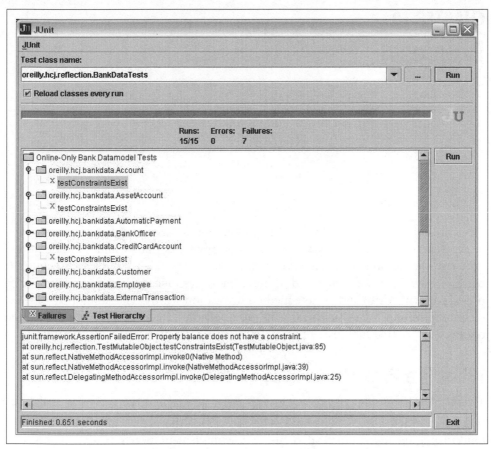

Figure 9-2. Testing an erroneous data model

CHAPTER 10
Proxies

The concept of a proxy is one of the most important aspects of modern programming. A proxy makes it possible to simplify many tasks that would be difficult and time-consuming otherwise. However, understanding proxies is often a difficult task because they are usually involved in much more complicated topics such as Enterprise JavaBeans (EJB) and remote method invocation (RMI). The developers of these technologies implement proxies for the users of these technologies, who are often not even aware that they are using a proxy.

What Is a Proxy?

To put it simply, a *proxy* is an object that stands in for another object and appears to perform the first object's functions. The object that the proxy imitates is called the *implementation object*. Instead of using the implementation directly, classes that want to access the features of the implementation use a proxy. For example, in an EJB system, the implementations are across the network from the clients that want to use them. The advantage of proxies is that they allow you to insert code between the implementation and the proxy. A proxy can hide complex tasks such as network communication and transaction management from the proxy user, all without changing the implementation object's functionality.

To better understand how proxies work, let's look at a class that implements two simple methods (see Example 10-1).

Example 10-1. An implementation object

```
package oreilly.hcj.proxies;
public class SomeClassImpl {

  private String userName;

  public SomeClassImpl(final String userName) {
    this.userName = userName;
  }
```

Example 10-1. An implementation object (continued)

```
  public void someMethod( ) {
    System.out.println(this.userName);
  }

  public void someOtherMethod(final String text) {
    System.out.println(text);
  }
}
```

Since you want a user to be able to use this class without having direct access to it, you need to create a proxy. Let's begin with a simple proxy; we'll add to it as we proceed. Implement a series of methods that are identical to the implementation (see Example 10-2).

Example 10-2. A simple proxy

```
package oreilly.hcj.proxies;
public class SomeClassProxy {
  private final SomeClassImpl impl;

  public SomeClassProxy(final SomeClassImpl impl) {
    this.impl = impl;
  }

  public void someMethod( ) {
    this.impl.someMethod( );
  }

  public void someOtherMethod(String text) {
    this.impl.someOtherMethod(text);
  }
}
```

This code creates a proxy to `SomeClassImpl` that looks exactly like `SomeClassImpl` itself. However, instead of providing the functionality of the class, `SomeClassProxy` forwards requests to `SomeClassProxy` to the implementation (stored in the `impl` member variable). Now that you have your proxy, you can work with it as if you were working with the implementation itself.

At this point, you may wonder why this special code isn't inserted into the implementation object itself. There are many reasons why you may not want to do this:

- The source code of the implementation class may not be accessible. This could be the case if third-party libraries were implemented by your company or provided by a separate department.

- The new functionality added is often not consistent with the functionality of the implementation object. Consider a class that models the functionality of a satellite. If you want to access this class remotely across a LAN or WAN, you need to write some networking code. However, placing the networking code inside the implementation violates the principle that an object should implement only one concept.

- The implementation could expose features that should remain hidden from various users. For example, the billing department doesn't need to access the shipping portion of an order. You can use several proxies to the same implementation object to show an altered implementation specifically for the billing department.

- You may want to hide the names of the implementation methods from the users of the implementation for security reasons. This would require a special view proxy in which the methods in the proxy have different names than those in the implementation.

- The functionality may be dependent on the context in which the object is being used. For example, a computer connected directly to a robotic arm in a factory does not need networking code to access the arm, but the control center on the other side of the factory does need this code.

- The functionality may be dependent on the development phase. For example, you can use a proxy to implement tracing behavior in a program that counts the number of times the object is called. This code may not be necessary in the deployed release of the software.

- The location of the implementation object may be changeable, as it is in enterprise programming. The objects performing the actual operations in an enterprise network often shift locations depending on load-balancing and fault-tolerance code. You would need an intelligent proxy to locate the object to provide the services of that object to the user.

There are other reasons to create proxies as well. However, these are some of the most common. In fact, the entire Enterprise JavaBeans programming paradigm is modeled on the last reason.

Network Proxies and CORBA

Life was hard before proxies. If a user wanted to call a remote object, he would have to set up a TCP connection to the remote object and then create a protocol to communicate with it. Finally, he would use the protocol to talk to the remote object, request an action, and get a response. The invention of the *network proxy model* made this all much easier.

The network proxy model is used throughout modern programming. It is the core functionality in CORBA, RMI, EJB, and Web Services programming. It makes all of these technologies easier by hiding the difficulties of managing the network communication protocols.

The invention of common object request broker architecture (CORBA) by the Object Management Group (OMG) was a turning point in the programming of network software. The programmer didn't need to invent protocols. Also, the problem of *marshalling* (flattening data to streams across the network and then reconstructing this data on the other side) was solved. CORBA managed all of this using proxies.

 CORBA and other Internet inter-orb protocol (IIOP) technologies have many other functionalities as well. However, these are far beyond the scope of this book.

Distributed systems such as CORBA, RMI, and EJB use network proxies in which the programmer defines the interface to an object and then runs a pre-compile-time tool to generate code based on that interface. From one interface definition, the user ends up with four different classes. However, the user on the client side simply uses one of these objects as if it were the actual implementation. The proxy class handles the protocol negotiation, data marshalling, and networking. This allows the business application programmer to concentrate on code for his company rather than reinvent the wheel. Figure 10-1 shows a UML deployment diagram of how this works.

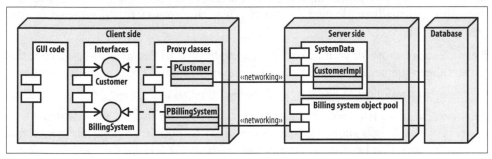

Figure 10-1. The distributed proxy model

In this diagram, the developer building the GUI component needs to concern himself only with the interfaces to the services on the server. The proxies convert the data to be sent over TCP/IP. The GUI developer doesn't need to worry about the fact that the billing system is implemented on the server side as a pool of objects that balance load. All he needs to know is that he has a box in which he can put something in and extract a result.

Using proxies is an example of *distributed programming*, which is one of the most significant advances in software engineering since the invention of object-oriented engineering. It takes object-oriented engineering to a new level by allowing the objects to be *distributed* around a network of computers transparently. Although this distribution is possible without proxies, it would be much more difficult and costly.

Following the example of CORBA, many other technologies that use the network proxy model sprung up. Among these technologies were EJB, JAX RPC, and other web services technologies. All of these would be unfeasible without the concept of proxies.

Factories

To get a proxy to an object, you usually have to use a factory object, which combines the proxy and the implementation into one unit. One reason why factories are used is because you don't particularly care which kind of object implements your functionality, as long as it implements it properly.

With EJB, the factory object finds the implementation on the network using another object or a unique identifier. The factory then binds the proxy to the implementation and gives you back the proxy. At this point, you can work with the proxy as if it were the implementation of the object, even though the implementation is on a different computer.

Factory objects are used to obtain proxies because they often do a great deal of work setting up proxies. They may need to allocate network resources to the proxy, or allow the proxy to perform initialization routines to prepare itself for use. Also, factory objects usually implement a security policy that prevents unauthorized or dangerous activity.

Let's create a factory for your proxy from Example 10-2. In Example 10-3, the code that creates the implementation object simply passes in the name "Fred" as the username:

```
SomeClassProxy proxy = new SomeClassProxy(new SomeClassImpl("Fred"));
```

However, you want to pass the actual username of the user in the constructor to SomeClassImpl. If you allow the user of the proxy to pass in anything he wants, you cannot be sure that he will pass in his real username. To make sure you get the real username, use a proxy factory (see Example 10-3).

Example 10-3. A basic proxy factory

```
package oreilly.hcj.proxies;
public class SomeClassFactory {

  public final static SomeClassProxy getProxy() {
    SomeClassImpl impl = new SomeClassImpl(System.getProperty("user.name"));
    return new SomeClassProxy(impl);
  }
}
```

In this code, the proxy factory sets up the object and binds to the implementation. In a real system, the user would simply not be able to create the actual implementation objects. For example, in an EJB system, the user simply doesn't have the actual class files for the implementation. Instead, he must ask the EJB server for a proxy to that object.

Using the proxy factory is quite easy:

```
package oreilly.hcj.proxies;
public class DemoProxyFactory {

  public static final void main(final String[] args) {
    SomeClassProxy proxy = SomeClassFactory.getProxy( );
    proxy.someMethod( );
    proxy.someOtherMethod("Our Proxy works!");
  }
}
```

Here, the proxy factory is used to create a proxy for the desired implementation class. Since this is the only way the user would be able to access the implementation in a real system, he can never submit a false username.

Whenever you access any EJB object, you take advantage of a factory called a home interface. Since a home interface is second nature to EJB programmers, many don't realize that this is actually a factory, nor do they realize that the object they are using on the client side is actually a quite sophisticated proxy.

Client and Server Objects

With proxies and distributed programming, the terms *client* and *server* take on a different meaning than what many client/server programmers are used to. In standard client/server programming, a client is the user interface and the server implements the business logic of the system. In this context, the clients never have any business logic at all.

In proxy-based programming, the client is simply an object that takes advantage of the services of another object, called the server (object). Therefore, a single object may be both a client to another object and a server to various clients, all at the same time.

For example, consider an object that provides billing in an online store. The Billing object is a client to the CreditCardVerification object since it uses this object to verify the credit card before billing begins. However, the Billing object is also a server to the Ordering object because the Ordering object requires the services of the Billing object so it can order products for the customer. In this case, the user interface is most likely a client (and not a server) to various server objects. However, it's not uncommon to see a mix of client and server objects at all levels of a distributed application.

Understanding the dichotomy between client and server is important when talking about proxies because the terminology often conflicts with terminology from the old method of client/server programming.

Two Kinds of Proxies

When working with proxies, there is a wide array of strategies available to you for implementing them. One strategy is the use of pre-compile-time tools such as those used by CORBA. Also, proxies can be manually written, reflexively driven, or dynamically generated.

Static Proxies

Proxies that are written manually are referred to as *static proxies*. Static proxies are programmed into the system at compile time. Example 10-2 shows a simple static proxy.

Programming static proxies is a just like programming any other class with a couple of new rules:

- The proxy can never extend the implementation (or vice versa). The proxy and implementation must form a delegation structure in which the proxy delegates to the implementation. This restriction exists because if the proxy simply extended the implementation, a user would be able to cast the proxy to the implementation and bypass the proxy altogether. For example, if you create a proxy to implement a security policy and the user can cast away the proxy, then you would have a huge hole in your security.

- The user of the proxy should never create the implementation. If the user can create an implementation directly, then he can bypass the proxy and simply use the implementation. For example, the following usage of the proxy from Example 10-2 would be a bad idea because it would bypass any checking code in the proxy:

  ```
  package oreilly.hcj.proxies;
  public class DemoClientGeneratedProxy {

    public static final void main(final String[] args) {
      SomeClassProxy proxy = new SomeClassProxy(new SomeClassImpl("Fred"));
      proxy.someMethod( );
      proxy.someOtherMethod("Our Proxy works!");
    }
  }
  ```

  Since there is nothing to prevent a user from ignoring the proxy and going directly to the implementation, proxies should always be obtained from a factory or through calls to other proxies. Furthermore, the implementations should be protected from access by the client.

When writing static proxies, the programmer introduces new code into the proxy to implement the new functionality. For example, you can alter the proxy from Example 10-2 to incorporate the ability to count how many times the methods of the implementation are called. The resulting class is shown in Example 10-4.

Example 10-4. A counting proxy

```
package oreilly.hcj.proxies;
public class SomeClassCountingProxy {

  private final SomeClassImpl impl;

  private int invocationCount = 0;

  public SomeClassCountingProxy(final SomeClassImpl impl) {
    this.impl = impl;
  }

  public int getInvocationCount() {
    return invocationCount;
  }

  public void someMethod() {
    this.invocationCount++;
    this.impl.someMethod();
  }

  public void someOtherMethod(String text) {
    this.invocationCount++;
    this.impl.someOtherMethod(text);
  }
}
```

This static proxy will keep track of the number of times the implementation's methods are invoked. You changed the original proxy and inserted content into the proxy to implement the required functionality. Using the proxy is virtually identical to using the SomeClassProxy object. Here's a modified factory-creation method:

```
package oreilly.hcj.proxies;
public class SomeClassFactory {

  public static final SomeClassCountingProxy getCountingProxy() {
    SomeClassImpl impl = new SomeClassImpl(System.getProperty("user.name"));
    return new SomeClassCountingProxy(impl);
  }
}
```

Just as before, get the proxy from the factory and then use it as if it were the class itself:

```
package oreilly.hcj.proxies;
package oreilly.hcj.proxies;
public class DemoCountingProxy {

  public static final void main(final String[] args) {
    SomeClassCountingProxy proxy = SomeClassFactory.getCountingProxy();
    proxy.someMethod();
    proxy.someOtherMethod("Our Proxy works!");
```

```
    System.out.println("Method Invocation Count = " +
                        proxy.getInvocationCount());
    }
}
```

Here, you access the methods in an identical fashion as the last proxy you wrote. However, this method counts the number of invocations to the methods of the implementation. In the emphasized code, you write out the invocation count. The output is shown here:

```
>ant -Dexample=oreilly.hcj.proxies.DemoCountingProxy run_example
run_example:
    [java] Robert
    [java] Our Proxy works!
    [java] Method Invocation Count = 2
```

This two-tier functionality gives you a great deal of power in designing strong applications. You can insert code in between the implementation of an object and the object itself to alter the functionality of the original implementation. Also, you can add more methods to the proxy class that did not exist in the original implementation class. For example, the getInvocationCount( ) method, which does not exist in the original implementation, was added. This technique is known as a *decorator pattern*.

Decorators are especially useful when you want to modify objects whose sources you do not control, such as third-party libraries. However, they can also be useful in creating extended functionality of an object within a particular context, as is done with method counting.

Proxy by Interface

In previous examples, the proxies that you created required that the user know which kind of proxy he wants. This is often not a desirable situation.

For example, a distributed program that could be spread across several machines would want to take advantage of a variety of proxies, depending on the location of the implementation. If the implementation is running on the same machine, the program shouldn't have to use the network to talk to the object; if the object is elsewhere on the LAN, then networking is required.

However, the user of the implementation is not interested in these details. He simply wants to use the object without worrying about where the actual implementation is. What you need is a way for the factory to give the user the correct proxy based on specific information, such as where the implementation is located within a network.

In Example 10-4, you created a proxy that counted the number of times the methods of the object was called. As an example of a proxy that behaves differently based on specific conditions, suppose that your counting proxy may be necessary during debugging but not during the deployment of the application. What you would like to do is give the user the counting proxy when debugging is activated and the non-counting proxy when debugging is turned off. However, the user won't know which proxy he is getting until runtime. Therefore, you need another way for the user to refer to the proxy. Java interfaces are ideally suited to solving such problems.

To isolate the implementation details of the proxy, you can use an interface that describes the functionality of the implementation. When you apply this technique to the implementation class from Example 10-2, you get the result in Example 10-5.

Example 10-5. An interface to an implementation

```
package oreilly.hcj.proxies;
public interface SomeClass {

  public abstract void someMethod( );

  public abstract void someOtherMethod(final String text);
}
```

Now that you have an interface to your implementation, you can enforce this interface by changing SomeClassImpl:

```
public class SomeClassImpl implements SomeClass {
  // same as before
}
```

Additionally, you can make the proxy classes implement the interface:

```
public class SomeClassProxy implements SomeClass {
  // same as before
}

public class SomeClassCountingProxy implements SomeClass {
  // same as before
}
```

Although the proxy classes implement the interface, this doesn't break the inheritance rule from earlier because the user will have only the proxy, which doesn't inherit from the implementation. If a user gets a proxy and casts it up to the interface, the virtual machine won't have a problem. However, if he tries to cast the interface to the implementation, the built-in RTTI mechanism will slap him with a ClassCastException. Casting an object doesn't change its type; it merely changes the view of its type. An instance of SomeClassProxy remains SomeClassProxy no matter how it is cast.

Now that both of the proxies and the implementation are using this new interface, you can create a factory that allows the user to ignore the actual implementation of the proxy itself. This factory is shown in Example 10-6.

Example 10-6. A factory that gives back various proxies

```
package oreilly.hcj.proxies;
public class SomeClassFactory {

  public static final SomeClass getSomeClassProxy() {
    SomeClassImpl impl = new SomeClassImpl(System.getProperty("user.name"));
    if (LOGGER.isDebugEnabled()) {
      return new SomeClassCountingProxy(impl);
    } else {
      return new SomeClassProxy(impl);
    }
  }
}
```

The new factory method simply gives back an object of type SomeClass. Since both of the proxies implement SomeClass, you can give back whichever one you want. In this example, if Log4J is set for debugging, return the proxy that counts invocations; otherwise, return the noncounting proxy.

To use the new factory method, the user simply needs to know he is getting an instance of SomeClass. Your new proxy scheme is shown here:

```
package oreilly.hcj.proxies;
public class DemoInterfaceProxy {

  public static final void main(final String[] args) {
    SomeClass proxy = SomeClassFactory.getSomeClassProxy();
    proxy.someMethod();
    proxy.someOtherMethod("Our Proxy works!");
  }
}
```

The user doesn't need to know (or care) if the proxy is counting. You can give him any proxy that conforms to the interface SomeClass. Using interfaces is clearly superior to using concrete classes because it decouples the client from the server object, allowing the developer to insert code between the client and server objects depending on various criteria.

In this example, the count of the method invocations in the demo program is not shown. You could, however, check to see whether proxy is an instance of SomeCountingProxy and output the count:

```
if (proxy instanceof SomeClassCountingProxy) {
  System.out.println(((SomeClassCountingProxy)proxy).getInvocationCount());
}
```

This code would allow you to print the count if the proxy is a counting proxy, or simply skip it if it is a noncounting proxy.

In real-life programs, the client of a proxy rarely needs to access the features of the proxy itself. Normally, third-party tools such as cache managers and network monitors need this extra information. Therefore, it's rare that a client would care which kind of proxy she had received from a factory.

Similarly, you could create additional interfaces that extend the SomeClass interface to implement dynamically returned decorators, each adding new methods that are specific to the proxy classes. Each of the proxy classes would implement the extended interface, which would be used by the clients of the implementation. This is an extremely powerful way to deal with a variety of implementations.

Dynamic Proxies

 The concepts in this section depend on the tools available in JDK 1.4. JDK 1.3 and below lack the proxy tools in the java.lang.reflect package.

While programming proxies to objects, you may notice yourself doing the same thing over and over again in a proxy class. For example, for each implementation for which you wanted a counting proxy, you would have to replicate all of the work that you had already done for each new implementation. The problem with this is that all these proxy classes with duplicated code are troublesome to maintain. If your proxy had 1,000 lines of networking code, and a bug was found in just one line, you would have to remember to change that line in each bit of duplicated code, throughout tens, or even hundreds, of additional proxies.

 Whenever you see words such as "you have to remember," then a warning light should go off in your head. The problem is that many times we *don't* remember. When pressed with deadlines, we sometimes forget to do these things, and they bite us later. Also, programmers new to your project may not know they need to remember these constraints. All dependencies in your code should be modeled (and documented), not stored in your head.

To alleviate this problem, you could create helper utility methods that each proxy could call, but you would still be stuck with multiple proxy classes that do essentially the same thing. What you need is a way to implement the method-counting code in one location, and a way to reuse it for any object.

Dynamic proxies can do this by using reflection. Dynamic proxies differ from static proxies in that they do *not* exist at compile time. Instead, they are generated at runtime by the JDK and then made available to the user. This allows the factory to bind an object to many different kinds of implementations without copying or duplicating code.

Invocation handlers

When writing a dynamic proxy, the principal task of the programmer is to write an object called an *invocation handler*, which implements the InvocationHandler interface from the java.lang.reflect package. An invocation handler intercepts calls to the implementation, performs some programming logic, and then passes on the request to the implementation. Once the implementation method returns, the invocation handler returns its results (along with any exceptions thrown).

Example 10-7 shows an invocation handler that implements your method-invocation counting.

Example 10-7. A method-invocation-counting invocation handler

```
package oreilly.hcj.proxies;

public class MethodCountingHandler implements InvocationHandler {

  private final Object impl;
  private int invocationCount = 0;

  public MethodCountingHandler(final Object impl) {
    this.impl = impl;
  }

  public int getInvocationCount() {
    return invocationCount;
  }

  public Object invoke(Object proxy, Method meth, Object[] args)
              throws Throwable {
    try {
      this.invocationCount++;
      Object result = meth.invoke(impl, args);
      return result;
    } catch (final InvocationTargetException ex) {
      throw ex.getTargetException();
    }
  }
}
```

This invocation handler provides the same functionality as static proxies. However, it uses reflection to do the job. When a user executes a method on the proxy, the invocation handler is called instead of the implementation. Inside the invocation handler, insert code to increment the invocationCount variable and then forward the call to the implementation using the invoke( ) method on the Method object. Once the invocation is complete, the implementation will return a value to the handler. You then pass that value back to the caller.

 When writing invocation handlers, be careful of methods that return primitive types. The JDK will wrap primitive types in their corresponding wrapper types to return them from a reflexive invocation. The problem is that your handler can return null, but the actual method being called on the implementation cannot. Therefore, if you try to return null after calling a method that returns a primitive, the proxy class will throw a NullPointerException. This NullPointerException applies to the *return value*, not to the parameters of the method.

The code inside the invoke( ) method can do a variety of things. In this example, you simply count the invocations of methods. However, you could write an invocation handler that would perform security checks or even implement IIOP protocol to send method calls across the network.

Generated proxy classes

Writing an invocation handler is only the first step in generating a dynamic proxy. Once you have an invocation handler, you must generate a proxy for the users. Furthermore, according to the proxy design pattern, you have to make sure that the proxy looks like the implementation; the user shouldn't be aware of the differences between the proxy and the implementation.

You can do this by using a java.lang.reflect.Proxy class in conjunction with your proxy factory. The resulting factory method is shown here:

```
package oreilly.hcj.proxies;
public class SomeClassFactory {

  public static final SomeClass getDynamicSomeClassProxy( ) {
    SomeClassImpl impl = new SomeClassImpl(System.getProperty("user.name"));
    InvocationHandler handler = new MethodCountingHandler(impl);
    Class[] interfaces = new Class[] { SomeClass.class };
    ClassLoader loader = SomeClassFactory.class.getClassLoader( );
    SomeClass proxy = (SomeClass)Proxy.newProxyInstance(loader,
                                                        interfaces,
                                                        handler);

    return proxy;
  }
}
```

In this version of the factory method, SomeClass is an interface implemented by the actual implementation, named SomeClassImpl. This allows you to tell the Proxy class to generate a new proxy that implements the interface SomeClass and uses the invocation handler.

One limitation of this system is that the implementation class must implement the interfaces used in the proxy. Therefore, if the implementation did not implement the interface in the first place and the source code is out of your control, this paradigm won't work.

The Proxy class plays a pivotal role in creating and managing new proxy classes in the virtual machine. Proxy got its enormous power from only four methods:

getInvocationHandler( )

This method gives the caller a reference to the invocation handler used in the proxy given as a parameter.

getProxyClass( )

This is the prime method in the creation of the actual proxy class. It takes an array of interfaces and a class loader as arguments and generates the byte code for the proxy class at runtime. Once the class is generated, it can be instantiated and used. It is then cached and returned the next time the method is called with the same parameters. Since the generation of the proxy class is relatively slow, this improves the performance of proxies significantly.

isProxyClass( )

This method tells you whether the proxy class was generated dynamically. It is used by the security engine to verify that the class is a proxy class.

newProxyInstance( )

This method is a shortcut to calling getProxyClass( ) and then calling newInstance( ) on the resulting class.

Generated proxy classes are required to conform to the following rules:

- All proxy classes are declared as public and final.
- All proxy classes extend the class java.lang.reflect.Proxy.
- When a proxy class is defined, it implements the interfaces stated in the same order as they are in the array.

There are several additional aspects of generated proxy classes of which you should be aware:

- The unqualified name of proxies is considered undefined, although the prefix $Proxy is generally reserved for proxy classes. This means that you can't depend on references to the class by name. For example, the following code would be dangerous:

```
package oreilly.hcj.proxies;
public class DangerousNames {

    public static final void main(final String[] args) {
        SomeClass proxy = SomeClassFactory.getDynamicSomeClassProxy();
        System.out.println(proxy.getClass().getName());
```

```
    try {
      Class cl = Class.forName("$Proxy0");  // <== Dangerous!
      System.out.println(cl.getName());
    } catch (final ClassNotFoundException ex) {
      ex.printStackTrace();
    }
  }
}
```

Since the unqualified name of a proxy is undefined, using the name literally (as was done in the emphasized line) could cause problems. This code may work on one virtual machine and fail on another, as the name may be correct on the first virtual machine, while the other virtual machine may generate $Proxy_SomeClass0 as the name of the proxy class. The best advice is simply not to rely on the names of proxy classes for anything.

- Proxy classes are just like other classes with respect to reflection. You can use reflection to get a list of their methods and interfaces and then execute them dynamically.

- The protection domain of Java proxy classes is the same as the protection domain of the Java bootstrap classes. This means that proxy classes can access *all* permissions in the JDK.

 A discussion of protection domains is far outside the scope of this book. For more information on protection domains, check out *Java Security* by Scott Oaks (O'Reilly).

- Proxy classes are generated with a single constructor that takes a single argument of type InvocationHandler. This allows you to create a new proxy if the proxy class object is already using the newInstance() method.

Using dynamic proxies

Now that you have your dynamic proxy class, you can use it in a new method:

```
package oreilly.hcj.proxies;
public class DemoDynamicProxy {

  public static final void main(final String[] args) {
    SomeClass proxy = SomeClassFactory.getDynamicSomeClassProxy();
    proxy.someMethod();
    proxy.someOtherMethod("Our Proxy works!");
  }
}
```

Using the proxy class is virtually identical to using the static proxy classes. However, there are a couple of important differences. First, the implementation of the proxy is generated by the Proxy class. Second, to get the method invocation count of the proxy, you would have to fetch the invocation handler and then ask the invocation handler for the count:

```
InvocationHandler handler = Proxy.getInvocationHandler(proxy);
if (handler instanceof MethodCountingHandler) {
  System.out.println(((MethodCountingHandler)handler).getInvocationCount());
}
```

The method `Proxy.getInvocationHandler()` is used to fetch the invocation handler from the proxy. You then make sure that the handler is in fact a `MethodCountingHandler`; remember that any invocation handler could have been used. Finally, output the invocation count.

Proxy Gotchas

As demonstrated in the previous sections, proxies are an extremely powerful tool in the creation of modern applications. However, as with any powerful tool, you can get into trouble if you aren't careful.

One of the prime dangers of using proxies is the performance hit they put on your application. When using a proxy, every call to the implementation goes through at least one extra method call. In proxies that perform more complex operations, each call may go through a large amount of code before it contacts the implementation and returns the result of the call. The accumulated performance hit in an application can be significant.

A major annoyance of dynamic proxies is that the class has to be designed with the dynamic proxy in mind. If the class does not implement an interface, you can't create a proxy to a class using that interface. Although this is not such a big deal in code over which you have control, in third-party libraries, it can be a pain.

As long as you keep the limitations of proxies in mind, judicious use of static and dynamic proxies can provide quite a bit of power to your development.

CHAPTER 11

References in Four Flavors

The java.lang.ref package is criminally underused in Java programming. Despite the enormous power of the classes within this package, you rarely see them in mainstream coding. Most likely, this is because using these classes properly requires a fairly deep understanding of the garbage-collection infrastructure in Java. However, once you understand garbage collection, you can create code that uses resources efficiently.

The Problem

One of the critical problems in the Online Only Bank data model from Chapter 8 is the high potential for memory leaks. In fact, the process of garbage collection is not enough to protect you from memory leaks. Garbage collection protects you from only one kind of memory leak, known as a *lost pointer*.

In languages such as C++, a memory leak resembles a lost pointer to an allocated block of memory. In this scenario, an object asks the runtime environment to allocate a block of memory. However, after this allocation, the pointer to the block is lost, perhaps through method return. There is a memory leak because there is a dead stack of allocated memory that the computer cannot use and to which the program can no longer get a pointer. In Java, this type of memory leak is not possible.

However, Java suffers from a different type of memory leak based on the garbage-collection paradigm itself. Since all objects in Java are references, they form an intricate web of associations; these associations can cause a memory leak. Consider the JavaBean data class in Example 11-1.

Example 11-1. A basic JavaBean data class

```
package oreilly.hcj.references;

import java.beans.PropertyChangeListener;
import java.beans.PropertyChangeSupport;

public class SomeDataClass {
```

Example 11-1. A basic JavaBean data class (continued)

```
  protected PropertyChangeSupport propertyChangeSupport =
    new java.beans.PropertyChangeSupport(this);

  private int age = 0;

  public void setAge(final int value) {
    final int oldAge = this.age;
    this.age = value;
    this.propertyChangeSupport.firePropertyChange("value", oldAge, this.age);
  }

  public int getAge( ) {
    return this.age;
  }

  public void addPropertyChangeListener(final PropertyChangeListener lst) {
    propertyChangeSupport.addPropertyChangeListener(lst);
  }

  public void removePropertyChangeListener(final PropertyChangeListener lst) {
    propertyChangeSupport.removePropertyChangeListener(lst);
  }
}
```

This class is a standard JavaBean with a single bound property named age. When the value of age changes, the listeners to the data object are informed of the change via normal property change events. Example 11-2 shows how the object is used in a GUI panel.

Example 11-2. A GUI panel that uses SomeDataClass

```
package oreilly.hcj.references;

public class SomeGUIPanel extends JPanel implements ActionListener,
                                                PropertyChangeListener {
  public SomeDataClass dataObject = null;

  JTextField valueField;

  public SomeGUIPanel(final SomeDataClass obj) {
    this.setLayout(new GridLayout(1, 2));
    JLabel label = new JLabel("Age: ", SwingConstants.RIGHT);
    this.add(label);
    this.valueField = new JTextField( );
    this.valueField.addActionListener(this);
    this.add(this.valueField);
    changeObject(obj);
  }

  public void actionPerformed(final ActionEvent event) {
    if (event.getSource( ) == this.valueField) {
      try {
```

Example 11-2. A GUI panel that uses SomeDataClass (continued)

```
        int temp = Integer.parseInt(this.valueField.getText());
        this.dataObject.setAge(temp);
      } catch (final NumberFormatException ex) {
        Toolkit.getDefaultToolkit().beep();
      }
    }
  }

  public void changeObject(final SomeDataClass obj) {
    this.dataObject = obj;
    this.dataObject.addPropertyChangeListener(this);
    this.valueField.setText(Integer.toString(obj.getAge()));
  }

  public void propertyChange(final PropertyChangeEvent event) {
    if (event.getSource() == this.dataObject) {
      this.valueField.setText(Integer.toString(this.dataObject.getAge()));
    }
  }
}
```

In this example, the GUI class gets a `SomeDataClass` object instance to manage at construction. However, it can also replace this instance with a different one. Furthermore, if someone else changes the data object, the GUI wants to be informed of that change so it can update its controls to reflect current data. Therefore, it registers itself as a property change listener with the data object to get these events.

This code, which is fairly typical in GUI systems, has a glaring problem. `SomeDataClass` and `SomeGUIPanel` both hold onto a reference to each other and refuse to let go. The flow of the resulting program works like the following:

1. The program starts up, and data objects are initialized.
2. The `SomeGUIPanel` object is created inside a `JFrame` window and is passed one of many data objects in the program, which we'll call data object A.
3. A user can now use the GUI panel.
4. While the user is working, he presses a button in the frame window that calls `changeObject()` on the GUI panel with a new object, data object B, to manage.
5. The user closes the GUI panel, and the program continues.

Voila! You now have a memory leak. Congratulations!

At the end of the process, both data objects A and B are still holding onto the panel in their listener lists. Therefore, the GUI panel cannot be garbage collected by the virtual machine. Consequently, neither can any of its buttons, layout managers, string variables, and so on. Furthermore, since the responsibility for removing listeners from the data object does not rest with the data object itself, the memory will never be released. This Java memory leak does not result from a lost pointer, but because circular references pin objects in memory.

Yes, this is a bug, and one that is very difficult to find. Yes, the programmer should have had the panel remove itself as a listener prior to changing objects or closing. Raise your hand if you've never written a bug. I wouldn't expect any honest software engineer to have his hand up. Professional Java code is plagued by these problems—in fact, it is plagued by them so much that there are several vendors that make software that helps you locate these kinds of errors (and they make a lot of money doing so).

Performance-tuning software can help you find bugs such as this, but it can take time (and cost money). To make the situation worse, you must know how to use the profiler, and what should be in memory (and when). To find a memory leak like this, you will have to search through the program, method by method, and examine the contents of the memory at each step to see whether everything is in place. If this sounds like a scary proposition, your instincts are dead accurate. Single-line problems such as this can consume weeks of resources and man-hours.

By using special techniques with references, you can prevent this problem before it starts. No, don't throw away that profiler; it's still quite useful. However, the less work you have to do with it, the faster you can place new features and requirements in a solid system. Your quest to get things right the first time will get a massive boost from coding with the `java.lang.ref` package.

Java Reference Concepts

Before you turn your attention to solving memory leak problems, it is important that you understand how Java references work. There are four different types of references in Java: strong, weak, soft, and phantom.

Strong References

Strong references are the mainstay of the Java world. As I look at the stacks and stacks of Java books on my desk, I can't find one code sample that uses anything other than strong references.

A *strong reference* is a reference type that pins objects in the memory so that the objects can't be garbage collected. Strong references are used whenever an assignment is made to a normal variable. For example, consider the following code:

```
String name = "Robert Simmons";
Set nameSet = new HashSet( );
set.add(name);
```

This code creates three different strong references. The reference `name` points to the memory location holding the contents of the immutable `String` object. The reference nameSet holds the memory location of the newly created Set. Finally, another strong reference to the same object that name points to is inside the HashSet. This third reference was created when the name was passed to the add( ) method.

In every virtual machine, there is a set of references called the *root set*, which is created and maintained by the virtual machine. From the root set, each of the objects in the virtual machine is referenced. When you create a main function in your program, all of the objects declared in this method are attached to the root set. Consequently, each of the objects declared in these objects are attached to the root set indirectly.

Whenever a path of strong references cannot be drawn from the root set to an object, the object is marked for garbage collection and is removed on the next pass. This process recurses throughout the network until all garbage-collectible references are gone. To make this a little easier to understand, consider the typical Java program shown in Figure 11-1.

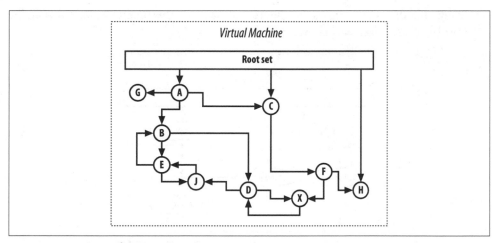

Figure 11-1. Strong-reference structure in a typical program

In this diagram, all of the objects can be traced with strong references to the root set. For example, the root set has a reference to object A, which in turn has a reference to object G, and so on. In this state, the garbage collector would have nothing to do. If you set the reference from A to B as null, you get the result shown in Figure 11-2.

When A drops its reference to B, the virtual machine checks to see whether it can trace a path from the root set to the object through strong references. It discovers that there is still a path. The path C → F → X → D → J → E → B satisfies the requirement. This type of construct is quite common in Java applications. You can think of E, J, and X as data objects with appropriate listener callbacks to the objects that are listening to them. In this structure, nothing is garbage collected.

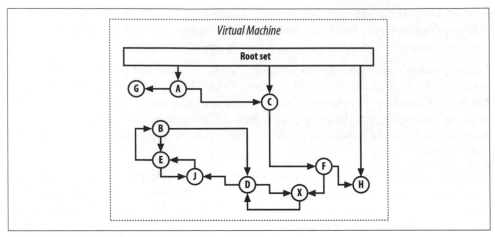

Figure 11-2. Strong references after reference deletion

To bring this discussion from the theoretical back to the practical, let's revisit the GUI problem discussed earlier. See Figure 11-3.

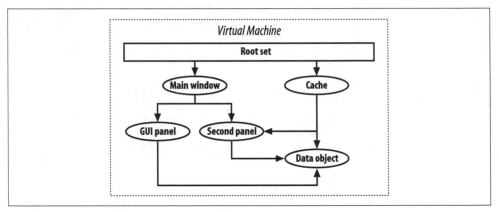

Figure 11-3. Strong references in a GUI application

Now it should be a bit clearer why the memory leak occurs. The data object has a list of registered property change listeners that are strong references. The data object is not responsible for adding or removing listeners from this list. The listeners themselves must do this through the addPropertyChangeListener and removePropertyChangeListener methods.

The second panel is still pinned in memory by the listener reference from the data object. The data object is pinned by the cache and GUI panel. Now, any memory associated with the second panel is not available. All of the buttons, menus, and other data objects it was holding are pinned in memory with it. The end result is a cascade that will increase your program's memory consumption throughout the execution until you restart it—all because of one line of missing code, which will be a pain to find in a large application.

You *can* solve the above problem with strong references—just don't forget anything. If you make even one tiny mistake in your code, or if you forget to remove just one listener, you could strand huge amounts of objects in memory. You would have to choose between a very long session with your profiler or explaining to your network administrators why every computer in the company needs to have a gigabyte of memory just for your application.

Weak References

A *weak reference* does not pin an object in memory. When an object is no longer referred to with any strong references and has only weak references remaining, it is eligible for garbage collection. In Figure 11-4, weak references end with a double empty arrow, and strong references end with a single solid arrow.

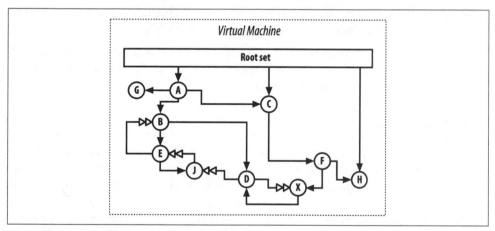

Figure 11-4. Weak references in an application

Note that there are many weak references breaking up those dangerous, circular, strong-reference patterns. This time, when A drops its reference to B, the result is the structure shown in Figure 11-5.

Deleting the reference from A to B causes B, E, and J to be garbage collected. When the strong reference from A to B is dropped, the virtual machine tries to find a strong-reference path from the root set to B, but it can't. The old path of C → F → X → D → J → E → B is blocked between D and J because the reference from D to J is a weak reference. The circularity is broken, and the objects without paths are garbage collected. Similarly, if you dropped the X-to-D reference, D and X would both be garbage collected.

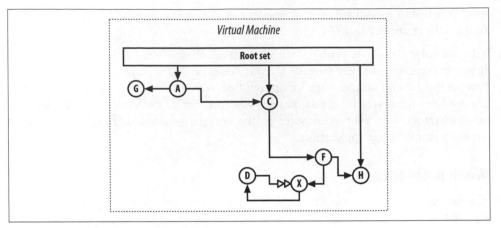

Figure 11-5. Weak references after deletion

By strategically distributing weak references in your program, you can eliminate circularity and thus remove memory leaks. Later in this chapter, we will discuss when to use weak references and when to use strong references.

Now you can make sure that an object is garbage collected whenever you remove references. This is useful. However, if you want only to clean out references when free heap memory is low, you need to use soft references.

Soft References

Soft references are similar to weak references except they are, theoretically, cleared only when the memory on the heap is low. Therefore, prior to allocating another heap block, the virtual machine attempts to clear memory by dropping all the weak references. If this still isn't enough for the requested new allocation, the virtual machine will clear soft references. So using a soft reference is a way of telling the virtual machine, "If you really need that memory, you can take that object, but don't do it unless you really need it."

Unfortunately, soft references are not implemented correctly on many virtual machines. Most virtual machines simply treat soft references like weak references; regardless of whether memory is needed, they wipe out these objects on a garbage-collection pass. You should consult the documentation for your virtual machine to see how it implements soft references.

Soft references are very useful for tools such as cache managers (at least when they are working correctly). As a non-Java example, consider your Internet browser. To speed up the loading of files, it caches the various files and images in your computer. It is convenient if these objects are available in the cache, but this is not necessary. If an object isn't in the cache, the browser would fetch the document from the Internet. This is a good example of how a soft reference would be used. Later in this chapter, we will examine an example of how to take advantage of soft references in your programs.

Phantom References

Phantom references are completely different from weak or soft references. They are references to data that has *already* been garbage collected. The fact that there can be references to data that has already been garbage collected may seem a bit counterintuitive. However, you don't access the object itself, only a reference to the object. Therefore, you cannot use a phantom reference to call methods or access fields of the object; it simply notifies you that the object has been garbage collected.

Phantom references are useful if you need to do some cleanup in your application. Suppose you have a class that is watching the contents of a container but doesn't want to interfere with the objects in the container; its job is to count the number of objects deleted from the container. You want a reference to the object when it is completely gone so you can modify your count. Phantom references do the job. Since they refer only to objects that are completely dead, you can be sure your count is accurate.

References and Referents

To implement weak references, the virtual machine uses a two-layered approach, as shown in Figure 11-6.

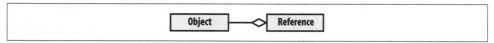

Figure 11-6. UML diagram of a reference structure

The object that is the target of the weak, soft, or phantom reference is known as the referent. The reference object itself is known as the reference. Furthermore, the referent does not know anything about the reference object.

Any object in the virtual machine can be a referent, but only the classes in the java.lang.ref package can be references. This is because the reference classes are tightly integrated with the garbage collector. You can extend the references to add more information, but you cannot create new kinds of references. We will discuss the actual implementation of the reference classes later in this chapter.

Reference Queues

A reference queue is used to notify the reference user of the various events that occur when objects in memory are altered. A programmer can use these reference queues to be notified when an object is marked for garbage collection or when it is garbage collected. With reference queues, you communicate with the virtual machine about memory management and garbage collection. References do not actually appear in the reference queue until the virtual machine decides to garbage collect the object, or the object is forcibly queued by a method call.

For example, if there is a weak reference to an object, and the object is garbage collected, the reference will appear in the queue. You can then act on that reference to remove the information from your collections. For this to work, you have to create a reference queue and give the reference to the reference queue when the weak reference is created. This allows the reference to register itself with the queue. Later, we will look at an example of how to use reference queues.

The Garbage-Collection Process

Garbage collection is one of the core processes of Java. However, it is not as simple as it may appear at first. The requirements of weak references, soft references, and reference queues complicate the process. To make garbage collection a bit clearer, let's examine the UML activity diagram in Figure 11-7.

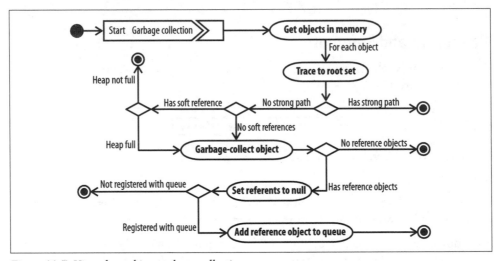

Figure 11-7. Virtual-machine garbage collection

This diagram shows all of the steps that are taken when a reference to an object is removed from the virtual machine. This happens whenever the user explicitly sets a variable to null, overwrites a reference variable to point to another object, or causes the class holding the reference variable to go out of scope. For each reference that the virtual machine has, it executes this process during its garbage-collection cycle.

First, the virtual machine tries to trace a path from the root set to the object. If it finds a path, no garbage collection takes place. If it doesn't find a path, the virtual machine removes the referenced object from memory. Next, the virtual machine determines whether there are reference objects pointing to the removed reference, including weak, soft, and phantom references. If there are reference objects, the virtual machine determines whether they are soft references. If so, it does a memory check. If the memory check indicates that there is no free memory or that the reference is a weak or phantom reference, the referent in the reference is set to null. Finally, if the reference objects are registered with a queue, the reference is added to the queue.

Note that this process happens only during garbage collection. Because of this, it appears that a second thread silently modifies the objects, which in fact does occur. Now it's time to put this thread to work in your application.

The Java Reference Classes

Now that you understand the concepts, let's reconsider the code. All of the reference types mentioned in the previous section appear in the java.lang.ref package.

Reference Classes

The majority of the java.lang.ref package is comprised of reference classes. These classes are the implementation of the actual references covered in the previous section, with one exception. There is no StrongReference class. Since a strong reference is a normal Java variable, there is no need for extra implementation. However, the other types of references all descend from the base class Reference.

java.lang.ref.Reference

The Reference class is an abstract class that defines the functionality of the reference classes. The implementation classes—WeakReference, SoftReference, and PhantomReference—implement the functionality of the base class. All of these classes have four methods that they inherit from Reference:

clear( )

> Clears the referent, which causes the referent in this reference object to be set to null without affecting the object itself. I have never found a use for this method, since there is no way to reset the referent after it has been cleared.

enqueue( )

> Registers a reference with a ReferenceQueue. This allows the user to receive updates about the status of the object in memory. A reference will be placed in a reference queue at garbage-collection time only if it was registered with that queue. If it succeeds in registering the reference, the method will return true; otherwise, it will return false. Keep in mind that a reference can be registered only with one queue at a time, and if you call this method on a reference that is already

registered with a queue, the object will be unregistered from the previous queue. If you call enqueue( ) with a null argument, you will unregister the object.

isEnqueued( )

Tests to see whether the reference has been queued.

get( )

Returns a strong reference to the referent object to the user. If you execute this after the reference has been queued or the garbage collection has been completed, null will always be returned.

There is no way to set the referent object via a method call. In fact, the referent can be set only when the reference object is constructed. At that time, you can also register the reference with a queue. Construct a reference object with the following code:

```
Object obj = new Object( );
WeakReference ref = new WeakReference(obj);
```

This code will create a new weak reference to the object obj. This reference won't be registered with any queue at creation time, so you won't be able to know when the object is garbage collected. You can always register it with a new queue later by calling the enqueue( ) method.

 I will show why you may want to create a reference without queueing it in the section "Practical Applications."

Alternatively, you could construct the reference, as in the following code:

```
ReferenceQueue clearedObjects = new ReferenceQueue( );
SoftReference ref2 = new SoftReference(obj, clearedObjects);
```

This code will create a new reference to obj and simultaneously queue it in the given queue.

Note that you can create multiple reference objects of multiple types to the same referent. In this case, there is a weak reference and a soft reference to the same object. In garbage collection, the strong reference takes precedence. Therefore, if all strong references to obj are gone, the soft reference will hold the obj in memory until the heap needs more memory.

java.lang.ref.WeakReference

This class implements the weak-reference paradigm. All of its methods, and even its code, are identical to Reference. The code inside the reference class does all of the work; this class merely provides a façade to the abstract class.

java.lang.ref.SoftReference

This class implements the soft-reference paradigm. It allows the base class to keep the referents in memory until the memory is low. To do this, the garbage collector timestamps the object so that the oldest soft references are purged first. Of course, this implementation is all under-the-hood. On the outside, there is no difference between this class and a WeakReference.

java.lang.ref.PhantomReference

This class implements the phantom-reference paradigm. Like SoftReference, the implementation of this is all under the hood. However, the phantom reference's get() method will always return null. Once you create this type of reference, you are hinting to the garbage collector to tell you when it is completely dead. For this to happen, there must be no way to retrieve a strong reference.

Reference Queues

The java.lang.ref.ReferenceQueue class implements reference queues, which are repositories for garbage-collection events. A reference queue consists of the following methods:

poll()
> This checks the reference queue to see whether there are any reference objects in the queue. If it finds one, it returns the first reference in the queue. This reference is left on the queue.

remove()
> This removes the first reference on the queue and returns it to the caller. If there are no references on the queue, it returns null.

remove(long timeout)
> This performs the same job as the remove() method, but it will wait up to the specified number of milliseconds for a reference object to arrive in the queue before returning null or a reference.

Its important not to forget that the reference queue is modified by the garbage collector directly. Therefore, it is impossible to determine when the references will arrive in the queue. If you destroy all strong references to an object, the related Reference object may not arrive in the queue until much later. Since garbage collection runs periodically, your reference won't be queued until the next garbage-collection pass. If you want to ensure that the reference arrives quickly, use remove(long) and set the timeout as a value that is longer than the duration of each garbage-collection pass. Consult your virtual-machine documentation for more information.

Practical Applications

In the Online Only Bank data model, the JavaBeans mechanism was employed to allow users of the data model to register for property change events. This gives you a great deal of functionality in these classes, but it also introduces the potential memory leak discussed earlier. Your data model objects will be referred to by various parts of the program that will then register themselves as listeners for property change events, creating a cycle of strong-reference dependencies.

A Weak Collection

Ideally, you should be able to alter your code so that the objects in the data model register their property change listeners in a nonbinding way. To do this, you need to create a different kind of collection in which to store your listeners—a collection based on weak references.

To store your listeners, create a class called WeakHashSet. If you look in the JDK source code for HashSet, you will see that it is implemented by using the keys in the HashMap class. You implement WeakHashSet in a similar way, using the java.lang.util.WeakHashMap class as the backing store for the WeakHashSet contents. The keys in WeakHashMap are stored in weak references instead of in strong references, so this class will fit your needs nicely.

 The fact that the class WeakHashSet isn't in the JDK already is something of a mystery. Sun implemented the WeakHashMap class but failed to finish the job with the WeakHashSet.

I won't bore you with all of the implementation details, since most of them are fairly trivial. If you want to read the whole source, you can find it in the oreilly.hcj.references package. However, there are some noteworthy aspects of your new WeakHashSet class. Consider this source snippet:

```
public class WeakHashSet extends AbstractSet implements Set {

  private static final Object DUMMY = new String("DUMMY");  // $NON-NLS-1$
  WeakHashMap backingStore = new WeakHashMap( );


  public boolean add(final Object o) {
    if (o == null) {
      throw new NullPointerException( );
    }
    return backingStore.put(o, DUMMY) == null;
  }
}
```

Items were placed in the backing store WeakHashMap by using a dummy object for the value. When you place this object into the backing store, the WeakHashMap class creates a new WeakReference object to o, and this reference is stored as the key.

Also note that unlike the HashSet class, you do not allow null in WeakHashSet. Since your set is meant to store only references to objects, there is no point in making a reference to null. Therefore, you disallow it.

The next point of interest in the WeakHashSet class is the operation of the set iterator. Fortunately, the WeakHashMap does most of the work:

```
public Iterator iterator( ) {
  return backingStore.keySet().iterator( );
}
```

Although this iterator seems normal, it's not. Normally, you expect to be able to iterate over the contents of a set, and to have that set be fixed for the duration of the iteration. For example, if you iterate over a HashSet, and during the iteration, call add( ), you will get a ConcurrentModificationException. However, when using WeakHashSet, you must remember that the contents of the set can change from second to second. Since the garbage collector is working in the background to remove objects, there is always a second thread that silently modifies the contents. As you iterate through the set, the object you encountered three iterations ago could have been garbage collected and removed from the set before the fourth iteration. Essentially, concurrent modifications are the rule rather than the exception.

 The WeakHashSet iterator will give you back strong references to the objects in the collection. However, you shouldn't store the actual reference object with the intention of using the referent later. If you store only the reference, the referent could be garbage collected between the time you store it and the time you actually try to use it.

Testing WeakHashSet

Since you will use the WeakHashSet class over and over again, it would be a good idea to test the class to make sure it performs its job properly. Conveniently, testing WeakHashSet will also give you the chance to explore ReferenceQueues. However, you first have to do a bit of setup work on your unit test.

To test the new WeakHashSet class, take advantage of the JUnit testing framework. Place all of your test cases in a subpackage of oreilly.hcj.references called _test. This is a good strategy for sorting test cases because it allows you to keep your tests with the code that is being tested. Also, the underscore prefix for testing packages separates them from nontesting packages, making it easy to filter the testing packages out of production builds.

The majority of the test, found in oreilly.hcj.references._test, is fairly standard JUnit test code. The testWeakRefCleanup method contains the fancy work. However, before you get to the testing method, you need to create some preliminary test objects. This is done in the static initialization code:

```
package oreilly.hcj.references._test;
public class TestWeakHashSet extends TestCase {
  private static final String A = new String("Object A");
  private static final String B = new String("Object B");
  private static final String C = new String("Object C");
  private static final String D = new String("Object D");
  private static final String E = new String("Object E");
  private static final String F = new String("Object F");
  private static final String G = new String("Object G");

  private static final Set TEST_SET;

  static {
    TEST_SET = new HashSet();
    TEST_SET.add(A);
    TEST_SET.add(B);
    TEST_SET.add(C);
    TEST_SET.add(D);
    TEST_SET.add(E);
    TEST_SET.add(F);
    TEST_SET.add(G);
  }
```

To prepare the test, create a master set of test objects that contain String objects. This will serve as your control group; the objects should never be removed from the set because their strong references will never be dropped. Later, you will use this set to compare the contents of the WeakHashSet and to make sure that these objects are still in the set no matter what you do to other parts of the set. Once this setup is complete, you can focus on the testWeakRefCleanup method.

The testWeakRefCleanup method is designed to test the weak-reference part of the set. Its purpose is to prove that objects will be removed if they go out of scope. To examine how this test works, we will examine each phase of the method. The setup phase is shown here:

```
public void testWeakRefCleanup() {
  try {
    String x = new String("Object x");
    String y = new String("Object y");
    String z = new String("Object z");
    ReferenceQueue queue = new ReferenceQueue();
    WeakReference refx = new WeakReference(x, queue);
    WeakReference refy = new WeakReference(y, queue);
    WeakReference refz = new WeakReference(z, queue);
    // *** add everything to the WeakHashSet
    WeakHashSet whs = new WeakHashSet();
    whs.addAll(TEST_SET);
    whs.add(x);
    whs.add(y);
    whs.add(z);
```

In this part of the test method, you instantiate several new objects with strong references (x, y, and z) to those objects. You then create a new WeakHashSet and weak references (refx, refy, and refz) to x, y, and z. While creating the weak references, you register them with a new ReferenceQueue. This queue will tell you when the objects are garbage collected by placing the reference object in the queue.

 The referent of a Reference object in a Reference queue will always be null because the object has already been garbage collected by the virtual machine before it is placed in the queue.

Finally, you add your static test set and all of the strong objects to the WeakHashSet. This causes the WeakHashSet to create internal weak references to these objects. Since there can be multiple weak references to the same object, this process will work properly.

You are finally ready to begin testing the class. Start by making sure that everything is actually in the set:

```
// *** validate everything in the WeakHashSet
assertEquals(CONTAINS_ALL, true, whs.containsAll(TEST_SET));
assertEquals(CONTAINS, true, whs.contains(x));
assertEquals(CONTAINS, true, whs.contains(y));
assertEquals(CONTAINS, true, whs.contains(z));
```

Now it's time to delete strong references. Throughout the test, you will use the reference queue (queue), which will tell you when an object is garbage collected. Once you destroy a strong reference to an object, it should vanish from the set and appear in the reference queue. The following code shows how this is done:

```
// *** nuke x from the JVM.
x = null;
System.gc();
while (queue.remove(1000) != null) {
}
```

x is set equal to null. This will break x's path to the root set and leave it connected by weak references only. It will then be garbage collected and will appear in the queue. Use a timeout of 1 second (1,000 milliseconds) to make sure that the garbage collector has a chance to complete its run before you poll the queue. Check the set to make sure that x is actually gone:

```
// *** make sure x isn't in the set anymore but all others are.
assertEquals(CONTAINS_ALL, true, whs.containsAll(TEST_SET));
assertEquals(CONTAINS, true, whs.contains(y));
assertEquals(CONTAINS, true, whs.contains(z));
assertEquals(SIZE, (TEST_SET.size() + 2), whs.size());
```

You can be sure that x is gone because y, z, and the TEST_SET are still in the WeakHashSet, and the set is only the size of TEST_SET + 2. You can make this determination because there can be no duplicates in a set, and you know that y and z are still in the set.

The rest of the method continues to create objects, dropping them into the set and then removing their strong references and waiting for them to be collected. Here is the creation of another strong reference to y and the destruction of z:

```
// *** build a double link, p, to y and nuke z.
String p = y;
z = null;
System.gc();
while (queue.remove(1000) != null) {
}
// *** make sure x, and z aren't in the set anymore but all others are.
assertEquals(CONTAINS_ALL, true, whs.containsAll(TEST_SET));
assertEquals(CONTAINS, true, whs.contains(y));
assertEquals(SIZE, (TEST_SET.size() + 1), whs.size());
```

This test succeeds because there are no more strong references to z. Now remove one of the strong references to y but not the other one. You can assume that y is still in the set.

```
// *** nuke y but leave p intact.
y = null;
System.gc();
while (queue.remove(1000) != null) {
}

// *** y should still be in the set as p.
assertEquals(CONTAINS_ALL, true, whs.containsAll(TEST_SET));
assertEquals(CONTAINS, true, whs.contains(p));
assertEquals(SIZE, (TEST_SET.size() + 1), whs.size());
```

Finally, null the final strong reference to y and make sure that it is removed from the method, then check the results:

```
// *** finally nuke p.
p = null;
System.gc();
while (queue.remove(1000) != null) {
}

// *** y should still be in the set as p.
assertEquals(CONTAINS_ALL, true, whs.containsAll(TEST_SET));
assertEquals(SIZE, (TEST_SET.size()), whs.size());
} catch (Exception ex) {
LOGGER.error(ex.getMessage(), ex);
fail(ex.getMessage());
}
}
```

Throughout the test, the TEST_SET elements are never removed because the test class always holds onto them with strong references. However, it has been shown that the WeakHashSet class does manage the references properly.

A Weak Listener

Now that you have a tested collection that doesn't hold objects in memory, you can use it to break the loop of strong references. Instead of holding the listeners in a normal set, put them in WeakHashSet. To do this, you will have to rewrite the property change support class and invent your own support class that does the same job with weak listeners. The code for PropertyChangeSupport is in the oreilly.hcj.references package.

This PropertyChangeSupport class implements the identical interface as the stock java.beans.PropertyChangeSupport class except that it uses weak references to store the listeners. It allows the same firing of events that the original JDK class does without pinning the listeners in memory. If one of the listeners decides to go away, the property change support class will simply note this fact and move on.

The class is implemented using a regular HashMap to store the listeners. The keys in the HashMap (listenerMap) are the named properties that the listener is interested in. The values in the HashMap are instances of WeakHashSet. This allows the listener to register to receive events on single properties. For listeners that want to receive events on all properties of the class, an ALL_PROPERTIES key is used to store the set. To avoid conflicting keys in your map, the value of the ALL_PROPERTIES key is a string that would be illegal to use as a property name:

```
package oreilly.hcj.references;
public class PropertyChangeSupport {
  private static final String ALL_PROPERTIES = "**GENERAL**";
```

The declaration of the constructor initializes the HashMap with the ALL_PROPERTIES key and the keys for the other properties in the class:

```
public PropertyChangeSupport(final Object producer) {
  try {
    final BeanInfo info = Introspector.getBeanInfo(producer.getClass());
    final PropertyDescriptor[] props = info.getPropertyDescriptors();
    for (int idx = 0; idx < props.length; idx++) {
      listenerMap.put(props[idx].getName(), new WeakHashSet());
    }
    listenerMap.put(ALL_PROPERTIES, new WeakHashSet());
    this.producer = producer;
  } catch (IntrospectionException ex) {
    throw new RuntimeException(ex);
  }
}
```

Reflection and the weak hash set are used in your constructor. To support named property listeners, create a HashMap of WeakHashSet objects. In addition to having one for each property of the object, add an extra object with the DUMMY key to the listeners of all properties. The end result is that the mirror.event.PropertyChangeSupport class is interchangeable with Java's java.beans.PropertyChangeSupport class. Let's interchange them in MutableObject. To do this, simply change one line:

```
import java.beans.PropertyChangeSupport;
public abstract class MutableObject implements Serializable {
  // ...same as before!!
}
```

becomes:

```
import oreilly.hcj.references.PropertyChangeSupport;
public abstract class MutableObject implements Serializable {
  // ...same as before!!
}
```

Using this class, break the loop of strong references. The GUI panel will now hold onto your data objects with strong references. However, the data objects will hold onto the GUI panels with weak references. Figure 11-8 shows how the resulting structure looks in a UML diagram.

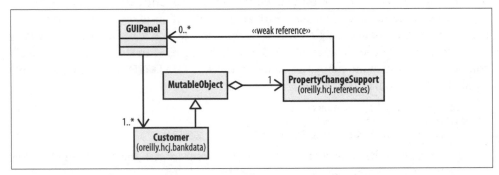

Figure 11-8. Using the PropertyChangeSupport object

Since the PropertyChangeSupport object holds onto the GUI panel with a weak reference, there is no loop of strong references such as those in Figure 11-3. If the panel removes itself from the PropertyChangeSupport, that is fine with the data object. If it forgets to remove itself, that is also fine because the weak reference won't hold the panel in memory, and the panel will be removed passively. The potential for memory leaks is zero. Now, no matter what happens, when the GUI panel goes out of scope, everything is released.

When to Use References

Now that you have learned how to create a weak listener, you can create weak key listeners, weak action listeners, and so on. In fact, the more strong-reference loops you can eliminate in your reference tree, the better your code will be. However, you should be careful. Like any other powerful tool, weak references can be dangerous if used improperly. Therefore, it is important to know when to use them and when not to. To make this decision, you need to know which stereotype the reference is. References from an object can be classified into one of four stereotypes:

Active references

> These need other objects to exist for them to do their job. For example, your GUI panel needs the data object before it can present it. If the data object suddenly went out of scope, the GUI wouldn't be able to display or modify its data. Active references should always be strong references.

Passive references

> These are indifferent to the presence of other objects. For example, the data objects are passive to the GUI. If the GUI panel exists, then the data object will do it the courtesy of informing it of its changes. However, the data object doesn't need the GUI object to do its job. Passive references should be weak references.

Convenience references

> These exist for the user's convenience but are not necessarily required. For example, in creating data cache management software such as that used by database persistence managers, the cache is designed to return the objects if they are in the cache and fetch them if they aren't. In this case, keeping the objects in memory is desirable because doing so lowers the number of expensive database fetches that the software has to do. However, it isn't required that these objects remain in the cache if they are not being used. Convenience references should be soft references.

Dead references

> With these, the object needs to be informed after it is cleaned up. For example, a tool that needs to keep track of the number of objects removed from the virtual machine doesn't particularly care about the objects until they are dead. Dead references should be phantom references.

You can create a wide variety of tools using these references. Passive listeners in objects are only the start of the story. References can be used to implement cache managers that centralize storage of data in GUIs and in many other applications. They are one of the gateways to truly advanced Java programming.

Tiger: JDK 1.5

A major source of debate in the Java community is whether the new release of the JDK, called "Tiger," should instead be called JDK 2.0. In many ways, Tiger represents a fundamental improvement in the Java language that hasn't been seen since the emergence of the Java Foundation Classes (JFC).

In addition to offering bug fixes and new classes, Tiger offers several new language features and an implementation of parameterized types called generics. The concept of generics brings Java collections into the world of strong typing and is one of the most conspicuous components missing from JDK 1.4. Generics will be covered later in the chapter; first, we will tackle the new language features.

Before you read on, note that the information presented in this chapter is in a state of flux. As of this writing, the information is current. However, the process of defining Tiger is still ongoing, and updates or changes may have been implemented between the writing and publication of this book.

New Language Features

Tiger has several new language features designed to eradicate some of Java's annoyances. Many of these features are borrowed from other languages such as Python or Perl, so if you have experience with these languages, these new features should be familiar to you. However, there are idiosyncrasies of these features that Python and Perl users may not be familiar with.

For Each

One useful feature of Tiger is the new for-each syntax. The purpose of this syntax is to make it easier to iterate through collections and arrays. For example, consider the following JDK 1.4 code:

```
package oreilly.hcj.tiger.
public class ForEach {
```

```
        public final static String[] importantPeople = new String[] {
                "Robert", "Jim", "Sacir", "Aida", "Alma",
                "Amila", "Selma", "Nefisa", "Mustafa",
                "Paul", "Debbie", "Marco", "Bettina", "Ana",
                "Maria" };

        public static void someMethod(final String prefix) {
            for (int idx = 0; idx < importantPeople.length; idx++) {
                if (importantPeople[idx].startsWith(prefix)) {
                    System.out.print(importantPeople[idx] + " ");
                }
            }
            System.out.println( );
        }
    }
```

Although this code works fine, the for statement is fairly wordy, which makes it annoying to type if it is used hundreds of times in an application. The new for-each feature makes this code much simpler:

```
package oreilly.hcj.tiger.
public class ForEach {
    public static void someTigerMethod(final String prefix) {
        for (String person: importantPeople) {
            if (person.startsWith(prefix)) {
                System.out.print(person + " ");
            }
        }
        System.out.println( );
    }
}
```

 If you are wondering why Sun didn't create a new keyword named foreach for the implementation of the for-each functionality, you are not alone. The official explanation from Sun is that they didn't do this because they didn't want to break the code of those who used foreach as an identifier.

You should read this code as "for each string importantPeople, assign it to the variable person and do the following code."

The first statement in the for-each loop must be an object initialization statement that specifies the variable that will be used to store the contents of the iteration. If you try to use the wrong type for the iteration variable, the compiler will give an error on the for line. For example, if you substituted Integer for String in the previous example, you would get the following errors at compile time:

```
>c:\j2sdk1.5.0\bin\javac -source 1.5 javac *.java
ForEach.java:44: incompatible types
found   : java.lang.String
required: java.lang.Integer
                for (Integer person: importantPeople) {
                ^
```

```
ForEach.java:45: cannot find symbol
symbol  : method startsWith(java.lang.String)
location: class java.lang.Integer
                    if (person.startsWith(prefix)) {
```

The second statement in the for-each loop must be an evaluation that evaluates to an array or an instance of the new interface java.lang.Iterable. Since the collection classes in the new JDK have been updated to implement this interface, you can use this syntax to iterate through them as well. The following example shows the old way of iterating through collections:

```java
public class ForEach {
  public static void someCollectionMethod(final String prefix) {
    List people = Arrays.asList(importantPeople);
    Iterator iter = people.iterator();
    for (String person = (String)iter.next(); iter.hasNext();
        person = (String)iter.next()) {
      if (person.startsWith(prefix)) {
        System.out.print(person + " ");
      }
    }
    System.out.println();
  }
}
```

Compare this to the new version using a for-each loop:

```java
public class ForEach {
  public static void someTigerCollectionMethod(final String prefix) {
    List<String> people = Arrays.asList(importantPeople);
    for (String person: people) {
      if (person.startsWith(prefix)) {
        System.out.print(person + " ");
      }
    }
    System.out.println();
  }
}
```

The second code sample is much more concise and easier to read than the first; the improved readability translates into easier debugging and maintenance.

Autoboxing with Variables

One of the persistent annoyances in Java is the frequent need to cast to other types:

```java
Integer x = new Integer(25);
Number y = (Number)x;
```

In this code, the casting between the types is superfluous. Since an Integer is a subclass of Number, you should be able to just assign y to x without casting. Because this is a deficiency that needlessly bloats code, the concepts of autoboxing and autounboxing have been added to the language.

 The boxing and unboxing features are broken in the prototype implementation at the time of this writing, so you may not be able to use them until Sun releases a new prototype or the beta. However, Sun has announced that a new prototype is on the way; furthermore, the beta of Tiger may come out before this book hits the shelves.

Autoboxing is the process of converting a type to a higher-order type, while *autounboxing* is the inverse of this process. Autounboxing is shown in the following code:

```
Integer x = new Integer(5);
int y = x;
```

In JDK 1.4 and below, this would not compile and give an "incompatible types" error. However, in Tiger, the compiler knows that it can convert the wrapper Integer type to an int and does so automatically. Similarly, you can go the other direction and autobox your int:

```
int x = 5;
Integer y = x;
```

This functionality avoids the interminable casting and intValue( ) calls that must be done if you want to use mathematics with wrapper types. This technique also works for all other primitive types in the JDK. However, one thing you cannot do is autounbox null:

```
Integer x = null;
int y = x; // <= Error
```

In this code, you attempted to autounbox null into a primitive type. If this error can be caught at compile time, the compiler will complain that you can't stuff a null into a primitive. However, sometimes this problem can't be resolved by the compiler at compile time, as in the following code:

```
public void someMehtod(final Integer x) {
    int y = x;
    // ...other code
}
```

In this case, the compiler doesn't know what the user of this method will pass at compile time, so it can't check the assignment. If the user sends null in the parameter x at runtime, the virtual machine will throw a NullPointerException to indicate the erroneous autounboxing attempt. Although you should check your methods for null in this case, not even the check for null would have altered the fact that the autounboxing attempt can't be checked at compile time.

Implicit casting

Primitives are not the only types to benefit from autoboxing and autounboxing. Constructed classes can also benefit:

```
String str = new String();
Object obj = str;
String str2 = obj;
```

In this code, the casts of type are implicit; instead of having to manually type in the casts, the compiler will do it for you. You can use this scheme to implement implicit type conversion. Furthermore, if it is possible to check for a legal conversion at compile time, the compiler will check and return errors on any illegal conversions. If the legality of the cast cannot be determined at compile time, then an illegal conversion would result in a `ClassCastException` at runtime. The following code shows an example of both in action:

```
public class SomeClass {
  public void someMethod(final Object obj) {
    String str = obj;  // <== can't be resolved at compile time because
                       //     user could pass you anything.
    Object obj2 = str; // <== resolved at compile time and OK.
    Integer x = 5;     // <== resolved at compile time and OK.
  }
}
```

Note that autoboxing and autounboxing don't let you convert a reference to a different type. Reference conversions must be supertype to subtype or vice versa; this complies with RTTI in Java. Similarly, you can't convert an array of one reference type to an array of another reference type unless the components of the array have a subtype/supertype relationship:

```
Integer[] values = new Integer[1];
Number[] nums = values;  // <== Legal
String[] strs = values;  // <== Illegal
```

Since there is a conversion between `Integer` and `Number`, the first cast works fine. The second one doesn't work because `String` and `Integer` don't share a supertype/subtype relationship.

In addition to manipulating variables, you can use the autoboxing mechanism for method calls:

```
public class SomeClass {
  public void someMethod(final Object obj) {
    // ...code
  }

  public void someMethod(final String obj) {
    // ...code
  }
```

```
public void someMethod(final Integer obj) {
  // ...code
}

public final static void main(final String[] args) {
  someMethod(5); // <== 1st:calls someMethod(Integer)
  someMethod("hello"); // <== 2nd:calls someMethod(String);
  someMethod(new Boolean(false)); // <== 4th: calls someMethod(Object);
}
}
```

The first two calls in the main method are easy to understand. In the third example, the Boolean is unboxed to Object and someMethod(Object) is called. This is a potential trap waiting to happen. The programmer of this class may not have intended to process Boolean arguments in someMethod(Object). The lesson to be learned here is that when defining methods using Tiger, you should try to be as specific as possible in your method signatures.

The problem of calling a method that takes Object accidentally is one of the biggest dangers of porting code from JDK 1.4 and below to Tiger. When you port your code in the future, make sure you watch out for this bug and use assertions liberally.

When it comes to autoboxing interfaces, there are a couple of more rules to learn. You can't autounbox a class to an interface type unless the class actually implements that interface, nor can you convert an interface type to another type that implements a method in the interface that has the same signature but a different return type:

```
interface ISomeInterface{
  public void doSomething( );
}

interface ISomeOtherInterface( ) {
  public int doSomething( );
}

public void someMethod(final ISomeInterface obj) {
  IsomeOtherInterface someObj = obj; // <== forbidden
}
```

 Remember that the signature of a method is composed of only its name and parameter types and does *not* include the return type.

In this example, both interfaces implement the method doSomething( ), but one implements it to return void and the other implements it to return an int. This means that you can't autounbox one to the other because both interfaces could never be implemented in the same class since every method in a class must have a unique signature.

It's unclear at this time why autounboxing to disparate interface types is allowed at all. I really can't see any potential uses for it. The rule should be simply that you can't autounbox anything to anything if the autoboxing doesn't comply with the rules of RTTI.

You can autounbox an array to the interfaces `Serializable` and `Cloneable` because these are the only interfaces that all arrays implement. Also, you can autounbox an array only to a type of `Object`—again according to the rules of RTTI.

Finally, all reference types can be autounboxed to `String` because all references implement a `toString( )` method declared in `Object`. However, you can also autounbox a primitive to a `String`. Therefore, the following code is completely legal:

```
int x = 25;
Set y = new HashSet( );
String x2 = x;
String y2 = y;
```

Ambiguous autoboxing

Since you have the autoboxing functionality of Tiger, you may be tempted to write code such as the following:

```
public class Boxing {
  public static void someMethod(final Float x) {
    System.out.println("Float");
  }

  public static void someMethod(final Integer x) {
    System.out.println("Integer");
  }

  public final static void main(final String[] args) {
    someMethod(5);
  }
}
```

The semantics of this code look harmless, but in fact, if you try to compile this code, you will get the following compiler error:

```
>c:\j2sdk1.5.0\bin\javac -source 1.5 oreilly/hcj/tiger/*.java
oreilly/hcj/tiger/Boxing.java:28: reference to someMethod is ambiguous, both method
someMethod(java.lang.Float) in oreilly.hcj.tiger.Boxing and method
someMethod(java.lang.Integer) in oreilly.hcj.tiger.Boxing match
                someMethod(5);
                ^

1 error
```

The problem here is that autoboxing can't decide whether to use the `Float` or `Integer` version of the method. There are two ways around the problem. The first is to specify which type of number 5 is using a suffix to the number, as in the following code:

```
someMethod(5f);
```

In this code, you specify that 5 is a `float`. This allows the compiler to call the `someMethod(Float)` version. Similarly, you can use the other single-letter suffixes to specify the type of a literal number, such as L for a long and d for a double.

 Although it is permissible to use the letter l to specify that a number is a long, it isn't a good idea because the letter l looks a lot like the number 1. Instead, I recommend you use a capital L when specifying long values.

There is no single-letter suffix that specifies that a number is an integer since the Java language specification dictates that if there is no appending suffix, the number is treated as an integer. However, there is a way around this that will let you call the `Integer` method; you just have to revert back to casts:

```
someMethod((Integer)5);
someMethod((int)5); // <== Compiler error!?!
```

The first cast works because the virtual machine knows how to use autoboxing to convert an `int` literal into an `Integer`. Strangely, the second call doesn't work, even though it should. The second call first specifies that the literal 5 is an `int`, which should indicate that you are calling the `Integer` method that can perform the autoboxing conversion. Unfortunately, the compiler can't handle the double autoboxing and indicates that the call is ambiguous.

Enums

Enums in Tiger are almost exactly like constant objects (see Chapter 7) with a shorthand for declaration. The following is an example of an enum:

```
public class SomeClass {
  public enum ErrorLevel { DEBUG, INFO, WARNING, ERROR };

  public void someMethod(final ErrorLevel level) {
    switch (level) {
      case ErrorLevel.DEBUG: // do debug code.
                break;
      case ErrorLevel.INFO: // do info code.
                break;
      case ErrorLevel.WARNING: // do warning code.
                break;
      case ErrorLevel.ERROR: // do error code.
                break;
      default: assert (false);
    }
  }
}
```

This class declares an embedded enum with the given names as instances of the enum. The use of an enum makes the level parameter to someMethod( ) type-safe. The user must pass an ErrorLevel to someMethod( ) and can't create anymore ErrorLevel instances without altering the ErrorLevel class. The only apparent difference between an enum and a constant object is the manner of declaration. You can declare an enum in its own file instead of embedding it in another class:

```
// File: ErrorLevel.java
public enum ErrorLevel {
  DEBUG, INFO, WARNING, ERROR
}
```

In this case, you use the keyword enum instead of class or interface. The identifiers immediately following the opening brace of the enum declaration are used to name the various instances of the class that will be created. The same concept could have been created with the constant-object pattern using the following code:

```
public final class ErrorLevel extends ConstantObject {
  public final static ErrorLevel DEBUG = new ErrorLevel("DEBUG ");
  public final static ErrorLevel INFO = new ErrorLevel("INFO ");
  public final static ErrorLevel WARNING = new ErrorLevel("WARNING");
  public final static ErrorLevel ERROR = new ErrorLevel("ERROR");

  private ErrorLevel(final String name) {
    super(name);
  }
}
```

This code does pretty much the same job as an enum. However, the constant-object class is much more verbose and subject to error. For example, if the user accidentally adds an extra space to the end of the name, there would be problems.

 Although you can use any legal identifier for an enum constant, I suggest you name your enums with capital letters to indicate that the enum identifier is an instance that can't be changed.

Unlike enums, constant objects cannot be used in a switch statement; this gives enums a bit more flexibility than constant objects have. Also, enums can work seemlessly with the for-each construct (discussed earlier in the chapter):

```
for (ErrorLevel level : level.VALUES) {
  // ...code
}
```

In this example, the special member VALUES was declared automatically by the compiler to access the list of potential values for the particular enum. The VALUES member holds an unmodifiable set of instances declared in the enum. Furthermore, these values are type-safe and the identifiers in an enum declaration are assigned an ordinal number in the order they are declared. In this example, DEBUG would be associated with the ordinal number 0, and ERROR with the ordinal number 3. This allows you to implement comparisons such as the following:

```
if (level > ErrorLevel.INFO) {
    // ...do some logging code.
}
```

There are other methods and fields automatically declared for enums. For example:

ordinal
> This field holds the ordinal value of the enum.

name
> This field holds the name of the enum that corresponds automatically with the identifier name.

compareTo( )
> Enums implement the comparable interface, which allows you to sort based on the order of the enums. This method sorts according to the ordinal value, not the name.

Finally, each enum has an equals( ), hashCode( ), and toString( ) method, which allows enums to act like objects. In fact, they can even be used as objects. You can place enums in a collection and pass them to methods that take a type of object.

Adding functionality to enums

In addition to declaring the enum values, you can declare other methods in an enum class. For example, here are some changes made to the ErrorLevel class:

```
public enum ErrorLevel {
  DEBUG, INFO, WARNING, ERROR;

  public ErrorLevel next(final ErrorLevel level) {
    return VALUES.get(level.ordinal + 1);
  }

  public ErrorLevel previous(final ErrorLevel level) {
    return VALUES.get(level.ordinal - 1);
  }
}
```

In this version of ErrorLevel, two methods were added to the class, which allows you to get the previous and next enum values. These methods work exactly like a method defined on a normal class.

Additionally, you can add constructors to an enum using the following code:

```
public enum ErrorLevel {
    DEBUG(0x1), INFO(0x2), WARNING(0x4), ERROR(0x8);

    final int bit;
```

```
    public ErrorLevel(final int bit) {
        this.bit = bit;
    }
}
```

In this example, each of the enums define a bit that may be used in a bit mask. When the enum instances are created at static initialization, they will call the constructor that takes an int. However, this doesn't affect the actual construction of the enum by the virtual machine. The name and ordinal fields will still be there. In fact, the compiler uses a code-generation paradigm to create an enum. Therefore, you can declare as many special constructors as you want without worrying about interfering with the enum mechanism.

Interfaces and hierarchies

Although an enum class can implement interfaces, it can't use inheritance. For example, the following would be illegal:

```
public abstract enum EnumBase {
  public ErrorLevel next(final ErrorLevel level) {
  }

  public ErrorLevel previous(final ErrorLevel level) {
  }
}

public enum ErrorLevel extends EnumBase {
  DEBUG(0x1), INFO(0x2), WARNING(0x4), ERROR(0x8);

  final int bit;

  public ErrorLevel(final int bit) {
    this.bit = bit;
  }
}
```

Unfortunately, this code is not allowed by the compiler because multiple inheritance is not allowed in Java, and all enums automatically and implicitly inherit from the built-in class java.lang.Enum. Also, you are not allowed to explicitly extend java.lang.Enum yourself. Therefore, if you want to add functionality (such as a utility method) to your enums, you are out of luck. This is one of the major problems with enums.

However, enums do offer another brand of inheritance that is rather strange:

```
public abstract enum EnumAttach {
  one {
    public void someMethod( ) {
      // ...code
    }
  },
```

```
    two {
      public void someMethod( ) {
        // ...code
      }
    };

    abstract void someMethod( );
  }
```

In this code, EnumAttach is a base class that declares an abstract method. Subsequently, each enum instance must implement the abstract method. The syntax is extremely peculiar, and I'm not convinced it is altogether useful. When using this syntax, you are conceptually defining a method on an instance. Such a definition is far outside the Java and object-oriented programming mainstream.

 I can't think of a situation in which I would use this syntax (if you find a good use for it, I would love to hear about it). In fact, the enum paradigm would be excellent if you could write base enums to contain functionality. Therefore, I believe that the functionality of attaching a method to an object should be changed to allow normal inheritance of enums as long as an enum can inherit only from an abstract enum.

Static Imports

The static-import facility of Tiger was designed solely for developers writing Java code. This feature allows you to import all of the static members of a particular class and use them without referring to their type. For example, consider the following class:

```
package oreilly.hcj.tiger.
import java.awt.Color;
public class StatusColors {
  public static final Color DEFAULT = Color.green;
  public static final Color WARNING = Color.yellow;
  public static final Color ERROR = Color.red;

  public static void someMethod( ) {
  }
}
```

If you want to use this class in your code the old way, you would need to access it using the following code:

```
package oreilly.hcj.tiger.
public class StaticImports {
  public void firstMethod(final Graphics g, final int errCode) {
    if (errCode >= 3) {
      g.setColor(StatusColors.ERROR);
    } else if (errCode == 2) {
      g.setColor(StatusColors.WARNING);
    } else if (errCode == 1) {
```

```
      g.setColor(StatusColors.DEFAULT);
    } else {
      assert (false);
    }
  }
}
```

The problem here is one of readability and ease of use. Whenever you want to use a color constant in the code, you must type out the full name of the constant. If there are only three constants, this isn't too bad. However, if you have a huge field of constants to work with, such as when you make constants for an XML DTD, using the constant type can get tedious.

To solve this problem, many developers declare their constants in interfaces instead of classes, and then have the classes they want to use the constants implement these interfaces. However, this can lead to messy classes that implement 20 interfaces that contain only constants. Also, if one of these classes has to use four or five different sets of constants, the number of types grows rapidly.

The static import facility allows you to declare your constants in classes; they can also be referred to without the fully qualified name. You can rewrite the previous example using static imports:

```
package oreilly.hcj.tiger.
import static oreilly.hcj.tiger.StatusColors.*;
public class StaticImports {
  public void secondMethod(final Graphics g, final int errCode) {
    if (errCode >= 3) {
      g.setColor(ERROR);
    } else if (errCode == 2) {
      g.setColor(WARNING);
    } else if (errCode == 1) {
      g.setColor(DEFAULT);
    } else {
      assert (false);
    }
  }
}
```

Adding the keyword static to import causes the compiler to import the static identifiers from the class. After they are imported, they can be used as if they were declared in the class.

Static imports import only static identifiers. Therefore, if you have methods in the class that are instance-based or static, you will have to use the instance-based methods, as you did before. However, since you shouldn't create mixes of constant and static elements in a class (see the section "Constant Encapsulation" in Chapter 7), this shouldn't be a big issue.

One nice feature about this mechanism is that it applies to static methods and static attributes equally. This is convenient when using sets of static functions such as those declared in the java.lang.Math class:

```
package oreilly.hcj.tiger.
import static java.lang.Math.*;
public class StaticImports {
  public void mathMethod(final int x, final int y) {
    int z = max(x, y);  // instead of Math.max();
    double sqrt = sqrt(z^5); // instead of Math.sqrt();
  }
}
```

Static imports make the code read much cleaner without sacrificing the benefits of modularity.

As long as companies continue to use outdated JDKs, the ConstantObject paradigm will remain important. In many companies, it is politically and physically impossible to adopt a new JDK immediately, no matter how good the JDK version is. I still work with JDK 1.3 quite often in my consulting career.

Variable Arguments

The purpose of Tiger's variable arguments (or varargs) facility is to allow a method to take any number of arguments and then act on them. It is modeled after a similar facility in C and C++. This technique is used in the printf() method, which the Tiger prototype implements in its test code:

```
printf("Addition: % plus % equals %\n", 1, 1, 2);
```

At the time of this writing, there is a limited amount of information publicly available about the implementation of varargs.

This method will print a formatted string to the console. It determines the format by using the % characters embedded in the string. Wherever it sees a %, the printf() method will substitute the corresponding argument after the format string argument. In this example, the first % would be substituted by the first additional argument to the method:

```
printf("Addition: % plus % equals %\n", 1, 1, 2);
```

Substitution continues until the all of the arguments are used. Once completed, this example would produce the following output:

```
Addition: 1 plus 1 equals 2
```

The problem with the printf() method is that the writer of the method never knows how many arguments you will send him. In this example, four arguments were sent:

the format string and the three values to use. You could have also called the method in the following way:

```
printf("Numbers: %, %, %, % \n", 6, 7, 8, 3);
```

Varargs allow you to declare a method that functions with this syntax. Using varargs, you can build a Java version of the printf() method. In the Test class that comes with the implementation of the prototype, there is an implementation of this method that you can use:

```
class Test {
    // ...other code

    // varargs
    public static void printf(String fmt, Object... args) {
        int i = 0;
        // foreach on primitive array
        for (char c : fmt.toCharArray()) {
            if (c == '%')
                System.out.print(args[i++]);
            else if (c == '\n')
                System.out.println();
            else
                System.out.print(c);
        }
    }

    public static void main(String[] args) {
        // ...other code

        // varargs and boxing
        printf("Addition: % plus % equals %\n", 1, 1, 2);

        // ...other code
    }
}
```

In the declaration of the printf() method, a new syntax declared the variable arguments. When you use the ... operator after an argument, you are indicating that the number of arguments is undefined. In this case, you indicate that the number of object arguments is undefined. Once the arguments have been passed to the method, they can be used exactly like an array of objects:

```
System.out.print(args[i++]);
```

When you call the method, you not only use varargs, but also the autoboxing functionality in Tiger:

```
printf("Addition: % plus % equals %\n", 1, 1, 2);
```

In this call to the printf() method, the second, third, and fourth arguments are autoboxed into Integer objects.

You can also use varargs with any other type, as in the following signature:

```
public static void printf(String fmt, int... args) {
}
```

This indicates that the variable arguments are all integers. If a user tries to pass anything other than an integer as the second argument or higher, the compiler will give her an error.

The varargs syntax is used merely as a convenience. Using the functionality in JDK 1.4, you could have written the method with the following signature:

```
public static void printf(String fmt, Object[] args) {
}
```

However, if you had used this signature, you would have had to call the method using the following:

```
printf("Addition: % plus % equals %\n",
        new Object[] { new Integer(1), new Integer(1), new Integer(2)});
```

This call would accomplish the same task as using varargs, but it is much more verbose and difficult to read.

Generics

The implementation of parameterized types in Tiger is called *generics*. Generics allow you to build parameterized types that are checked at compile time. In addition to the new parameterized collection types that are implemented as part of Tiger, you can define new parameterized types to fit your needs.

> For those who want to look up the specifications of generics, they can be found under JSR 14. However, as of this writing, the version included in the public prototype implementation is old, and some parts of it are inaccurate.

One of the most persistent problems in Java is the lack of type safety in collections. For example, you can declare a new Set that should contain Address objects in the following manner:

```
Set addresses = new HashSet( );  // Component type Address
```

Once this set is declared, you are basically trusting your users never to place anything other than an Address in the set. If a user adds something other than an address to the set, the most fortunate result that could occur would be your program crashing outright on a ClassCastException. However, if you are not so fortunate, you could end up with irreparable data corruption. If this set is used as a part of a business-critical data model, such as the Online Only Bank data model in Chapter 8, you could end up destroying the entire business by implementing this software. Therefore, whenever someone calls a method to set your addresses property, you should check every member of the collection to make sure that it is a legal type (see Chapter 8).

The problem with checking elements in a collection at runtime is that it is extremely expensive; the order of efficiency is only O(n). If you have only 10 addresses in your collection, checking elements is easy. However, if the collection contains 15,000 addresses, then you would incur a significant overhead whenever someone calls the setter.

On the other hand, if you can prevent users from placing anything other than an address in your collection at compile time, then you wouldn't have to check the types at runtime. If they try to give you something that isn't an address, then the compiler will reject the attempt. This is exactly what parameterized types do.

Parameterized types allow you to declare a type that requires an additional parameter of another type to be complete. Using parameterized types, the addresses property can be declared in the following manner:

```
Set<Address> addresses = new HashSet<Address>( );
```

Now, if anyone tries to use another type as a component to addresses, the compiler will indicate an error on that line:

```
addresses.add(new Integer(5));  // <== Compiler error.
```

When compiled, this would produce the following result:

```
>javac oreilly/hcj/tiger/GenericSyntax.java
oreilly/hcj/tiger/GenericSyntax.java:24: cannot find symbol
symbol  : method add(java.lang.Integer)
location: interface java.util.Set<oreilly.hcj.tiger.Address>
                addresses.add(new Integer(5));
                     ^
```

The error specifies that the compiler cannot find an add method appropriate to the type. Since the user can't put anything into the set that doesn't belong there, you shouldn't have to check the values within the collection to make sure they are the right type.

 Unfortunately, the error message is a bit difficult to read. It should probably say that Integer is not applicable to the add method. This would be far more intuitive. In the meantime, watch out for this error message and make sure you don't spend hours checking methods in your generic classes before you check to see whether the user called them with the correct type.

The Syntax of Generics

The general syntax of generics has two parts: the declaration and the usage. You have already seen how to use a generic type. To declare a generic type, use the following basic syntax:

```
class SomeClass<Type> {
  Type value = null;

  public Type getValue() {
    return this.value();
  }

  public void setValue(final Type value) {
    this.value = value;
  }
}
```

This syntax declares a generic type that works with the type that the user passes when the instance is constructed. The Type parameter can be any constructed type in Java, but you can't use primitives as component types for generics. This is considered to be a major limitation of the generics implementation. In the declaration of SomeType, wherever the compiler sees the word Type in the body of the class, it will substitute Type with the type parameter given at the time of construction. For example, consider how this generic type is used:

```
SomeClass<String> someVar = new SomeClass<String>();
someVar.setValue("Hello");
```

This code would cause the compiler to consider your generic type in the following expansion:

```
class SomeClass<String> {
  String value = null;

  public String getValue() {
    return this.value();
  }

  public void setValue(final String value) {
    this.value = value;
  }
}
```

 You may have noted that I didn't use the word "generated" here. This is because the generics mechanism in Tiger doesn't generate anything. This topic is covered later in the chapter.

Not only does this give you type safety with your generic class, it allows you to reuse code. The implementation is rather simple. However, some generic types can easily have thousands of lines of code.

Nested generics

In your implementation, note that you can use any nonprimitive type as the Type argument to SomeClass. This includes other generic types:

```
SomeClass<Collection<String>> someVar = new SomeVar<Collection<String>>();
```

If you use this syntax for SomeClass, the code will be expanded properly so that you can call setValue() only with collections of strings. This nesting can extend as deep as you want. However, for the sake of readability, I recommend you keep generic nesting to a minimum.

In addition to nesting generic type declarations, you can use the Type parameter to create other generic instances:

```
class SomeClass<Type> {
  List<Type> value = null;

  public List<Type> getValue() {
    return this.value();
  }

  public void setValue(final List<Type> value) {
    this.value = value;
  }
}
```

Just as before, the word Type is expanded wherever it is seen inside the class. This scenario includes the creation of the generic list instance for setValue().

Multi-generics

When declaring generics, you aren't limited to one generic type. In fact, you can declare several parameters to your generic type using the following syntax:

```
public class Pair<LeftType, RightType> {
  private LeftType left = null;
  private RightType right = null;

  public LeftType left() {
    return this.left;
  }

  public void left(final LeftType left) {
    this.left = left;
  }

  public RightType right() {
    return this.right;
  }

  public void Right(final RightType right) {
    this.right = right;
  }
}
```

Once declared, the class is used as follows:

```
Pair<String, Integer> nvp = new Pair<Integer, String>();
nvp.left("John");
nvp.right(25); // <== note the use of autoboxing.
```

This class works just like generic types that have only one parameter. Wherever the compiler sees LeftType, it substitutes the type given in the construction of the generic instance—String, in this case. Similarly, RightType is substituted with the second type given in the construction. If the user of the generic class gives only one parameter within the angle brackets, the compiler will indicate an error.

Bounds

When creating a generic type, it is often useful to restrict the type of object that is passed to the generic. For example, if you are developing a generic type that works with the MutableObject class from Chapter 8, you should make sure that the user can use MutableObject classes only as a parameter to your generic type. These restrictions are called *bounds* and are defined with the following syntax:

```
public class SomeClass<Type extends MutableObject> {
  // ...
}
```

This syntax restricts the user, allowing him to give only subclasses of the MutableObject class in the Type parameter to the generic class. Similarly, you can use this syntax with interfaces as shown here:

```
public class SomeClass<Type implements Comparable> {
  // ...
}
```

With this declaration, the user must give a type for Type that implements the Comparable interface. In addition to restricting the user to one type, the bounds syntax allows you to call methods on the type without knowing exactly what it is. For example, you can declare a class in the following manner:

```
public class SomeClass<Type implements Comparable> {
  Type value = null;

  SomeClass(final Type value) {
    this.value = value;
  }

  public void someMethod() {
    Integer someInteger;
    // ... code
    int result = this.value.compareTo(someInteger);
    // ... other code
  }
}
```

Since this generic type knows that all users will implement the Comparable interface, it can safely call the compareTo( ) method declared in Comparable.

Sometimes it may be necessary to declare bounds that implement a type and extend another type. This can be done with a special syntax:

```
public class Bounds<Type extends Number & Comparable> {
}
```

The users of this class must give a type that extends Number and implements Comparable. Any other types will result in an error. Within the class body of Bounds, you can use any members of Number or Comparable. If you don't declare bounds on your types, you can't use any of the methods within that type. Essentially, you can't assume anything about Type that isn't declared, with one exception. The second bounds constraint is called an *additional bound*. You can add as many additional bounds as you want to specify other interfaces that you want to implement:

```
public class Bounds<Type extends Number & Comparable & Serializable> {
}
```

In this code, the type used as a parameter must be a subclass of Number and implement Serializable and Comparable. You can use only one extends bound. This is consistent with the prohibition of multiple inheritance in Java. Since no class can ever extend two different types, it makes no sense to allow declaration of multiple extends bounds.

All generic types implicitly declare the bound of extends, java.lang.Object, as normal classes do. Therefore, the following declarations are equivalent:

```
public class SomeClass<Type> { ... }
public class SomeClass<Type extends Object> { ... }
```

The fact that these declarations are equivalent has two implications. First, it allows the programmer of the generic type to call methods such as hashCode( ) and equals( ) from the Object class on instances of Type. Second, this bounds restriction prevents the user of the generic type from using primitive types as a parameter.

 Given the autoboxing functionality in Java, I don't see why Sun would prevent someone from declaring a generic to use primitives. It would seem that the compiler could simply convert List<int> to List<Integer> automatically, since accessing the methods would autobox the ints.

Wildcards

One problem with generics is figuring out how to deal with the passing of generic classes to other generic classes. For example, suppose a class is designed to manage a collection of list objects. Each of the lists may be a different generic type:

```
public void someMManagerMethod( ) {
    ListManager<List<Integer>> integerMgr = new ListManager<List<Integer>>( );
```

```
ListManager<List<String>> stringMgr = new ListManager<List<String>>();
// ...other code.
}
```

In this case, you may want to use your list manager to manage a list of String objects and a list of Integer objects. However, you should make sure that the manager is given only a List and not something else, such as a Class object. This is not a problem, since you can declare a wildcard bounds on an interface. To do this, use the wildcard in the definition of ListManager:

```
public class ListManager<Type extends List<?>> {
}
```

The emphasized syntax means that the type the user gives you must be a parameterized version of the List class. Furthermore, in the class body, it doesn't matter what the contained type in the List is. You can declare bounds on wildcards as well:

```
public class ListManager<Type extends List<? extends Number>> {
}
```

This syntax allows your list manager to work only with List types that were parameterized using a subtype of Number. The semantics are identical to the bounds discussed earlier.

Lower bounds

Earlier, we discussed a type of bounding called an *upper bound* of a type. However, there is another type called a *lower bound*, which can be used on a wildcard:

```
public class ListManager<Type extends List<? super Integer>> {
}
```

This syntax allows the user to use the list manager with any List that was parameterized with Integer or a supertype of Integer. In this case, you can use List<Integer>, List<Number>, or List<Object>.

However, as with upper bounds, you can't use any of the information implied by a lower bounds.

Raw types

Raw types are collection classes that are not parameterized. These correspond to old types used in JDK 1.4 and earlier. There is no difference in how these old types and raw types are used.

```
List list2 = new ArrayList();
list2.add(new Integer(3));
list2.add(new String("Hello"));
```

However, if you use this code in your program, the compiler will spit out the following warning:

```
>c:\j2sdk1.5.0\bin\javac -source 1.5 oreilly/hcj/tiger/*.java
Note: oreilly/hcj/tiger/ErasureDemo.java uses unchecked or unsafe operations.
Note: Recompile with -Xlint:unchecked for details.
```

If you want more specific information about this warning, you can add the -Xlint: unchecked flag to the invocation of the compiler. Compiling with this flag results in the following:

```
>c:\j2sdk1.5.0\bin\javac -source 1.5 -Xlint:unchecked oreilly/hcj/tiger/*.java
oreilly/hcj/tiger/ErasureDemo.java:57: warning: unchecked call to add(E) as a member
of the raw type java.util.List
                    list2.add(new Integer(3));
                    ^
oreilly/hcj/tiger/ErasureDemo.java:58: warning: unchecked call to add(E) as a member
of the raw type java.util.List
                    list2.add(new String("Hello"));
                    ^
```

Since these warnings come whenever you use a raw type, cast anything to or from a raw type, or pass a raw type as a parameter, they are not particularly useful. Although they give you information about holes in your type safety, in a large project using legacy libraries, you will get hundreds of them. If there is a hole in your type safety (such as the one discussed in the next section), it isn't likely that the relevant warning will stand out in the crowd.

Erasure

Generics exist only for compile-time type safety. They provide absolutely no runtime type safety, which is one of the major drawbacks to the generics proposal. The reason why there is no runtime type safety is because of *erasure*.

After the compiler has resolved the type safety introduced by generics, it erases the parameterization from the type. Therefore, the information is not available at runtime. The purpose of erasure, as stated by Sun, is to allow class libraries built with an older version of the JDK to be able to run on the JDK 1.5 virtual machine.

Erasure is an important concept because it impacts runtime type safety as well as function-based polymorphism. For example, consider the following snippet of code:

```
public void someMethod(final List<Integer> list) {}
public void someMethod(final List<String> list) {}
```

Although both of these methods seem distinct, they actually are identical in the mind of the virtual machine. This is because the parameters to the generic classes are erased at runtime, and you end up with the following:

```
public void someMethod(final List list) {}
public void someMethod(final List list) {}
```

Since two methods cannot have the same signature, this would cause a compiler error:

```
C:\dev\hcj\tiger\src>c:\j2sdk1.5.0\bin\javac -source 1.5 -Xlint:unchecked oreilly/
hcj/tiger/*.java
oreilly/hcj/tiger/ErasureDemo.java:28: name clash: someMethod(java.util.List<java.
lang.Integer>) and someMethod(java.util.List<java.lang.String>) have the same erasure
        public void someMethod(final List<Integer> list) {}
               ^
oreilly/hcj/tiger/ErasureDemo.java:29: name clash: someMethod(java.util.List<java.
lang.String>) and someMethod(java.util.List<java.lang.Integer>) have the same erasure
        public void someMethod(final List<String> list) {}
               ^

2 errors
```

The compiler complains because both types "have the same erasure." Basically, this means that after the erasure process, both methods look identical. Another naming conflict resulting from erasure is a bit less obvious:

```
public static Comparable someOtherMethod(final Comparable obj) {
   return null;
}
public static <Type extends Comparable> Type someOtherMethod(final Type obj) {
   return null;
}
```

Both of these types look radically different, but let's look at them after erasure takes place. With the first version of someOtherMethod( ), no erasure is needed because there are no abstract types. However, erasure needs to be done on the second version. The compiler knows that Type must be of type Comparable, so it erases the emphasized parts in the following snippet:

```
public static <Type extends Comparable> Type someOtherMethod(final Type obj) {
   return null;
}
```

This results in:

```
public static Comparable Type someOtherMethod(final Comparable obj) {
   return null;
}
```

Since this method is identical to the first version of someOtherMethod( ), the compiler issues an error saying that two methods have the same erasure.

Unfortunately, there is no way to fix these problems short of a variety of complicated mechanisms. You could, for example, declare a useless boolean parameter on the second method or give the second method a different name than the first method. This problem is one of the major limitations of the Java generics implementation. Method overriding is one of the cornerstones of developing good quality software. Unfortunately, it cannot be done to methods that use generic types.

Cracking type safety

However, erasure introduces another, even more serious problem. See Example 12-1.

Example 12-1. Cracking type safety with reflection

```java
package oreilly.hcj.tiger;

import java.util.*;
import java.lang.reflect.*;

public class ErasureDemo {
  private static List<Integer> someList;

  public static void someMethod(final List<Integer> list) {
    for (Integer element : list) {
      element.intValue();
    }
  }

  public static void main(final String[] args) {
    someList = new ArrayList<Integer>();
    someList.add(new Integer(123));
    someList.add(new Integer(456));
    someList.add(new Integer(789));

    // Break type safety on a field.
    try {
      List list = (List)ErasureDemo.class.getDeclaredField("someList").get(null);
      list.add(new String("Hello"));
      for (Object element : list) {
        ((Integer)element).intValue();
      }

    } catch (final Exception ex) {
      System.out.println();
      ex.printStackTrace();
    }

    // Break type safety on a method.
    try {
      List list2 = new ArrayList();
      list2.add(new Integer(3));
      list2.add(new String("Hello"));

      Class[] paramTypes = new Class[] {List.class};
      Object[] methargs = new Object[] {list2};
      Method meth = ErasureDemo.class.getDeclaredMethod(
                                          "someMethod", paramTypes);
      meth.invoke(null, methargs);
    } catch (final Exception ex) {
```

Example 12-1. Cracking type safety with reflection (continued)
```
    System.out.println( );
    ex.printStackTrace( );
  }
 }
}
```

This example shows how you can completely crack the type safety of a generic field and a generic method without being blocked by the compiler. Here is the output of this program:

```
>c:\j2sdk1.5.0\bin\java oreilly.hcj.tiger.ErasureDemo

java.lang.ClassCastException: java.lang.String
        at oreilly.hcj.tiger.ErasureDemo.main(ErasureDemo.java:47)

java.lang.reflect.InvocationTargetException
        at sun.reflect.NativeMethodAccessorImpl.invoke0(Native Method)
        at sun.reflect.NativeMethodAccessorImpl.invoke(NativeMethodAccessorImpl.java:
39)
        at sun.reflect.DelegatingMethodAccessorImpl.
invoke(DelegatingMethodAccessorImpl.java:25)
        at java.lang.reflect.Method.invoke(Method.java:326)
        at oreilly.hcj.tiger.ErasureDemo.main(ErasureDemo.java:63)
Caused by: java.lang.ClassCastException: java.lang.String
        at oreilly.hcj.tiger.ErasureDemo.someMethod(ErasureDemo.java:32)
        ... 5 more
```

The first `ClassCastException` is caused by the breaking of `someList`'s type safety. To accomplish this, follow these steps:

1. Declare a type-safe field called `someList` in the class scope.

2. At the start of the main method, fill `someList` with 50 `Integer` objects.

3. Retrieve `someList` using reflection. Since the resolution of the type happens at runtime, `list` is a plain old raw `List` object and therefore isn't type-safe.

4. Add a `String` to `list`, which then adds it to `someList`, since they both are references to the same list.

Now when you loop through the elements of the list using the for-each loop, the program expects all the members of `someList` to be type-safe and of type `Integer`. As it goes through the list, it trips over the string you forced into the list, which causes a `ClassCastException`.

The process of cracking `someMethod` is similar:

1. Declare a method called `someMethod( )`, which takes a type-safe list of `Integer` objects as its list parameter.

2. Declare a new list called `list2` and fill it with one `Integer` and one `String`.

3. Retrieve a reflective reference to `someMethod( )`.

4. Invoke `someMethod( )` with reflection and pass the corrupted list to `someMethod( )`.

During the execution of someMethod( ), the Java runtime trips over the String value in the list and throws the ClassCastException.

Throughout this process, the compiler gives you only a warning telling you that you are using an unchecked type. Compiling the program produces only the following warnings:

```
>c:\j2sdk1.5.0\bin\javac -source 1.5 -Xlint:unchecked oreilly/hcj/tiger/*.java
oreilly/hcj/tiger/ErasureDemo.java:45: warning: unchecked call to add(E) as a member
of the raw type java.util.List
                    list.add(new String("Hello"));
                    ^
oreilly/hcj/tiger/ErasureDemo.java:57: warning: unchecked call to add(E) as a member
of the raw type java.util.List
                    list2.add(new Integer(3));
                    ^
oreilly/hcj/tiger/ErasureDemo.java:58: warning: unchecked call to add(E) as a member
of the raw type java.util.List
                    list2.add(new String("Hello"));
                    ^
3 warnings
```

 If you hadn't added the -Xlint:unchecked flag to the compiler, you would have received even less information (see the section "Raw types").

Since you get these warnings whenever you deal with raw types, it is likely that the programmers of your application wouldn't pay much attention to them. Furthermore, in a large project in which you access legacy libraries that use only raw types, the likelihood that your programmers will pay attention to these warnings is extremely remote.

Currently, Sun Microsystems does not have a solution to this massive hole in reflection. Therefore, generics are useless for enforcing type safety throughout a program; they are merely a mechanism to catch errors at compile time. When it comes to critical data models, such as the Online Only Bank data model from Chapter 8, you must still check each of the members of your collections individually. Since corruption at the business data model level can easily kill a business, you simply can't ignore them.

 There have been many proposals to implement runtime type safety in which this problem as well as the function polymorphism problem would be prevented. However, they have all been rejected by Sun. In fact, in the generics specification, Sun emphatically states that runtime type safety is not a desirable thing. Obviously, I disagree.

Casting Generics

To cast a generic type from one type to another, it must share a subtype/supertype relationship with the type to which you want to cast it. This is no different from the normal rules of Java casting. However, there is one common mistake that programmers often make:

```
List<Integer> intlist = new ArrayList<Integer>();
List<Number> numList = (List<Integer>) intlist;  // <== Compiler error
```

It may seem that the second cast should work, but it doesn't. Although `Integer` is a subtype of `Number`, `List<Integer>` is not a subtype of `List<Number>`.

Furthermore, you can always cast a generic to `Object`. However, if you try to subsequently cast it back to the generic type, the compiler will tell you that it can't resolve this at compile time by giving you a warning that the cast is unsafe. This also applies to casting a generic `List` to a nongeneric `List`.

Finally, since all parameter types are erased at runtime, you can't cast a generic type to another type if there isn't a unique erasure for the cast. To illustrate, here is the example from the JSR 14 specification available from the Java Community Process home page:

```
class Dictionary<A,B> extends Object { ... }
class Hashtable<A,B> extends Dictionary<A, B> { ... }
Dictionary<String,Integer> d;
Object o;

// Then the following are legal:

(Hashtable<String,Integer>)d // legal, has type: Hashtable<String,Integer>
(Hashtable)o // legal, has type: Hashtable

// But the following are not:
(Hashtable<Float,Double>)d // illegal, not a subtype
(Hashtable<String,Integer>)o // illegal, not a unique subtype
```

Since `Dictionary` and `Hashtable` form a hierarchy in this example, you can cast a `Dictionary<String, Integer>` to a `Hashtable<String, Integer>` because they are in the same inheritance structure. However, you can't cast a `Dictionary<String, Integer>` to a `Hashtable<Float, Double>` because these two types are on different branches. Figure 12-1 shows the relationship between these two hierarchies.

Casting with the last class is a little different. In previous casts, the compiler could resolve the legality at compile time. However, with o, the compiler starts out as a plain `Object`, so it could be anything. Since the parameters of a generic type are erased at runtime, you essentially have two `Hashtable` classes in memory, and the compiler doesn't know which to choose. Therefore, the cast is ambiguous.

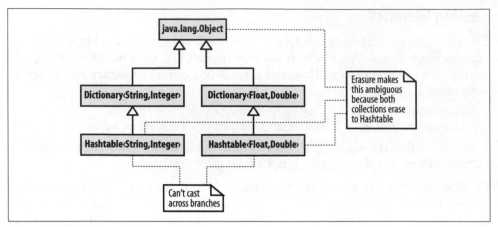

Figure 12-1. Casting in generic hierarchies

Generic Methods

In addition to defining generic types, you can define methods that are generic. For example, you may want to define a method that prints the contents of any numerical list to the console:

```
public class ListUtil {
  public void dumpList(final List<? extends Number> list) {
    int idx = 0;
    for (Object obj : list) {
      System.out.println("[" + idx + "] " + obj.toString());
      idx++;
    }
  }
}
```

This method can take any parameterized List that conforms to the bounds and then print the object to the console. The rules for defining bounds and other semantics are identical to those of generic types.

You can also define methods with which you access the enclosed type of the parameterized type using the following syntax:

```
public final class ListUtil {
  public <Type extends Number> void dumpList2(final List<Type> list) {
    int idx = 0;
    for (Number num : list) {
      System.out.println("[" + idx + "] " + num.intValue());
      idx++;
    }
  }
}
```

In this case, you want to access the type of the component of the List, so you have to declare a name to hold the type that is used to call the method. To do this, place a name in the angled brackets after all of the method modifiers but before the return type of the method. Also, you can use normal bounds rules for types in these declarations.

Inference

Inference is the process by which a runtime environment guesses (infers) the best method to call based on the types of parameters supplied at runtime. Java does not allow inference; instead, you are required to explicitly state the types of your objects when you make a call. The opposite is done in languages such as Lisp, which allow you to define variables without indicating their type and then determine their type at runtime. Another example of a language that uses inference is Python:

```
C:\dev\jython-2.1>jython
Jython 2.1 on java1.4.2_02 (JIT: null)
Type "copyright", "credits" or "license" for more information.
>>> someVar = 5;
>>> print someVar
5
>>> someVar = "Hi there";
>>> print someVar
Hi there
>>> print someVar[0];
H
```

 To run this example, use the Jython interpreter. Jython is a free Java implementation of Python that can be found at *http://www.jython.org/*.

In this Jython session, the variable someVar starts off as an int. Unlike Java, you don't have to declare the variable's type on the declaration line. Its type is inferred by the value given to it. Furthermore, you can change the variable's type in mid-session by assigning it a String value. Finally, you can treat the whole variable as an array by accessing it using square brackets. This is a perfect example of inference. The compiler determines the variable's type by figuring out how it is used.

On the other hand, Java would require you to declare the type of someVar and would not allow you to change the type or use it as anything that isn't explicitly declared. However, generics muddies the water. With generics, it is difficult to know which method to call based on the types being sent to the method. Tiger solves this problem with a limited implementation of inference.

Simple generic inference

In Tiger, inference is difficult to understand because there is no runtime manifestation of inference; inference rules are used simply to pick the right method but aren't represented in code at all. To understand the concept of generic inference, study the declaration of the InferenceDemo class in Example 12-2.

Example 12-2. The InferenceDemo class

```java
package oreilly.hcj.tiger;
public class InferenceDemo {
  static int callCount = 0;

  /** First. */
  public static <Type> Type someMethod(final Type obj) {
    System.out.print(" First==> ");
    System.out.println(obj.getClass());
    return obj;
  }

  /** Second. */
  public static <Type extends Number> Type someMethod(final Type num) {
    System.out.print(" Second==> ");
    System.out.println(num.getClass());
    return num;
  }

  /** Third. */
  public static <Type> Type someMethod(final Type obj, List<Type> list) {
    System.out.print(" Third==> ");
    System.out.println(obj.getClass());
    for (Type element : list) {
      System.out.println(element);
    }
    return obj;
  }

  /** Third. */
  public static <Type> Type someMethod(final Type obj, List<Type> list) {
    System.out.print(" Third==> ");
    System.out.println(obj.getClass());
    for (Type element : list) {
    }
    return obj;
  }

  /** Fourth. */
  public static <Type> List<Type> someMethod() {
    List<Type> result = new ArrayList<Type>();
    System.out.print(" Fourth==> ");
    System.out.println(result.getClass().getComponentType());
    return result;
  }

  /** Fifth. */
  public static void someMethod(final Object obj) {
    System.out.print(" Fifth==> ");
    System.out.println(obj.getClass());
  }

  /** Sixth. */
  public static void someMethod(final String str) {
```

Example 12-2. The InferenceDemo class (continued)

```
        System.out.print(" Sixth==> ");
        System.out.println(str.getClass());
    }

    private static class A {
    }

    private static class B extends A {
    }

    private static class C extends B {
    }
}
```

Try to call some methods within this class and see what happens. First, start with something simple:

```
    someMethod("Hello");
```

 For the sake of the following examples, assume that the code calling your methods is inside the main( ) method of InferenceDemo.

In this call, the compiler has a choice of three methods that would take a String; the First, Fifth, and Sixth methods can all take a single String parameter. The First method can take a String because a String can be a parameter to Type. The Fifth method can take a String because a String can be converted to an Object. The Sixth method specifically declares that it takes a String. The compiler will choose to call the Sixth method because the Sixth method is the most specific to the given parameters. Another example illustrates this behavior even more clearly:

```
    someMethod(new Integer(5));
```

In this example, the compiler has two options: the First and Second methods. Since the compiler chooses the most specific method, it will pick the Second method because a generic type with a bounds constraint of extends Number is more specific than a generic type with no bounds constraints. This also works for primitives:

```
    someMethod(5);
```

In this example, the compiler picks the Second method because the int parameter can be autoboxed into an Integer.

Masking methods with inference

There are some circumstances in which resolving the correct type is impossible:

```
    someMethod(new C());
```

In this case, there is no specific method that accepts a parameter of type C. Therefore, the compiler looks for methods that can take a variable of type Object and finds two: First and Fifth. Since it doesn't have enough information to make a decision, the compiler gives up and issues an error stating that the call is ambiguous. Similarly, the following would fail:

```
someMethod(new Object());
```

This is a major problem with inference.

In fact, the First and Fifth methods can never be called in this code. It would be beneficial if the compiler could tell you this with an error message such as "Method x and method y mask each other and can never be called." Unfortunately, it doesn't issue this error, but persistently issues errors on the attempts to access the Fifth method. However, this applies only to methods that work with the type Object.

If you try make this type of masking declaration with another type, such as Comparable, you would get a different compiler error:

```
/** Seventh. */
public static <Type extends Comparable> void someOtherMethod(final Type num) {}
/** Eighth. */
public static void someOtherMethod(final Comparable num) {}
```

This would cause the compiler to complain that both types have the same erasure. This error is a little bit more intuitive than the previous error involving the masked methods.

Inference based on return type

One interesting example of inference occurs when there are no parameters to a generic method, such as with the Fourth method in Example 12-2:

```
/** Fourth. */
public static <Type> List<Type> someMethod() {
    List<Type> result = new ArrayList<Type>();
    System.out.print(" Fourth==> ");
    System.out.println(result.getClass().getComponentType());
    return result;
}
```

If you call this method, the type of the return value of the method is used to determine the type in the list:

```
List<Integer> listOne = someMethod();
listOne.add(new Integer(5));
```

In this situation, listOne is a list of Integer objects. Therefore, the Type parameter to Fourth becomes the type Integer. The method returns a List parameterized with Integer that can subsequently be filled. Similarly, you can make the method return a List of String objects with similar syntax:

```
List<String> listTwo = someMethod();
listTwo.add(new String("Hello"));
```

In this example, the call to someMethod( ) produced a list of strings because the return type is a List of Strings. Taking this idea further, what would happen if you didn't give a list as a return type:

```
Object listThree = someMethod( );
System.out.println(listThree.getClass( ));
//listThree.add( ... );  // Can't put anything into this list
```

Although this call will return the expected ArrayList, you can't actually place anything in the ArrayList, not even null. In a way, it's an orphaned parameterized type.

Generic parameter-based inference

In addition to using inference with normal types, you can use it with parameterized types. Here is the Third method of the InferenceDemo class:

```
/** Third. */
public static <Type> Type someMethod(final Type obj, List<Type> list) {
  System.out.print(" Third==> ");
  System.out.println(obj.getClass( ));
  for (Type element : list) {
    System.out.println(element);
  }
  return obj;
}
```

In this method, the type of the list has to be inferred from the types embedded in the parameterized type passed to the list. For example, you can call the method with the following syntax:

```
someMethod(5, new ArrayList<Integer>( ));
```

In this call to the method, Type is inferred to be an Integer because an Integer can be used to autobox the literal number 5. Also, the parameter list will be of type Integer because the Integer type is used to parameterize the ArrayList that is passed to the method. However, just because Type appears in both parameters doesn't mean they have to be the same type:

```
// -- Make some lists --
List<A> listOfA = new ArrayList<A>( );
listOfA.add(new A( ));

List<B> listOfA = new ArrayList<B>( );
listOfB.add(new B( ));

someMethod(new B( ), listOfA);
```

In this example, Third is called with two different types. The type of obj is B, but the type of list is List<A>. This works because B objects can always be demoted to A objects. However, opposite presents a different situation:

```
someMethod(new A( ), listOfB);
```

Since an A object is not necessarily a B object, the compiler can't choose either to use for the inference, so it infers Object for both types. It then calls the method that infers Object and a List<Object> for the parameter types.

Context-sensitive inference

In some situations, inference is based on the context of the call to another method. For example, consider the following calls:

```
someMethod(5, someMethod());
someMethod("Hello", someMethod());
```

In both of these calls, the Fourth method is called to produce a list that can be passed to the Third method. In the first call, the Fourth method produces a List of Integer objects, but in the second call, the Fourth method produces a List of String objects.

The Fourth method makes a decision based on the needs of the Third method. Since the Third method needs a List of the type of the first parameter as the second parameter, the Fourth method gives it back a List of the first parameter's type.

Avoiding inference through explicit declaration

The specification for generics says that ambiguities in method calls can be cleared up with the following syntax:

```
A value = SomeClass.<A>someMethod(new B(), new ArrayList<A>()).getClass();
```

This says that the compiler should treat the B object as an A object and explicitly demote it. This syntax can be used to clear up ambiguities in which one or more types could fit the bill.

 You have to use the class name for a static method or the keyword this for an instance method before the <A>, or the code won't compile:

```
A value = <A>someMethod(); // <== won't compile!!!
```

Generic Gotchas

Now that you have mastered the intricacies of generics, you should be aware of their limitations, especially those introduced by erasure. There are several gotchas to watch out for when using generics, especially for a former C++ programmer.

Going overboard

You can do a lot of things with generics, both beneficial and damaging. While you can solidify your code into something approaching compile-time type safety, you can also easily turn it into an unreadable disaster by overusing generics and bounds on types. Using generics that have other nested generics is a prime target for bugs. For example, consider the following nested declaration:

```
public class Crazy<T extends Set<? extends List<? super Integer>> {}
```

To determine exactly which parameters Crazy takes may seem like a difficule task. But, in fact, it takes any class that extends a Set class that was composed of lists with types of Integer, Number, or Object. So the all of the following would work:

```
Crazy<Set<List<Integer>>> crazy;
Crazy<Set<List<Object>>> crazy1;
Crazy<Set<List<Number>>> crazy2;
Crazy<HashSet<List<Integer>>> crazy3;
Crazy<TreeSet<ArrayList<Number>>> crazy4;
Crazy<Set<LinkedList<Object>>> crazy5;
// ...and more...
```

Although this syntax is hard to read, compared to some of the things I have seen on generics forums, it is relatively easy.

Although type safety is an important concern in your code, you should watch out for complicated constructs such as the previous syntax and break them into smaller pieces if possible.

Compile-time class conformance

A common misconception about generic types is that they are generated at compile time into new classes. Unlike C++ templates, generics have no runtime analogy. This introduces limitations to generic classes. For example, consider the following code:

```
public class X {
  public void meth( ) {
    // ...code
  }
}

public class Y {
  public void meth( ) {
    // ...code
  }
}

public class SomeClass<Type> {
  Type value = null;

  public SomeClass(final Type value) {
    this.value = value;
  }

  public void someMethod( ) {
    value.meth( );
  }
}

public class MainClass( ) {
  public static void main(final String[] args) {
    SomeClass<X> x = new SomeClass<X>(new X( ));
  }
}
```

This code would work properly in C++ because during preprocessing, which occurs *before* compilation, the type of X would be replaced in SomeClass, and a new class would be generated with the result of the replacement. At the compilation phase, the value.meth( ) line resolves properly to call the meth( ) member of X. This type of late structure checking is called *compile-time conformance checking*. During this process, it is confirmed that the types used in the parameterized types conform to how the parameterized type uses them.

However, in Java there is no preprocessing phase and no generated classes. Therefore, there is no way for the compiler to do compile-time conformance checking. The solution to this problem is to use a bound for the generic type that requires classes being used to implement a specific interface:

```java
public interface LetterClass {
  public void meth( );
}

public class X implements LetterClass {
  public void meth( ) {
    // ...code
  }
}

public class Y implements LetterClass {
  public void meth( ) {
    // ...code
  }
}

public class SomeClass<Type implements LetterClass> {
  Type value = null;

  public SomeClass(final Type value) {
    this.value = value;
  }

  public void someMethod( ) {
    value.meth( );
  }
}

public class MainClass( ) {
  public static void main(final String[] args) {
    SomeClass<X> x = new SomeClass<X>(new X( ));
  }
}
```

In this case, the interface LetterClass defines meth( ), and classes implementing LetterClass have to implement meth( ). Furthermore, since the generic class knows that all types used in the generic class must implement LetterClass, it can call meth( ) without a problem.

Other Improvements in Tiger

There are many improvements in Tiger other than those covered in this chapter. Many of these improvements are under the hood and involve thread scheduling or other virtual-machine issues that are outside the scope of this book. For those of you interested in learning more about Tiger, take a look at JSR 176, which is available on the Java Community Process page at *http://www.jcp.org/en/jsr/detail?id=176*. These specifications will provide you with all the details you could possibly want about the implementation of the various components of Tiger.

Index

We'd like to hear your suggestions for improving our indexes. Send email to *index@oreilly.com*.

G

garbage collection, 257, 266
generated proxy classes, 253
    rules, 254
generic methods, 306
generics, 293–314
    bounds, 297
        lower bounds, 299
    casting, 305
    compile-time class conformance, 313
    erasure, 300–304
        cracking type safety, 302–304
    inference, 307–312
        based on return type, 310
        context-sensitive, 312
        explicit declaration, avoidance
            with, 312
        generic parameter-based
            inference, 311
        masking methods using, 309
        simple generic inference, 307
    lack of runtime type safety, 300–304
    multi-generics, 296
    nested generics, 296
    raw types, 299
    risks associated with, 312
    syntax, 295–300
    wildcards, 298
get( ) method, 268
getClass( ) method, 4
getInvocationHandler( ) method, 254
getProxyClass( ) method, 254
getString( ) method, 155
ghost classes, 192
greater reflection, 222
GUI builder tools, limitations, 217

H

hashCode( ) method, 105, 200
HashMap class, 99
HashSet class, 102
Hashtable class, 97

I

identity versus equality, 89
IdentityHashMap class, 99
IDEs (integrated development environments)
    Eclipse 3.0M4, xiv
    warning options, 49

if statement, 6
ignoring exceptions, 117
illegal forward references, 30
IllegalAccessException, 118
IllegalArgumentException, 115
immutability versus mutability, 83
immutable objects, 74
immutable types, 74–83
    cracked immutables, 76
    creating, 75
    false types, 77
    nonimmutable parameters, handling, 79
    string trap, 80
implementation objects, 240
implicit casting, 282
IndexedPropertyDescriptor class, 226
inference, 307–312
    based on return type, 310
    context-sensitive inference, 312
    explicit declaration, avoidance with, 312
    generic parameter-based inference, 311
    masking methods with, 309
    simple generic inference, 307
InferenceDemo class, 307
inheritance versus aggregation, 193–195
initialization, 27–32
inner classes, 131–145
instances, natural ordering, 91
instance-scoped variables, 60–63
integrated development environments (see
    IDEs)
interfaces, 85
    advantages of coding with, 86
    to implementations (proxies), 248
    nested interfaces, 149
        in classes, 149
        in interfaces, 150
internationalization with substitution
    constants, 154
Introspector class, 64, 224
invocation handlers, 252
isEnqueued( ) method, 268
isProxyClass( ) method, 254
Iterable interface, 280
iterating collections, 103
iteration through collections, 280
Iterator class, 104
iterators, 104–105
    fail-fast iterators, 104

About the Author

Robert Simmons, Jr. started programming when floppy disks were really floppy and 64 KB of RAM was considered state of the art. From his early days of programming BASIC and Logo on an Apple IIe, he advanced through Pascal and C to arrive in the object-oriented realm of C++. When Java was first introduced, he knew that the infant language would become a serious player among corporations; Robert learned Java and began using it as his primary language for programming in 1997. He lives and works as a senior software architect in Germany.

Colophon

Our look is the result of reader comments, our own experimentation, and feedback from distribution channels. Distinctive covers complement our distinctive approach to technical topics, breathing personality and life into potentially dry subjects.

The animal on the cover of *Hardcore Java* is a lion. The lion (*Panthera leo*) is the largest of the African carnivores. Males, distinguished by their tawny manes, can weigh up to 500 pounds; the smaller, maneless females can weigh up to 300 pounds. Both sexes are powerfully built. Their muscular bodies can take down such large prey as buffalo, giraffe, and young elephants, but they usually hunt medium- to large-sized herd animals, such as antelopes and gazelles.

The regal designation "king of the jungle" is a misnomer. Lions tend to live on the open plains throughout sub-Saharan Africa. Nor are they the ferocious, man-eating beasts portrayed in old stories and movies. Though lions have been known to attack humans when provoked, their lifestyle is surprisingly laid-back. They love to lie around and snooze in the sun, and are active for only two to four hours a day. They hunt in groups, usually at night. A pride consists of 12 females that are closely related and up to 6 males.

While their day-to-day life may be easygoing, the mating rituals of lions are often savage and deadly. Males mate with females of their pride. The toughest males can take over a pride by expelling other males in bloody, often fatal, fights. These males are then expelled by younger, stronger males within 1 to 10 years. New males not only kill off their rivals, but they also kill the pride's cubs to ensure that the females will once again be ready to breed, thereby guaranteeing that their genes will be passed on.

The lion's most prominent trait, its bloodcurdling roar, is used by both males and females during mating and to keep other predators at a distance. A roar will often begin with a low rumble and slowly build to a deafening crescendo before subsiding.

Matt Hutchinson was the production editor and copyeditor for *Hardcore Java*. Mary Brady proofread the book. Sarah Sherman, Mary Brady, and Claire Cloutier provided quality control. John Bickelhaupt wrote the index.

Ellie Volckhausen designed the cover of this book, based on a series design by Edie Freedman. The cover image is a 19th-century engraving from the Dover Pictorial

Archive. Emma Colby produced the cover layout with QuarkXPress 4.1 using Adobe's ITC Garamond font.

Melanie Wang designed the interior layout, based on a series design by David Futato. This book was converted by Julie Hawks to FrameMaker 5.5.6 with a format conversion tool created by Erik Ray, Jason McIntosh, Neil Walls, and Mike Sierra that uses Perl and XML technologies. The text font is Linotype Birka; the heading font is Adobe Myriad Condensed; and the code font is LucasFont's TheSans Mono Condensed. The illustrations that appear in the book were produced by Robert Romano and Jessamyn Read using Macromedia FreeHand 9 and Adobe Photoshop 6. The tip and warning icons were drawn by Christopher Bing. This colophon was written by Matt Hutchinson and Genevieve d'Entremont.

Related Titles Available from O'Reilly

Java

Ant: The Definitive Guide

Eclipse: A Java Developer's Guide

Enterprise JavaBeans, *3rd Edition*

Head First Java

Head First Servlets & JSP

Head First EJB

J2EE Design Patterns

Java and SOAP

Java & XML Data Binding

Java & XML

Java Cookbook

Java Data Objects

Java Database Best Practices

Java Enterprise Best Practices

Java Enterprise in a Nutshell, *2nd Edition*

Java Examples in a Nutshell, *3rd Edition*

Java Extreme Programming Cookbook

Java in a Nutshell, *4th Edition*

Java Management Extensions

Java Message Service

Java Network Programming, *2nd Edition*

Java NIO

Java Performance Tuning, *2nd Edition*

Java RMI

Java Security, *2nd Edition*

Java ServerPages, *2nd Edition*

Java Serlet & JSP Cookbook

Java Servlet Programming, *2nd Edition*

Java Swing, *2nd Edition*

Java Web Services in a Nutshell

Learning Java, *2nd Edition*

Mac OS X for Java Geeks

NetBeans: The Definitive Guide

Programming Jakarta Struts

Tomcat: The Definitive Guide

WebLogic: The Definitive Guide

O'REILLY®

Our books are available at most retail and online bookstores.
To order direct: 1-800-998-9938 • *order@oreilly.com* • *www.oreilly.com*
Online editions of most O'Reilly titles are available by subscription at *safari.oreilly.com*

Keep in touch with O'Reilly

1. Download examples from our books

To find example files for a book, go to:

www.oreilly.com/catalog

select the book, and follow the "Examples" link.

2. Register your O'Reilly books

Register your book at *register.oreilly.com*

Why register your books?
Once you've registered your O'Reilly books you can:

- Win O'Reilly books, T-shirts or discount coupons in our monthly drawing.
- Get special offers available only to registered O'Reilly customers.
- Get catalogs announcing new books (US and UK only).
- Get email notification of new editions of the O'Reilly books you own.

3. Join our email lists

Sign up to get topic-specific email announcements of new books and conferences, special offers, and O'Reilly Network technology newsletters at:

elists.oreilly.com

It's easy to customize your free elists subscription so you'll get exactly the O'Reilly news you want.

4. Get the latest news, tips, and tools

www.oreilly.com

- "Top 100 Sites on the Web"—PC Magazine
- CIO Magazine's Web Business 50 Awards

Our web site contains a library of comprehensive product information (including book excerpts and tables of contents), downloadable software, background articles, interviews with technology leaders, links to relevant sites, book cover art, and more.

5. Work for O'Reilly

Check out our web site for current employment opportunities:

jobs.oreilly.com

6. Contact us

O'Reilly & Associates
1005 Gravenstein Hwy North
Sebastopol, CA 95472 USA

TEL: 707-827-7000 or 800-998-9938
      (6am to 5pm PST)

FAX: 707-829-0104

order@oreilly.com
For answers to problems regarding your order or our products. To place a book order online, visit:

www.oreilly.com/order_new

catalog@oreilly.com
To request a copy of our latest catalog.

booktech@oreilly.com
For book content technical questions or corrections.

corporate@oreilly.com
For educational, library, government, and corporate sales.

proposals@oreilly.com
To submit new book proposals to our editors and product managers.

international@oreilly.com
For information about our international distributors or translation queries. For a list of our distributors outside of North America check out:

international.oreilly.com/distributors.html

adoption@oreilly.com
For information about academic use of O'Reilly books, visit:

academic.oreilly.com